For Alison & Curt,

who probably know all about
this already & are writing the
definitive history!

with love & best wishes,

Jim

Christmas 1994

Theatre in the Cotswolds

*The Boles Watson Family
and the Cirencester Theatre*

by
Anthony Denning

Edited and extended by
Paul Ranger

THE SOCIETY FOR THEATRE RESEARCH

First published in 1993
by The Society for Theatre Research
c/o The Theatre Museum, 1E Tavistock Street
Covent Garden, London WC2E 7PA

© 1993 The Society for Theatre Research
ISBN 0 85430 054 6

Typeset by EMS Photosetters, Thorpe Bay, Essex
Printed by Woolnough Bookbinding
of Irthlingborough, Northants.

Contents

Illustrations

Anthony Denning

The author of this book was a prime example of the type of researcher whose enthusiasm and scholarship has advanced the study of theatre history in England. These are, typically, men and women of wide cultural interests who – in the absence until very recently of any formal academic studies in this discipline – have made time in the course of busy careers to collect evidence about and to study aspects of the history of the theatre either on a national or a local level. Later students are deeply indebted to them.

Anthony Denning was born in Chard, Devon, in 1916 and was educated at Ilminster Grammar School and for a year at the University College of Exeter. He served as a captain in the Army during the War, and was awarded the Military MBE for services in the North African Campaign. After the War he joined the War Office and then moved to the Foreign Office, where he served as a Visa Officer in many European countries. He was a fluent linguist, speaking Dutch (his wife was Dutch), German, French, Italian and Swahili, and with a sound working knowledge of Polish, Swedish, Russian and Serbo-Croat. It was rumoured that he was associated with the Intelligence Service.

He had a great love of Opera. He kept written notes of all the performances that he attended, and collected many recordings of live performances on disc. Many operas he knew by heart. Additionally he felt a great love for theatre scenery, and this led to him forming a fine collection of plays whose characters and scenery have been preserved in the toy theatre sheets of the English Juvenile Drama and the German Papiertheater. Particularly, he was able to take advantage of his posting to Austria to acquire an unrivalled collection (at least as far as England is concerned) of the superb sheets of scenery issued by the Viennese publisher Matthias Trentsensky between about 1820 and 1860. This collection was eventually presented to the Derby Museum, there to complement the fine collection of English stages and plays formed by Frank Bradley. It is currently displayed in a Georgian mansion, Pickford House, at Friar's Gate, Derby.

After retirement, Anthony Denning and his wife settled in the attractive country town of Cirencester, in the Cotswolds. He took a keen interest in the local musical life, and was an enthusiastic member of the Cirencester Archaeological and Historical Society. Above all, he was fascinated by the history of the eighteenth-century theatre in Cirencester, the exterior of which still stands, and he was inspired by a collection of old playbills in the town's Bingham Library. He set himself to learn all he could about the theatre, the actors who had played there, and the productions that had been staged in it. He discovered that it had been part of a chain of theatres, in the ownership of the Boles Watson family, that had extended over a large part of the West Country. The story of this circuit encapsulates a hundred years of the British Theatre. Anthony had certainly intended to make a book from this research, but first the illness of his wife, and then his own failing health prevented him from completing the work. He left an incomplete text at his death in 1987.

Few of his friends knew that Anthony Denning was a man of any wealth, but his will revealed that he had left substantial and generous bequests to the Musicians Benevolent Fund, the Wireless for the Blind Fund, a Sick Animals organisation, and the Society for Theatre Research. The Society has used part of its bequest to improve its service to its members, and has devoted the interest on the remainder to establishing an annual research grant in Anthony Denning's name for topics substantially concerned with the history and practice of the British Theatre. Additionally the Society was determined, if at all possible, to complete Anthony's history and to publish it. We were fortunate to find in Dr Paul Ranger a theatre historian well qualified to bring Denning's book to a state of completion in a form that we hope he would approve. With this publication we honour both the rich history of the theatre in

Cirencester and its associated circuit, and the memory of a man who has made a great contribution not only to the theatre in the Cotswolds but to the general study of theatre history in these islands.

George Speaight

The following Anthony Denning Research Awards have been granted to date by The Society for Theatre Research:

1990–91 Jane Mederos Baldwin, 'Michel Saint-Denis and Actor Training'
1991–92 Terry Lane, 'Stephen Joseph, his Life and Legacy'
1992–93 Sarah McCleave, 'Handel's Operas, including Dance, in the context of contemporary dance and theatre practice'
1993–94 Gabriella Dideriksen, 'From Play to Opera: The Second Covent Garden Theatre, 1809–1856'

Information regarding the annual research grants awarded by the Society may be obtained from The Chairman, Research Sub-Committee, The Society for Theatre Research, c/o The Theatre Museum, 1E Tavistock Street, London WC2E 7PA.

Anthony Denning

ix

Anthony Denning: A Personal Memoir

Tony Denning (also known affectionately by some of his friends as 'Denny') taught at a number of small private schools before joining, as a tutor, a Berlitz language school on the Dutch–German border. The knowledge of the area that he gained was to be of great influence on his subsequent career.

At the beginning of the Second World War, Tony returned to Britain and joined the Pioneer Corps as a private. Hearing that he knew the Dutch–German border, his Commanding Officer asked Tony to present a talk about the area. Command Headquarters then summoned him to give the talk there. His General was so impressed that he instructed that Tony should be given an immediate Commission.

Tony was later posted to North Africa, where a surprise manoeuvre by Rommel led to him being taken prisoner. However, both he and a fellow captive managed to jump from the truck in which they were being transported and escape. Tony's German was so good that he succeeded in talking himself through the German lines to rejoin the British Army: an exploit for which he was decorated.

After the war, success in applying for a Foreign Office appointment took Tony to Copenhagen, Bucharest, Belgrade, Vienna, with a final posting to Berlin as Third Secretary. His decision to settle in Cirencester after retirement is said to have been prompted by the similarity of the town's Roman name, Corinium, to that of his wife, Corinne, who was at one time secretary to a Dutch minister.

Following his wife's death Tony contributed a considerable sum on her behalf towards the repair and rehanging of the bells in Cirencester's splendid Perpendicular Parish Church, both their names being recorded on the tenor bell which had to be recast. Tony himself suffered ill health and died as a result of a brain tumour. His last years were eased for him by the companionship of his pet rabbit, Toby: the resurgence of an affection for these animals which he first had as a youngster, when he would read with his rabbit sitting on his lap. At that time, also, his interest in model theatres had begun, when he shared the production of plays with his brother.

Tony Denning was a somewhat reticent man and this portrait of him has been possible only by bringing together reminiscences of his friends: friends who recall him in his prime as a robust, charming, erudite and engaging man.

Alan Welsford

Foreword

For the latter part of his life Anthony Denning lived in Cirencester, a small market town in the Cotswolds. The visitor to this place is astonished first of all by the magnificence of the Parish Church towering above the Market Place and then, as he makes his way around the fascinating warren of streets, he is amazed by the sheer variety of Georgian architecture still standing in the town. One of the most attractive of these thoroughfares is Gloucester Street and along this Anthony Denning often made his way to a domestic building which was for almost forty years Cirencester's first professional purpose-built theatre. Exploring the remains of its interior on many occasions, he determined to write the history of this place. His intricate researches (for the piecing together of the story is in the nature of a jig saw made up of minute scraps of information) led him to the knowledge of John Boles Watson, the manager not only of this small theatre but also of a circuit of great magnitude. The character of Watson fascinated Denning and he managed to get inside the mind and heart of this man with an amazing degree of sympathy. Watson's son, John Boles Watson II (Denning refers to him as Jack Watson in this book) was less of a challenge and dealt with only sketchily. But a theatre is more than a manager with a building and Denning revelled in his knowledge of the plays which were staged here, the members of the company and the names of the many visitors who came to Gloucester Street for a night of entertainment.

Before his death Denning committed much of this story to a typescript. He painted his picture of the theatre on a large canvas: history, gossip, plots of dramas, anecdotes of personalities, notes on far-flung playhouses, all jostled for attention. I was delighted by Anthony Denning's enthusiasm for the subject when I first read the script and highly honoured when I was asked by the Society for Theatre Research to prepare it for publication. My own work on the circuits of Thomas Collins, playing in the Hampshire and Wiltshire area, and on Henry Thornton, a manager who built his circuit along the roads to Bath and Portsmouth, prepared me in some measure to deal with John Boles Watson and his sprawl of theatres across the western counties of England and through Wales. Studying the original work, I felt that certain alterations were needed in order to make the plethora of material assimilable to the non-specialist reader and it is only fair to Anthony Denning to account here for the changes I have made to his typescript.

The story of the establishment and growth of the Cirencester Theatre was Denning's principal interest and I have extracted this from the script so that the chronology progresses unhindered by other considerations. The theatre at Cheltenham was Watson's administrative centre and a certain amount of the history of that playhouse impinged on the Cirencester Theatre. Material on the repertoire I have placed in separate chapters and to some extent I have cut down on the retelling of the plots of plays, although I trust that these remain clear. I have also tried to place information about the actors, whether members of the company or visiting celebrities, within clearly defined bounds. Thus there has been a restructuring of the original script. Nevertheless, the material within the sections of the book designated 'chapters' consists of Anthony Denning's own words, although rearranged and with the addition of a few minor linkages. The notes to each chapter I have supplied myself and the discerning reader will realise that sometimes these are tentative. Unfortunately none of Mr Denning's working notes and references are extant and I had to reconstruct his research before any primary sources could either be given or suggested as possibilities. In undertaking this my previous studies of other provincial managers served as a foundation.

The script contained many casual references to other theatres on the circuit; these I filleted out and discovered in the process that John Boles Watson I had set up theatres in around forty locations. To attempt to weave all of this material into some kind of continuous narrative seemed an impossibility; yet the Cirencester Theatre existed as part of a circuit and a false impression could be given if the background were to be ignored. I decided to use information about the circuit by developing it into a Gazetteer, adding considerably to it from my own researches. In this way the chronology of each particular theatre can easily be followed and the frequent stating of dates allows the reader to compare events in other places with those at Cirencester.

Why Anthony Denning chose the date 1819 as the conclusion of his typescript is a mystery. All that can be said is that at the time the management of John Boles Watson II was in the doldrums. Maybe Denning's illness prevented further progress. My decision has been to continue the story to the end of the management of John Boles Watson III, even though the latter is a shadowy character. I have also followed the fortunes of the building which was the Cirencester Theatre through its two conversions – to a public house and later to a domestic residence. In order to differentiate my writing from Mr Denning's this part of the story is told in the Epilogue.

The Prologue represents my attempt to set Denning's account of the Cirencester Theatre in the context of the conventions and developments of the Georgian theatre. During the lifetime of John Boles Watson I the scene changed from the hazardous adventures of strolling players to the establishment of permanent playhouses and the rise in the social status of the performer. The working lives of John Boles Watson II and III cover days of war and subsequent economic recession. It is important to bear this background in mind as the narrative unfolds.

Acknowledgements

When death interrupts work on a book the subsequent editor must deal with numerous loose ends. My task in completing this volume has been greatly eased by the patient help many librarians, archivists and curators have given me and I would like to thank the following for their help: Trevor Allen, librarian at Cirencester; M E Arnold, librarian at Northampton; J M Baillie, archivist at Leicester; Roger Beacham, librarian at Cheltenham; Paul Bolitho, librarian at Warwick; V J Booler, librarian at Droitwich; Jennifer Broomhead of the State Library of New South Wales; Anthony M Carr, librarian at Shrewsbury; R A Chamberlain-Brothers, archivist at Warwick; Brian J Chesney, librarian at Moreton in the Marsh; Alun Edwards, archivist at Llandrindod Wells; Victoria Gabbitas, curator at Daventry; S V Helm, librarian at Stourbridge; Andrew Helme, curator at Monmouth; R J H Hill, librarian at Hereford; D R Hughes, librarian at Mold; J V Hughes, librarian at Swansea; Liz Kotlarz, librarian at Tamworth; Chris Latimer, archivist and local studies officer at Walsall; Helen Maund, librarian at Brecon; K A Morris, librarian at Brecon; J North, archivist at Worcester; Frank Olding, archivist at Abergavenny; Helen Palmer, archivist at Carmarthen; E L Pettitt, archivist at Hawarden; C Price, librarian at Brecon; Elizabeth Rees, archivist at Wolverhampton; Margaret Richards, librarian at Gloucester; J E Rimmer, librarian at Welshpool; J Robertson, librarian at Daventry; Margaret Sanders, librarian at Worcester; Jennifer Smallman, librarian at Ludlow; Sue Smith, library manager at Michinhampton; Clare Spruce, librarian at Coventry; Aubrey Steventon, information officer at Leicester; Richard Sulima, curator at Tamworth; Helen Taylor, librarian at

Acknowledgements

Lichfield; Elizabeth Teiser, librarian at Ross-on-Wye; Marina Thomas, librarian at Wrexham; Maria Twist, librarian at Birmingham Central Library; Rachel Watson, archivist at Northampton; Carolyn Watts, librarian at Flint; D R Williams, librarian at Oswestry; Pamela Williams, librarian at Birmingham Central Library; S Williamson, librarian at Evesham; D Woodhouse, librarian of the Powysland Local History Club; M W Yorke, archivist at Worcester; Robert Bearman, archivist at Stratford-upon-Avon.

I must also thank the following people for written or verbal information: Mr Charles Calvert of Stratford-upon-Avon; Mr and Mrs Peter Davies of Cirencester; Mrs B Drake of Gloucester; Mr Brian Firth FSG of Gloucester; Mrs Jenkins of Cirencester; Sr Bonaventure Kelleher of Brecon; Mr George Speaight of the Society for Theatre Research; Ms Susan Wallin of Stourbridge. The Revd E M Chappell, Miss Beryl Kingan and Mrs Margaret Thorpe have kindly contacted experts to answer my enquiries.

I must record a debt of gratitute to the staff of the libraries and record offices where I undertook the major part of my investigation: the Bingham Library, Cirencester; Birmingham Central Library; the Bodleian Library, Oxford; the British Library, London; Cheltenham Public Library; The Gloucestershire Collection, Gloucester Public Library; the Library of the Society of Antiquaries; Warwick Public Library and the County Record Offices at Gloucester, Warwick and Worcester. I must thank Mr David Viner of the Corinium Museum, Cirencester, and Dr Stephen Blake of Cheltenham Museum and Art Gallery for their help in arranging for me to see materials.

In my initial preparation of this project I was greatly aided by notes Dr Arnold Hare had made on Anthony Denning's writing.

My especial thanks go to George Speaight for his meticulous and perspicacious help in preparing the work for publication. His encyclopaedic knowledge is a constant joy to any theatre historian and, as have many others, I have benefited greatly from his kindly wisdom.

Paul Ranger
Oxford
October 1992

Prologue:
The Georgian Theatre in the Provinces

The story told in this book is about one theatre in Cirencester and yet it is set against the wider terrain of a circuit of theatres which stretched from the home base of Cheltenham, across the western Midlands, through to Wales, reaching at its most westerly point to Carmarthen. The fortunes of this unwieldy circuit play an important role in the history of the Cirencester Theatre. One must also be aware of the general day to day activity of a Georgian theatre so that as the narrative of the Cirencester Theatre unfolds, such distinctive qualities as it possessed may be appreciated.

Too often in the past it has been assumed that the acquisition of playhouses on a circuit was a haphazard affair, at best determined by the ease of journeying from one town to another. Anthony Denning's account clearly shows that other factors existed. John Boles Watson I (the name ultimately covered three generations of the family) inherited much of his circuit from an older actor manager, Roger Kemble, who in turn had worked for a similar manager, John Ward. Ward became his own master in the early 1740s and toured his company around an area which encompassed Warwickshire, parts of Herefordshire such as Leominster and the county town, and the Welsh border towns such as Brecon. Roger Kemble acted in John Ward's company and married his daughter Sarah in 1753. Eventually Kemble took over the Ward company and circumstances led him to become domiciled at either Hereford or Worcester for parts of each year and so he consolidated the company's presence in these towns but without neglecting the regions to the west of them. The other important towns on Kemble's circuit were Ludlow, Leominster, Droitwich and Bewdley. John

1

Boles Watson I had taken over much of Roger Kemble's company by June 1781 (Henry Masterman also inherited some interests) and one of his earliest independent acts was to set up a playhouse in Cheltenham, naming his company the 'Cheltenham Company of Comedians'.[1] Busy here from June to September, the social season for the spa town, he used Cheltenham as a base from which to visit Gloucester and Cirencester. The winter and spring of each year was a time in which he could work his way over to Wales, following Ward's original 'walk', usually visiting each of his theatres once every three years and playing for as many weeks as interest would prompt the townspeople to attend the playhouse. Thus his personal pattern of working was built up.[2]

The methods of travel and the places in which the three companies – those of Ward, Kemble and Watson I – performed changed over the years. Ward established a company of strolling players and tramping was their way of getting from one town to another. Elizabeth Farren, when a child actress in another troupe, carried the drum whilst other members of the company bodily hauled the scenery from town to town, and this was not an isolated instance, although a horse and cart were often used.[3] Privileged members of the company would travel on the cart, others would walk. By Watson's managership, although the scenes were still carried privately, actors tended to rely on public forms of transport. Although this was an improvement, one must bear in mind the limitations. The Cirencester entry in the *British Universal Directory* (1790–8) advertised that a stage coach set out for London each Tuesday, Thursday and Sunday evening at 6.00 pm; a good rate of progress would have been sixty miles a day during the summer, a distance which could be halved in the wintertime. This was the time of year, inauspicious for travelling, in which Watson visited the Welsh hill towns.[4]

In Ward's day a strolling company would use temporary accommodation as a theatre. Barns in the yards of inns were often favoured although, as at Tewkesbury, pavilions would sometimes be set up in fields outside the town, possibly a necessity if permission to perform within the built-up area were lacking. The stage would consist of little more than trestles and bales of hay at floor level would serve as the box partitions; a gallery, if one were provided, would be improvised from a cart or waggon.[5]

An intermediate provision was the fit-up, a popular method of creating a theatre in the early days of Watson's management. The company would arrive at a building, such as a town hall, the assembly rooms situated in a hotel or an indoor tennis court, with a wooden pre-fabricated structure which dove-tailed together to form stage, proscenium arch, rudimentary boxes and sometimes a gallery. Refinements 'such as a pit for the half-dozen violinists who accompanied' were lacking although traps in the stage floor seem to be indispensable for performances. Gradually more permanent arrangements were made in such spaces as malthouses or market halls.[6]

In the 1780s the arrival of the players had become a popular feature in the social round, surmounting evangelical condemnation, and many towns, or even villages, discovered that they were destined to contain a purpose-built theatre. The cost of these was often met by subscriptions (for which each subscriber would be given a free pass for himself and his family), shares or a tontine. Denning describes in detail the purpose-built theatre in Cirencester and although this has been altered beyond recognition, a working theatre similar to the original in Cirencester may be visited at Richmond in Yorkshire. Sometimes these buildings were dedicated solely to use as a theatre, at other times they served a dual purpose, often leased for use as a warehouse in the absence of the company.[7]

An elaborate system was soon employed of leasing and even sub-letting these permanent buildings to other managers for a season of entertainment or to people who wished to stage some sort of function, whether it were simply a lecture on astronomy (a very popular winter use and topic) or, with the pit floored over at box level, for an assembly in which the boxes made convenient 'sitting-out' apartments for non-dancers.[8]

This progression from the transitory to the permanent indicates changes in the acceptance of the players in society. In 1737 Robert Walpole, finding his cabinet lampooned on the stage of the Little Theatre in the Haymarket, passed an Act of Parliament which forbade the setting up of playhouses other than those with a royal patent, the Theatres Royal at Drury Lane and Covent Garden and half a dozen provincial playhouses which had a royal connection.

ACTING OFF THE STAGE. *The well fed Magistrate listening to the request of the half famished Player to perform in a Barn*

*And then the justice
In fair round belly with good capon lind,
With eyes severe and beard of formal cut,
Full of wise saws and modern instances.*

The manager of a touring company requests permission to perform from a local magistrate, as depicted by Theodore Lane for Pierce Egan's *The Life of an Actor* in 1825.

Given time, the players came to be tolerated in the country towns: it was incumbent on the manager of a company to visit the magistrate to obtain permission to perform, which was usually, but illegally, given provided that the takings of a stipulated number of nights were given to a charitable cause. However, if a formal objection were lodged with the magistrate, then the manager would be fined £50.00 for each performance given. This anomaly was eventually recognised and the Act of 1788 allowed a manager to perform in a given place for up to sixty days provided he obtained a licence from the magistrate. As many companies performed only three or four nights in the week a season could last as long as twenty weeks. The building of permanent playhouses is an indication of the security afforded to Georgian managers by the passing of the Sixty Day Act.

Consideration has been given here to the manager as the person responsible for setting up a theatre, but he had other duties. His was the hiring and recompense of the actors. One must remember that most companies were family affairs with the manager often performing alongside his wife and children together with sundry

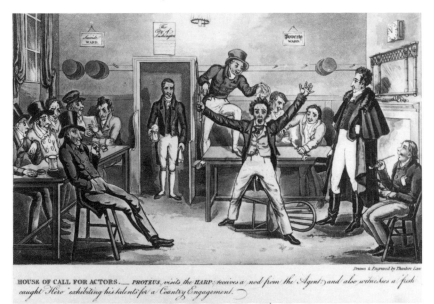

HOUSE OF CALL FOR ACTORS.__ *PROTEUS, visits the HARP; receives a nod from the Agent; and also witnesses a fresh caught Hero exhibiting his talents for a Country Engagement.*

A touring manager inspects applicants for his company at a 'house of call' in Covent Garden, as depicted by Theodore Lane.

blood relations as well as those by marriage. These formed the nucleus of the company. Other actors were hired and fired. Popular places for the former were the 'houses of call', taverns in the Covent Garden area, where applicants who had noticed the manager's advertisement would be interviewed. At other times an actor would approach the manager, either by letter or in person, to enquire if a vacancy existed. The manager was on the look-out for people to play stock roles as these would satisfy the demands of most plays, including those of Shakespeare. Thus a young male actor would be suitable to play the light hero and, because of the large number of operettas in the repertoire, would need to be able to sing. Similar criteria also applied to young women who wished to take the role of the heroine. Other accomplishments, such as the ability to dance the hornpipe or recite poetry, would come in useful. Or, to take another example, the manager might wish to find an elderly performer to take on such roles as Sir Peter Teazle or Squire Hardcastle. One of the enquiries a manager would make was the number of lines an actor could learn in an evening. One must remember that normally a different play was given each night and so a wide range of parts had to be assimilated. The sickness of a colleague or the advance choice of a play by an important member of the audience would mean that occasionally a complete role would have to be mastered in a short space of time.[9]

By the time that John Boles Watson I took up the reins of management most actors were paid a weekly salary.[10] This would be augmented at intervals by the inclusion of a benefit night in which, after the deduction of the customary house expenses for the evening (such considerations as the cost of the lighting, heating and the wages of the front of house staff), the beneficiary would receive the remainder of the box office takings.

In addition to hiring the run-of-the-mill actors, the manager would also invite, for an agreed fee, celebrity performers whose fame would draw larger audiences to the theatre. Letters of Sarah Siddons and Dorothy Jordan show that a star, making a tour of a number of theatres, would hope to amass an appreciable lump sum in a short period of time.[11] The two patent houses in London closed during the summer months when society decamped to the country and this left the Covent Garden and Drury Lane performers free to accept engagements. Here was an opportunity to take on new roles in the provinces. Older performers had established a number of roles in London which provincials would also wish to see in their own locality. Both John Boles Watson I and his son enjoyed entertaining a selection of such theatrical virtuosi.

The manager would also choose the repertoire of the theatre. He would wish to obtain the text of a London success as soon as possible to stage at his theatre.[12] Anthony Denning seems to make the tacit assumption that if a play succeeded at Cheltenham it would work its way around the rest of the circuit, but the extent to which the taste of the audience shaped the repertoire in each geographical location is open to question. A considerable number of genres were tackled by a theatre company. The metropolitan performances of the 'tragic triumvirate' of Siddons, Kemble and Cooke, ensured that Shakespearean plays such as *Macbeth*, *Othello*, *Richard III* and *King Lear* were regularly staged in the lesser playhouses. Only a few of Shakespeare's comedies were popular; one often repeated was David Garrick's adaptation of *The Taming of the Shrew* under the title *Katharine and Petruchio.* More often, though, the comedies of Richard Sheridan were played at the start and ending of a season and *She Stoops to Conquer* by Oliver Goldsmith kept its popularity alongside them. Thunderous dramas in which blood was spilt and villainy finally put down were a great attraction and many a performance of *de Monfort, The Castle Spectre, Timour the Tartar* and *Blue Beard* were given on the Watson circuit. But most popular of all were the light, musical, often sentimental, pieces (*Inkle and Yarico, The Will, The Honey Moon, Speed the Plough,* to name but several) which would end an evening spent in the playhouse.

Two other people held positions of responsibility in the theatre, the acting manager and the prompter. The first of these corresponds to the role of the director in the modern theatre although he was allowed, in comparison, only a modest amount of rehearsal time in which to put on an effective production. The acting manager would work in with the scene painter and the machinist (under whom were such departments as the costume makers and wardrobe mistress) in creating a homogenous entertainment. A certain amount of drilling (the procession in *The Shakespeare Jubilee* or military procedures in *Pizarro* are examples) was essential but much seems to have been left to the performers' knowledge of the conventions of the stage (such as the avoidance of up-staging a prestigious visitor) and to their innate sense of stage decorum.[13]

The work of the prompter was considerably more important than the title suggests. In his hands were the engagement of the backstage staff (scene-shifters, candle snuffers, machinists, amongst others), the writing up and keeping of the prompt copy, the responsibility of ensuring that actors were waiting for their entrances in the greenroom, the provision of lighting equipment and, of course, the prompting.[14]

The stage of a Georgian theatre was in two sections, the acting and the scenic areas. Nearest to the audience was an apron, the proscenium, jutting into the house. This was flanked on either side by one or two pairs of proscenium doors through which all of the entrances and exits from the outside world were made. The greater part of the action took place on the proscenium until about 1790 with actors standing in a straight line to address each other and, somewhat directly, the audience which tended to resemble an extra character in the piece so regularly was it recognised. Behind the actors was the proscenium arch from which hung the green proscenium curtain, a prized possession – resembling the flag of a regiment – which in the days of the strollers was taken from theatre to theatre by the company.

The arch separated the two areas of the proscenium and the scenes. The scenery in provincial theatres was based on the system, the groove and shutter, employed at Covent Garden and Drury Lane. A series of five sets of grooves cut in the stage floor, with corresponding overhead pieces, provided a runway for pairs of shutters of which the locations of the scene were painted. Scene hands pushed or pulled these into place. In order to work the system only the area in front of a pair of shutters was used so that scenery and properties could be set up behind them and at the right moment in the progression of the play the stage-hands would draw aside the shutters were series of wing pieces which could be, but were not required, then shutters downstage of the current scene were pushed along the grooves until they met. Masking the outer edge of the shutters were series of wing pieces which could be but were not always, changed to correspond to the scene on the shutters. Thus, if a manager were negligent and owned only several wings, the shutters might be painted as a woodland but the offending wings could show a couple of pillars on either side of the stage. The pushing and pulling of wings and shutters were controlled by the prompter who gave a blast on a whistle when the scenes were to be changed. It has to be understood that the green proscenium curtain was drawn up at the beginning of the play and stayed thus until the end, so that all transformations were visible to the audience. Where well organised, the change could be effected whilst the actors in the former scene made their exit and new characters entered the stage. At a time when each theatre had plenty of stagehands, this method of scene change offered a speedy and flexible way of mounting the drama.[15] After 1790 there was a tendency for the actors to perform greater sections of the play within the scenic area than formerly. Often the nature of the play dictated this; castle ramparts were stormed, caverns and underground tunnels were entered, rock faces were the backdrop to a fall.

During the management of Ward the stage would have been lit by candles with several sconces hanging above the proscenium and stands of candles in the wings casting some light on the shutters. A trough, which could be lowered beneath the deck level to give a darkening effect, ran along the front of the stage and in this further candles burnt. In the middle of the eighteenth century patent oil lamps, Argands, were utilised at Drury Lane and these gradually spread to the provinces. The lamps evenly lit a greater area so making the candle sconces redundant. They had the further advantage that with the turn of a single handle the shades on the footlights could change from colourless opaque to green, allowing mysterious night lighting to flood the stage. The auditorium was lit by candles which remained burning the whole evening.[16] The introduction of the Phantasmagoria into theatres necessitated that the house was in complete darkness for about twenty minutes and audiences were prepared for this unusual event in the advertising.

I have remarked that the actors were highly conscious of the audience in their performances and it is time to consider this important factor in the life of the playhouse. The auditorium was divided into three areas each reflecting a different strata of society. The pit, in purpose-built theatres, was often excavated below ground level and a series of steps built on which backless benches were set for the occupants. The pittites usually entered through the lobby at the front of the house from where they were diverted by means of a long passage running down the side of the theatre to an entry into the pit near the stage. In the London patent houses tradesmen, writers, artists, members of the legal profession all tended to sit in the pit. Very little research has been undertaken though on the composition of the pit in the comparatively cheaper seats of the provincial theatre. The gallery, built above the boxes, was the haunt of the lowly waged such as apprentices, uncommissioned soldiers and sailors and manual workers.[17] Up there it tended to be rough and noisy but many a witty aphorism rang from the gallery down to the stage. Missiles also were hurled on occasion from the top shelf to the proscenium and a manager would be forced to employ the Peace Officers to stand guard at times of unrest.[18] The boxes were, of course, for the more affluent members of society. Landed gentry, the principals of schools and colleges, commissioned members of the military, members of masonic orders were all to be found here.

When members of the royal family visited the theatre it was to this part of the house, with special chairs substituted for the benches, that the manager conducted them. Each theatre employed a box-keeper and his box-book could be consulted to make bookings (confirmed by circular box-tokens) in advance of the performance.[19] Servants would be sent ahead for popular presentations in order to 'keep places' (sit on the seats in the boxes) until their employers arrived at the theatre shortly prior to curtain-rise. The boxes nearest the stage often stood on either side of the proscenium so that their occupants were in the closest proximity to the performers and conversations could, and did, ensue.

Some occupants of the boxes might wish the company to perform a particular play and this would be noted on the playbills and in the newspaper as 'By desire of X'. In return the requester would buy blocks of seats in the surrounding boxes and make presentations of the places to his aquaintances. This was a popular method of ensuring a fuller house and managers lent on many a wealthy patron to help finance an evening. In the course of this history Anthony Denning tells of the various individuals in the locality of Cirencester who gave their support in this way. As a general rule, one finds that well-worn plays are 'desired' and a person inviting other patrons would usually be unwilling to sponsor a new play or an untried writer.

Audiences were informed of the theatrical fare by means of newspaper advertisements and sometimes in the columns by means of 'puffs', seemingly editorial matter either giving advance notice or an adulatory retrospect but in fact written by the manager who then paid the newspaper office for the entry.[20] Older than newspaper advertising was the use of playbills. In strolling days these were distributed as soon as the company arrived at a location and, to draw attention to them, accompanied by one of the company banging a drum. Later, when a manager was settled in a town for his sixty days' season, he had an arrangement with the town printer to produce his bills for him. One finds over a long spread of years that the same printer would be employed by a manager. It is worth mentioning that often there was a discrepancy between the plays advertised in the newspapers and those on the bills, an indication of the hand to mouth nature of the daily administration of the theatre.

When an actor prepared for his benefit he would often undertake extra advertising, sometimes producing attractive cards which would be left at houses as an invitation to take seats for the night.

In detailing from whom tickets could be purchased, especially for benefit nights, playbills often give an indication of the places at which actors lodged. Many shopkeepers gained an extra income by letting a room in their residential accommodation above the premises to one or two actors. Sometimes the manager, if the town were one which he infrequently visited, would also find a similar lodging. It was extremely rare that accommodation in an inn was chosen, a reflection of the difference in the prices these and private landlords charged. A theatre at which a manager regularly spent a long season would often be provided with a house for him and his family either as an integral part of the building, or adjacent, or as a separate dwelling in the town. This was a highly convenient amenity although, as in the case of John Boles Watson II, it could lead to many legal wrangles. Lastly, in considering accommodation, we must not forget that often people other than the manager would live in the theatre building. To this end tenements were enclosed in the front part of the theatre, not always evident to the casual observer.[21] The box-keeper tended to be given internal accommodation and there are instances in which his wife would act as house-keeper or the provider of the audience refreshments.

The small building in Gloucester Street gives slight indication today of the evenings of romance and gaiety which the Cirencester townspeople once found there. An evening at the theatre was a full one. It began as soon as one had found one's seat in the building for refreshments could be bought whilst one waited for curtain rise.[22] The small orchestra would provide a musical item and the theatre's green curtain would be drawn up revealing one of the company at the ready to speak the prologue to the main piece of the evening. Once this was finished other entertainments would ensue, often individual numbers, in which all or any amongst singers, acrobats, dancers, reciters and fire-eaters would perform. The after-piece, usually light and bubbling with musical numbers, would bring the evening to a satisfying conclusion, providing much to talk about during the following days. That building, which today coyly presents the passer-by with a domestic front, was once a haunt of magic and good cheer, giving an extra dimension to living and widening the vision of the people of a remote Cotswold town cut off from their neighbours by rolling hill country.

Why then did it all end? As this history shows, the Napoleonic Wars had taken a toll of British finances and an economic recession set in after 1815. The decline of the provincial theatre was a slow and, to some extent, barely perceived process at first. There were longer periods of time in which buildings were dark. Costumes and scenery became shabby and undistinguished with age. But new interests were at work also. The third and fourth generations of Wesleyans were becoming a force to contend with and they, together with evangelical Anglicans, provided a significant opposition to the theatre, protesting against the expected immorality of its fare and its exponents, viewing the process as wasteful of time and money. By the 1840s a new earnestness could be sensed; the gospel of self-improvement was at work. Literary and Scientific Institutes, Mechanics Institutes and other educational forums were setting up courses of lectures, 'improving' entertainments, such as readings from Shakespeare, and classes for those who had lacked formal education. Sometimes the very theatre buildings were used for series of lectures as at Banbury in 1836.[23] Poverty, religion and education were three formidable forces for an unsophisticated manager to contend with. Could they offer, though, the colour, the popular culture and the life which that constricted stage had given to people in the theatre's heyday?

Notes

1   Much of the preceding information is based on a series of newspaper cuttings of articles by H W Gwilliam in the County Record Office, St Helen's, Worcester and also on Cecil Price, *The Professional Theatre in Wales* (Swansea, 1984). Details of the establishment of the Cheltenham Theatre are given in Chapter 2 and the Gazetteer.
2   The story of the relationship of the three actor managers is told in some detail in: Cecil Price, *The English Theatre in Wales* (Cardiff, 1948).
3   'Petronius Arbiter', *Memoirs of Elizabeth, Countess of Derby* (1797), p. 9.

4   For several studies in which journeying times are considered see: John Copeland, *Roads and their Traffic, 1750–1850* (Newton Abbot, 1968); W T Jackman, *The Development of Transportation in Modern England* (Cambridge, 1916); 'Stage Coaches', *The Times*, 2 January 1813.

5   An account of barnstorming is given in George Parker's *A View of Society and Manners in High and Low Life* (1781) and a fictionalised version is to be found in Thomas Mozeen's *Young Scarron* (1752). At Chelmsford a barn was fitted up as a theatre in which the gallery consisted of a waggon hanging by ropes from the rafters: this is described in an epilogue spoken at the end of the season printed in the *London Magazine*, September 1773.

6   As an example of a fit-up on the Watson circuit the temporary theatre in Little Water Street, Carmarthen, may be cited; see the Gazetteer for details. Indoor raquets (or tennis) courts belonging to the various colleges were a popular base for fit-ups in Oxford, in spite of the university's disapproval of the professional theatre. Those at Merton College (still in use), Christ Church and St Mary Hall (now part of Oriel College) were all put to theatrical usage during long vacation.

Charles Knight gives a brief description of a provincial theatre orchestra, that at the Theatre Royal, Windsor, in *Passages of a Working Life* (1873), p. 46.

7   The theatre in Rawlins Lane, Andover, Hampshire, where the company arrived to perform only once every two years, is an example of a building put to another use for part of the time. It became a honey store. See: James Winston, *The Theatric Tourist* (1805).

8   The Royal Opera House was similarly floored over in the 1930s for dinner dances; during the second world war it was used by Mecca Dancing and very popular amongst service personnel. See: Andrew Saint, *et al*, *A History of the Royal Opera House, Covent Garden, 1732–1982* (1982).

9   A fictionalised description of managers at a 'house of call' is given in Pierce Egan's *The Life of an Actor* (1825), p. 41. On lengths (the number of lines an actor could learn in an evening), see: George Parker, *A View of Society and Manners in High and Low Life* (1781), V, 43.

10   Edmund Kean may serve as an example. In 1808, whilst employed in Watson's company, he was paid one guinea a week. See: Giles Playfair, *Kean. The Life and Paradox of the Great Actor* (1950).

11   A Aspinal, *Mrs Jordan and her Family* (1951), pp. 54, 55, 186; Thomas Compbell, *Life of Mrs Siddons* (1834), II, 318.

12   A manager could obtain a copy of a play by several means. Let us take Richard Sheridan's comedy *The School for Scandal*, first performed in May 1777 at Drury Lane, as an example. The official edition of the text was not published until 1821; a country manager, therefore, wishing to stage the

play immediately after the metropolitan presentation had to rely on a handwritten version which could usually only be obtained with the playwright's permission. In the year of the London production Sheridan presented the Bath company with a manuscript copy of the text and later gave Tate Wilkinson at York and Joseph Younger at Liverpool permission to stage the piece. See: *Felix Farley's Bristol Journal*, 8 November 1777; *York Courant*, 21 April 1778; Williamson's *Liverpool Advertiser*, 26 June 1778.

Managers sometimes obtained pirated editions of this play. A series of these issued from Dublin, the first in 1780. Alternatively, with the help of a shorthand writer, several members of the company would sit in the gallery of the London theatre, transcribing the play during a performance as Thomas Ryder did from the two-shilling gallery of Drury Lane. This text was staged at the Crow Street Theatre, Dublin, on 8 January 1778. See: Thomas Snagge, *Recollections of Occurrences*, ed. Harold Hobson (1951).

13   Compared with modern theatre practice rehearsal on the Georgian stage was skimped. The complaint was made that actors muttered their lines in rehearsal and merely noted the entrances, exits and stage positions. 'To make any display of passion or energy' wrote Macready, 'would be to expose oneself to the ridicule . . . of the greenroom.' When a perfectionist such as John Philip Kemble attempted to work in detail and drill actors, Walter Scott noted that the result confused and terrified the performers. See: Aaron Hill, 'An Essay on the Art of Acting' in the *Collected Works* (1753), IV, 413; Charles William Macready, *Reminiscences*, ed. Frederick Pollock (1875), I, 145; *Quarterly Review*, XXXIV (1826), 230.

14   The details in this paragraph are based on remarks of Richard Cross, prompter at both the London patent houses. See: Richard Cross, *An Early Diary of Richard Cross, Prompter to the Theatres*, ed. H W Pedicord (Manchester, 1955), p. 507 and Paul A Hummert, 'The Prompter: An Intimate Mirror of the Theatre in 1789', *Restoration and Eighteenth Century Theatre Research*, III (May 1964), 37–46.

15   Information in this paragraph is based on the following works: Sybil Rosenfeld, *A Short History of Scene Design in Great Britain* (Oxford, 1973); Sybil Rosenfeld, *Georgian Scene Painters and Scene Painting* (Cambridge, 1981); Richard Southern, *Changeable Scenery* (1952); Richard Southern, 'Trick Work in the English Theatre', *Life and Letters Today* XXI (1939), 94–100; Michael Wells, 'Spectacular Scenic Effects of the Eighteenth-Century Pantomime', *Philological Quarterly*, XVII (1938), 67–81.

16   Further details on stage lighting may be found in: Gusta M Bergman, *Lighting in the Theatre* (Stockholm, 1977); Terence Rees, *Lighting in the Age of Gas* (1978).

17   The composition of the audience is fully considered in James Jeremiah Lynch's *Box, Pit and Gallery* (Berkely, 1953).

18   A variety of events would induce managers to install Peace Officers. At Winchester a fight broke out between two women at the back of the gallery over a seat and members of the audience were thrown into a panic when the cry of 'Fight!' was thought to be 'Fire!' At Portsmouth a stage carpenter was killed in an affray with members of the navy. Sporadic trouble in the gallery followed and Wheeler, the manager, pledged to make special provision for maintaining order there. See: *Hampshire Chronicle*, 22 July 1799; British Library, Playbill Collection, 426, 22 February 1782.

19   Some of the box books still exist, such as those at the Theatre Royal, Bristol. The Theatre Royal, Windsor, has a number of box tokens.

20   Issues of the *Chelmsford Chronicle*, kept at the newspaper offices in the city, have the editorial copy referring to the previous week's performances at the theatre overwritten with the charge the printer would bill the manager.

21   A noteworthy example of this, shown in one of the plates of James Winston's *Theatric Tourist* (1805), occurs at Newbury, Berkshire. The doors on either side of the central entrance to the theatre proper lead to tenements, the windows of which, on two levels, can be seen at the front of the premises.

22   A range of refreshments were sold in theatres. Oranges were common. At Croydon in the gallery mutton pies were available, the crusts of which, wrote Benjamin Webster, were hurled at the orchestra. In Windsor the Queen's Ale was sold and porter was the favoured drink at the patent theatres. See: Horace Foote, *A Companion to the Theatres* (1829), p. 138; Charles Knight, *Passages of a Working Life* (1873), p. 46; Croydon Central Library: Notes of J C Anderson referring to the Croydon Theatre.

23   A set of four lectures was organised by the Mechanics Institute on 'Elements of Chemical Science' and given by John Murray whose work *A Manual of Chemical Experiments* was on sale at the Banbury Theatre. Banbury Museum: handbill.

Chapter 1:
Early Theatres in Cirencester

Towards the middle of the eighteenth century Cirencester enjoyed all the diversions the age could offer: public breakfasts, cock fighting, evening assemblies with music, dancing and cards, horse racing, entertainments with tea included, subscription balls, acrobats on the slack wire, dancers on the tight rope, artificial and mechanical fireworks, jugglers, the musical glasses, phantasmagoria, gardens, organ recitals, travelling cabinets of waxworks, hawkers of chapbooks, ventriloquists, ballad singers, snippers of silhouettes, popular science demonstrators, infant phenomena to recite, make music and sing, obedient cats, performing dogs, astronomical lecturers, mountebanks, itinerant quacks, fire-eaters, imitators of birds, in season, year in, year out, And, of course, there were theatricals.[1]

Companies of comedians had, once the winters were over, 'gone upon their progress' from Bath and Bristol during the 1720s and 1730s, bringing their folding stages and collapsible benches as near as Wotton Under Edge, Stroud, Minchinhampton and Gloucester. Cirencester, 'the very good town, populous and rich' Defoe had found during his tour in 1724, would have been visited and given the chance to admire the Bath Company's 'four Suits of Men's rich Cloaths, and three of Women's left off by the Royal Family, with a Sett of Roman Shapes, and a Falstaff's Dress' all sewn by a Dress-maker to the Court. This finery was paraded in 'some of the choicest Plays in Vogue'.[2]

In either 1746 or 1749 Charlotte Charke, the disowned daughter of Colley Cibber, playwright, actor and London theatre manager, came to Cirencester more than once. On one occasion an incident, 'an odd affair' she called it, occurred. While the troupe was acting Dryden's tragi-comedy *The Spanish Friar* one night Mrs Charke accepted favours from an elderly gentleman, 'extremely pleasing, and his Company entertaining', who gave himself out to be a wealthy grazier. Considering such a suitor to be 'dropped from Heaven', she proceeded to hand the manager of the troupe, Mr Linnett, a month's notice to quit but almost immediately he heard from the townspeople that Mrs Charke's revered friend was a housebreaker, gambler and rogue. 'About a year after, the old Man dangled into the next World, either at Salisbury or Oxford, which, I cannot positively affirm, but that was his deserved fate', she wrote.[3]

Charke left Cirencester with Mr Linnett's company, heading for Bath, and after varied buffetings of fate under ever changing constellations came to Cirencester again in Richard Elrington's troupe. On arrival in the town Elrington promptly decamped, taking a place on the stage-coach to London leaving Charlotte Charke stranded at Cirencester in charge of the company of six. 'One Scene and a Curtain, with some of the worst of their Wardrobe, made up the Paraphanalia – of the Stage of which I was Prime Minister', she wrote in her autobiography. They paid their way, however, borrowed money to finance the next leg of their wanderings in the direction of Minchinhampton 'and were then left to proced [*sic*] upon fresh Credit, and contract the strongest Friendship we could with each believing Landlord.'

Cirencester saw Mrs Charke in a different guise on her third visit. She had deserted the stage for a time and was making her way back to the pastry shop she had opened in Bristol, travelling on foot, as she had been wont in her strolling days, after victory in an expedition into Oxfordshire to collect a legacy for a friend. 'Our Journey Home was expedited by taking a Double-Horse from Whitney [*sic*] to Cirencester; and now and then, for the rest of the Way, mounting up into a Hay-Cart, or a timely Waggon.'

In 1753 the yard of the Three Cocks Inn, one of the Cirencester hostelries which stood just off the Market Place in Castle Street, contained a theatre. The size and the style of its advertising speaks of a superior company of players bringing their own booth theatre with them.

To make up for the omitted traditional crying of the bill through

18

The Market Place in Cirencester in the eighteenth century. The King's Head, hired for theatrical entertainments in 1816 (see chapter 12), is on the left. Some way behind this inn, in Castle Street, lay the Three Cocks, in theatrical usage from 1753.

the streets preceded by the beating of a drum, the following persuasive announcement for a season of plays appeared in the *Gloucester Journal* (12 June 1753):

At the THEATRE in the Three-cocks Yard
in CIRENCESTER
On WEDNESDAY EVENING, being 13th. of this instant June,
will be performed a CONCERT of MUSIC, Pit 2s. Gallery 1s.
A celebrated COMEDY called
The Provoked Husband; Or, A Journey to London.

To which will be added a Farce, called Miss in her Teens. The kind Applause of our Audiences while in Gloucester is an Instance of their Willingness to encourage a Good, Moral, Theatrical Performance, when conducted with Decency and Order; both being in our Power, our Spectators may depend on our making THEM our Guides, as well in our Private as our Public Station, and that we shall omit neither Expense nor Industry (as far as in us lies) to make the Evening's Entertainment Rationable and Agreeable, and worthy the Attention of a Thinking Audience. Our Stay in Cirencester will be six weeks and (positively) no longer; during which we shall perform

19

every Monday, Wednesday, and Friday, beginning punctually at Seven O'Clock. We shall take care to have sufficient Number of Bills delivered, therefore hope the Ceremony of a Drum will be excused. During the Races we shall perform every Night, beginning as soon as the Race is over.

The Races at that time lasted three days. Mornings were spent by enthusiasts at the King's Head Inn, to be found across the Market Place from the Parish Church, where the cock-fighting sported thirty-one birds in a main fight and twenty-one in a bye, stakes being generally ten guineas a battle with two hundred guineas for the odd one. Wild betting and excitement in plenty were assured since the opposing owners were the Gentlemen of Gloucester on the one hand and the Gentlemen of Wiltshire on the other. Lunch at one o'clock could be had at the inn for one shilling, a separate room being provided to spare ladies sporting language and over-gallant attention.

In the afternoons there was a general exodus in gig or phaeton, astride sleek horse-flesh or on shanks' pony to the downs at North Cerney, a few miles distant, to witness the running of the races. The district was fanatically devoted to horse racing. Bibury, a few miles to the east, had seen the formation of the first flat-racing club in England. For the Cirencester races the finest horses in the district gathered on the nearby flat-topped uplands. Bets and private wagers were laid right into the final lap and the humbler crowd were entertained by puppet shows, conjurers and buffoons as they milled around. A multitude of tents offered a variety of hearty food and all kinds of wine and beer. Carts and waggons were not allowed on the course and the selling of liquor permitted only after a contribution of one guinea to the purses. The races began at four o'clock and obviously racegoers were not back in Cirencester dined and ready by the stroke of seven. The curtain at the Three Cocks was therefore held until the house was sufficiently full to make a start. This was a common theatrical practice and a source of great annoyance.[4]

The play that opened the six week season was an old, well tried comedy *A Journey to London* by Sir John Vanbrugh, left incomplete at his death. Colley Cibber, Mrs Charke's unforgiving father, used some of the scenes and gave it an ending of his own, adding the new title, *The Provok'd Husband*. The new name indicates the fresh turn he gave to the plot. The farce that followed, *Miss in her Teens*, altered by David Garrick from a French play, was a sparkling comedy that had been a stock favourite ever since its first presentation in 1747 at Covent Garden.

On the first day of racing (20 July 1753) the company gave another Concert of Music 'to begin as soon as the Race is over', between the parts of which was presented a comedy, *The Constant Couple*. The couple proved a scruple less than constant and none of the characters made the slightest attempt to get to Rome for the Pope's jubilee, the subject of the subtitle, *A Trip to the Jubilee*. This piece, George Farquhar's second play, originally brought out in 1699 when he was twenty-one, would have needed some toning down to make of it a moral, theatrical performance for it was as licentious as any of the works from which the situations were borrowed. George Farquhar, son of an Irish clergyman, left Trinity College, Dublin, to become an actor. Alexander Pope, whose frequent visits to Lord Bathurst at Cirencester helped improve his fragile health, had not time for 'peeled, patched, piebald' mummers and even less esteem for the quick pen that wrote *The Constant Couple*. He called Farquhar 'a farce writer' and spoke of his 'pert, low dialogue'.[5]

If the company at the Three Cocks made anything good and moral out of the play then an early casualty would have been the song by Sir Harry which ends:

> At last his tears and sighs made way:
> She rose and softly turned the key:
> "Come in", said she, "but do not stay;
> I may conclude
> You will be rude:
> But if you are, you may."

This lyric had music by Henry Purcell's younger brother, Daniel, and, with Sir Harry's importunate knocking at the door deftly incorporated into the ditty, became an early action song for the stage. The prototype of Sir Harry is reputed to have been the young Farquhar himself and the role gained added spice when its indelicacies were spoken by a thigh-slapping actress *en travestie* to produce a revengeful satire on all fops and gallants.

Other celebrated pieces in the company's repertoire, advertised at the Gloucester Theatre and so presumably played in Cirencester, included *The Merry Wives of Windsor*, Cibber's *Careless Husband*, his Shakespeare adaptation *King Richard Third*, *King Lear and his Three Daughters* in Nahum Tate's version with a happy ending, and the favourite musical farce *The Devil to Pay*.

The company of players entertaining the holiday makers was sufficiently well known to require no naming in the advertisements and it is the register of Cirencester Parish Church that provides a statement of their identity. On 6 June, while the company was preparing to open, the marriage took place of Roger Kemble of Hereford, thirty-two years of age, and Sarah Ward, aged eighteen, of Gloucester; he was a Catholic, she a Protestant. Kemble had been an actor in the company for a year and is described as a suave, genial man. Young Miss Ward, a dignified and determined girl, was daughter of John Ward, leader of Ward's or the Warwick Company of Comedians, which had been making visits to towns on both sides of the Welsh border since 1746. Cirencester, if an advertisement did not need the company's name, must have been on its regular circuit.

Two years after the marriage, while the company was in Wales at Brecon, the first of the couple's twelve children was born and christened Sarah after her mother. All children were expected to help early in life and were put to work at the age of eight, preferably to learn a trade, and children in theatrical families found themselves thrust before an audience at a very tender age, their presence calculated to draw compassion from softened pit and gallery. Sarah gave her first performance if not at the age of two, as sometimes claimed, then as soon as she was able to repeat a simple story. The girl appeared in juvenile and minor parts in her early years when the company consisted largely of the Ward–Kemble family so Cirencester must have seen her in several parts during the formative period of her career. She appeared at Worcester, aged eleven, as a fully fledged Ariel.[6] Like her mother, she married an actor in the company at the age of eighteen, much against her father's will, and so was known from the start of her adult career as Mrs Siddons. This illustrious tragic actress was to renew her association with Cirencester many years later when at the height of her London fame.

Each of John Ward's performances was advertised as 'A Concert of Music'. This subterfuge of giving a play, gratis, between the parts of a musical entertainment for which admission was charged was necessary in order to remain on the right side of the law, even though by 1753 a company such a Ward's, 'conducted with Decency and Order', would encounter little difficulty from the magistrates in a town on its regular circuit. None the less, the company's activities were against the law of the land. All acting in the provinces was illegal from 1737 to 1788. Actors could suffer a fine, any informer getting one half of the amount and the parish poor the other. Distraint could be placed on an actor's goods and, failing cash, he could be gaoled for up to six months. Hard labour could be added if the judge disliked theatricals and, though appeal to the quarter sessions was admissible, that took precious time and offered little hope of a lighter visitation. No wonder, therefore, that strolling companies volunteered a charity performance for the parish poor when attending at the magistrate's residence, three weeks in advance, to seek permission to put on a season of plays.[7]

The ceremony of the drum was dispensed with by Ward to help keep on the right side of local justice. Drumming caused a gathering of idle folk and magistrates saw in any crowd the threat of sedition and the seed of public disturbance. Thus fell away a very old theatre practice. From a colourful entry into the town of the actors in costume preceded by trumpet and drum, it had first dwindled to the less exuberant use of the two instruments accompanying the distribution of handbills. Eventually a drum alone announced one actor clad in the company's best suit of clothes and armed with a supply of the opening bill. By 1753 Ward was distributing bills without even benefit of drum and the sheets were passed from hand to hand rather than posted up for fear of magisterial suspicion.[8] Bills, accordingly, remained small and were often printed on a company's own portable hand press. An advertisement in a local newspaper, where such existed, was made only for some distinctive occasion, an opening declaration or the presentation of some speciality, literary or human.

When allowing his daughter to marry into the profession, much against his better judgement, John Ward has squared his conscience by declaring that Roger Kemble was, in any case, no actor. It was nevertheless the son-in-law who, after a few years on his own, took over Ward's circuit and the leadership of the Warwick Company of Comedians. When Roger Kemble ultimately died in 1802 the *Gentleman's Magazine* judged that Ward's Company had been 'a respectable body of comedians'.[9] Ward's claim that he brought 'London tastes and diversions to the country' had been justified but in 1753 his declamatory style was already old-fashioned. He was fortunate in that most of his patrons had never been to London and seen the 'naturalistic' acting then being pioneered by David Garrick, the manager of the company at the Theatre Royal, Drury Lane.

When in 1754 Ward purchased from London 'a quantity of modern and Roman Habits so that the characters may be properly dressed' he was not buying togas in an early attempt to dress his tragedies in a historical style. Rather he was buying up old London stock to use in the provinces. A 'Roman Habit' consisted of a short, skirted coat which stood out from the legs and was richly embroidered. On both the French and English stages this was the accepted dress for classical tragedy. Ward up-dated his newly acquired tragedy costumes by removing the stiffening from the coat skirt, impressing his country audiences with the new grandeur and at the same time retaining a stage convention they understood. A helmet indicated that the wearer was a Greek 'capital'; a plume in the helmet made the wearer a Roman.[10]

Sarah Kemble's first son, John Philip, was born two years after her daughter. The boy appeared early with the company as usual and of necessity as soon as he could be a frightened prince in the Tower huddling against his self-confident sister but Roger Kemble had no intention of allowing his son to make acting a career. In due course he sent him to the English Benedictine seminary at Douai in northern France to train as a Roman Catholic priest, the parents having agreed that the boys should take the father's religion and the girls their mother's. John Philip had other ideas. He abandoned his studies and returned to England to become an actor.[11] In the course of his wanderings he acquired a friend in John Boles Watson, an Irishman nine years his senior and equally fanatical about a life in the theatre. Watson, born at Clonmel, the popular hunting centre in County Tipperary came, it was said, from Quaker stock. His family had intended him as a merchant. The two strolling friends ate raw turnips by the wayside in periods of thin theatrical fortune and presented themselves as reciter (Kemble) and supporting conjurer (Watson) the better to line both stomach and pocket.[12]

Returning home, John Philip met with a cold reception from his father. After the members of the company had raised a subscription for him, to which his father contributed a parting guinea, he went off to Birmingham to see if his sister could help him to a place in the company there. Watson was taken into Roger Kemble's Warwick Company. Due probably to early privations, John Boles Watson always suffered impaired health so he turned from acting to management and, proving an efficient and astute man of business, took over the circuit when Roger Kemble retired. According to his own statement in the *Gloucester Journal* (1 June 1801) he began his venture into theatrical mangement in 1779 but he always remained, in both speech and dress, the inveterate Irish actor, unable to resist appearing on stage from time to time, especially to enliven a Watson family benefit night. He was to be the main source of theatrical entertainment in Cirencester for more than twenty years.

Notes

1   The mid-eighteenth century entertainments popular in Cirencester mentioned throughout the chapter are gleaned from the columns of the *Gloucester Journal*, first published in 1722.

2   Daniel Defoe's visit to Cirencester is described in *A Tour through the Whole Island of Great Britain* (1724–7).

Kathleen Barker outlines the early days of the Bristol and Bath companies in several of her works, notably *The Theatre Royal, Bristol. The First Seventy Years* (Bristol, 1961) and *The Theatre Royal, Bristol, 1776–1966. Two Centuries of Stage History* (1974).

3   The biography of Charlotte Charke (1713?–1760) was first published in 1775 as *A Narrative of the Life of Mrs Charlotte Charke (Youngest daughter of Colley Cibber, Esq.)*. The second edition of the same year has been reproduced in facsimile with an introduction by Leonard R N Ashley (Gainersville, Florida, 1969). See: Fidelis Morgan with Charlotte Charke, *The Well-Known Trouble Maker* (1988).

Mr and Mrs Linnett had worked briefly in London in 1740; otherwise the couple's career was undistinguished. Richard Elrington started his career as a child actor in Dublin, later, in 1746, marrying Elizabeth Martin. The couple toured the south of England in 1749. The Elringtons were successful enough to play at Bath and at Covent Garden.

4 Many theatres in addition to Cirencester functioned during the respective race weeks and the variable gap between the end of the racing and curtain rise sometimes caused those waiting to complain. At Winchester, where the course was several miles away at Worthy Down, 'the uncertainty of what time the performance is likely to begin, we are inclined to think, keeps away a good deal of company' (*Hampshire Chronicle*, 22 July 1797). Thomas Collins (d 1806), the manager, solved the problem by hiring the Royal Flintshire Military Band to play as the audience arrived (*Hampshire Chronicle*, 18 August and 8 September 1800).

5 The remarks of Alexander Pope (1688–1744) concerning George Farquhar (1678–1707) are taken from his 'Imitations of Horace: the First Epistle of the Second Book of Horace'.

6 The two principal biographers of Sarah Siddons (1755–1831) are James Boaden, *Memoirs of Mrs Siddons* (1827) and Thomas Campbell, *The Life of Mrs Siddons* (1834). Details of the early years of Mrs Siddons are given in Roger Manvell's *Sarah Siddons* (1970).

7 For elaborations of Denning's summary of the Walpole Act of 1737 which sought to restrict drama to the two patent Theatres Royal at Covent Garden and Drury Lane, see W M N Geary, *The Law of Theatres and Music Halls* (1885) and, more recent, Clifford Leech and T W Craik, *The Revels History of Drama in English*, V (1972), under the article by John Loftis, 'The Social and Literary Context'. The latter suggests various papers for further reading.

8 Abandoning the drum in the mid-eighteenth century was common. For a different reason the practice ceased in Birmingham. *c* 1740 the theatre was situated in Moor Street and performances were advertised during the day by a bellowing drummer. On the removal of the theatre to King Street in 1751 the visiting company from the London patent houses requested that the drum should not be used. Attendances did not suffer. See: Thomas Gilliland, *The Dramatic Mirror* (1808).

9 The obituary of Roger Kemble (1722–1802) is to be found in the *Gentleman's Magazine*, LXXII, part 2 (1802), 1169–70.

10 'The ordinary method of making a Hero, is to clap a huge Plume of Feathers on his Head,' wrote Joseph Addison (1672–1719) in the *Spectator* (18 April 1711). It is in this guise that James Quin (1693–1766) in the title role appears in the frontispiece of James Thomson's *Coriolanus* (1749). He wears a stiff, wide skirted *tonnelet* and buskins. As a late comparison, see the caricature by Thomas Rowlandson (1756–1827) published in 1805 and 1811, 'John Bull at the Opera'. In this the size of the plume atop the hero's

helmet is exaggerated. The *tonnelet* is still worn. Both are examples of slow change in the theatre, especially in the staging of opera.

11   Early biographies of John Philip Kemble (1757–1823) are John Ambrose Williams', *Memoirs of John Philip Kemble, Esq.* (1817) and James Boaden's *Memoirs of the Life of John Philip Kemble, Esq.* (1815). A more recent, fully annotated work is by Herschel Baker, *John Philip Kemble. The Actor in his Theatre* (Cambridge, Mass., 1942).

12   The *Thespian Dictionary* (1805) gives brief notes of John Boles Watson's Irish origins and early life. In the eighteenth century, and since, Clonmel has been a Quaker stronghold; the pleasant burial ground of the Society of Friends in the town may be viewed through locked iron gates. *The Reminiscences of Michael Kelly* (1826), edited by Theodore Hook, contains an account of the early professional partnership of Watson and Kemble.

Chapter 2:
John Boles Watson I's Headquarters at Cheltenham

John Boles Watson entered upon management with an energy that never flagged as long as his health held out and, with an eye to any town large enough to provide an enthusiastic play-going public, he was soon seeking to extend the old Ward–Kemble circuit. At one time and another over a span of fifty-odd years he and the theatrical line he founded were sending companies, even if only for a race week or an assize fortnight, to Gloucester, Cirencester, Stroud, Wotton Under Edge, Tewkesbury, Ross-on-Wye, Hereford, Leominster, Monmouth, Abergavenny, Merthyr, Brecon, Swansea, Carmarthen, Welshpool, Llandrindod Wells, Kington, Wrexham, Holywell, Oswestry, Ludlow, Worcester, Evesham, Stourbridge, Wolver-hampton, Warwick, Leamington, Coventry, Birmingham, Daventry, Walsall, Tamworth, Lichfield and to Abington. This last was the place on the outskirts of Northampton where Shakespeare's grand-daughter had lived and where Garrick had for that reason planted a mulberry tree in 1776 during his last active year after retirement from the London stage.[1]

Watson treated Cheltenham as his headquarters and chose to call his players 'The Cheltenham Company of Comedians', eventually spending the summer months there and touring during the early winter and spring. The increasing number of people drawn to the town's curative waters brought him a widening public of quality which could appreciate his endeavour to mount productions of some standard. His first theatre consisted of a converted malt house situated in Coffee House Yard off Pittville Street. But it was a hallowed building for during the tenure of its former managers Chamberlain and Crump, Sarah Siddons, Roger Kemble's daughter,

Entrance to Cheltenham Theatre,

The entrance to the first purpose-built theatre in Cheltenham, opened in 1782. The house on the extreme left was Watson's private residence; the door beneath the rounded arch gave access to a passage leading to the auditorium; the third door to the right of this served as the stage door. A drawing by James Winston.

had played in the company.[2] It was not long after assuming the role of manager that Watson was building a new theatre and engaging leading players from the metropolitan houses in the closure during the London summer recess.[3] By May 1782, when the season opened, the reputation of Cheltenham as a resort for pleasure as much as for healing was increasing.

The event that fixed Watson in this pattern of business was undoubtedly the descent on Cheltenham in July 1788 of George III, accompanied by Queen Charlotte, the Princess Royal and the Princesses Augusta and Elizabeth. They stayed at Earl Fauconberg's residence on Bay's Hill.[4] After a week's rest they made an excursion into the country on Saturday 19 July. George III, at his most informal, visited Cirencester where, with a retinue of twenty instead of the usual hundred, he called on Lord Bathurst in holiday mood. The king, erect and rolling his prominent blue eyes, rode a horse at the side of the carriage of the Queen and Princesses and after a sumptuous breakfast at the Earl's mansion they all drove out to view the park and the progress on the construction of the new canal linking the Thames with the Severn. Its tunnel at Sapperton was the longest canal tunnel in Britain, over two miles in length, and five years of work on it was nearing completion. The Royals were duly impressed by such enterprise and were delighted with the woods, groves and gardens that Pope had helped Lord Bathurst to devise in the open, Arcadian style.[5]

Dinner had been prepared but the meal remained untouched. His Majesty was unfortunately on a diet and was determined to return later to Cheltenham to receive its purgative waters. From Cirencester outings into the Cotswolds, varied with visits to neighbouring boroughs and the Three Choirs Festival at Worcester, filled the holiday until the King had winded so many mounts and carriage bays that owners began to hide their horses. His Majesty, often accompanied by the Queen and the Princesses, walked in the town as freely as on the terrace at Windsor and when these outdoor diversions began to pall the King signified that he was ready to honour Watson's Cheltenham playhouse.

A royal box was prepared in the centre facing the stage and 'this village theatre', as Fanny Burney called it, became henceforth the Theatre Royal and the players 'His Majesty's Servants'. The King was delighted with the entertainment offered and made further visits. Finally, on the eve of departure, he attended a veritable gala to which Earl Bathurst and his eldest son, Lord Apsley, rode over from Cirencester. The house was packed to suffocation and the manager's wife attended their Majesties in the interval with tea. The programme for this auspicious occasion was printed on silk and Watson composed a 'Farewell Address' which was spoken from the stage by his leading actor, Mr Charlton. Illness deprived Watson of the opportunity.[6] Everything went off magnificently. Watson had laid his plans well. He had travelled up to London beforehand to make sure he had all he would need to ensure success, particularly engaging Becky Wells, the King's favourite actress at the time. Mrs Jordan, not yet the mistress of the king's third son, William, was also brought to Cheltenham to give her spanking Sir Harry Wildair in a pair of shapely breeches.[7]

The King was in an excitable mood on the night and, making a quip on the title of the piece, *The Chapter of Accidents* ready to enjoy anything. On reading the name of the company's leading comedian, Shuter, on the playbill presented to him, he exclaimed that from the name alone the actor must be a damned droll dog.[8] Shuter obviously lived up to expectation. Fanny Burney, attending as Second Keeper of the Robes to the Queen, so enjoyed Shuter's performance as to remark, '. . . and, without flattery, an excellent Gawky he is'. This judgement on the local comic after the condescending remark is highly complimentary for Shuter earned it in the small role of Jacob Gawky on the very side-lines of the piece. The whistled jig, the comical gait, the corduroys, brass buttons, smock and thumbstick would all proclaim the village dolt warmly enough for the London visitors to deign a round of laughter on initial acquaintance. Shuter, however, with his knowing look around the house turned to the royal box on his god-given line, 'Od rabbit it, if I ben't desprate glad to zee thee!'

Watson had started to call his theatre 'Royal' before the Monarch arrived in Cheltenham and it was rumoured afterwards that the King had pronounced that 'Charlotte would have it royal before it received my sacred person'.

Notes

1   The principal towns on Watson's circuit in the last decade of the eighteenth century are listed in the *Gloucester Guide* (1792) and the *Cheltenham Directory* (1800). According to these at this time he regularly visited Worcester, Hereford, Gloucester, Stourbridge, Coventry, Leicester and Cirencester. Some of the towns on Anthony Denning's list, such as Welshpool, were visited only briefly on one or two occasions with the company playing in makeshift locations.

The tree which David Garrick (1717–79) planted stands in the grounds of the Abington Museum, Northampton. This was formerly Abington Hall and belonged to Lady Wantage.

2   Weedon Butler in *The Cheltenham Guide* (1781) mentions this barn theatre in Coffee House Yard with its company 'chiefly from Worcester', a reminder that Roger Kemble's company were the original regular visitors. In Watson's time performance nights were Tuesday, Thursday and

Saturday. There was no elegance in the dresses or scenery but yet the company exerted its 'best endeavours to deserve approbation'. Admittance to the gallery was 1/- (5p) and 2/- (10p) to the pit. The building was 'not sufficiently spacious to seat a large audience' and seemingly too narrow to contain boxes. John Goding in *Norman's History of Cheltenham* (Cheltenham and London, 1863) places the building and its activities in their social context. *The Secret History of the Green Rooms* (1790) by Joseph Haslewood claims that John Philip Kemble made his theatrical debut at Coffee House Yard but other writers give this palm to Wolverhampton. William and Sarah Siddons were performing here in the 1774 and 1775 seasons (Florence Mary Parsons, *The Incomparable Siddons*, 1909); an appreciative review of *As You Like It* with Sarah as Rosalind was written by the Revd Henry Bate who saw the performance from the wings. This appeared in the *Morning Post*, 12 August 1775. Dinah Maria Mulock (1826–87) gives a fictional description of the arrival of Sarah Siddons at the Coffee House Yard in Chapter 6 of *John Halifax, Gentleman* (1856). John refers accurately to the building as a 'poor, barn-like place'. In the novel Cheltenham figures as Coltham. Mulock, keen to capture genuine local colour, wrote part of the work at Detmore House near Cheltenham.

3 The intention to form a 'society of gentlemen' and raise cash for a new and more commodious playhouse is mentioned in the *Cheltenham Guide* of 1781.

The theatre of 1782 was situated in York Passage, Grosvenor Terrace, off the High Street, and a plaque commemorates the building. According to Theodore Hannam-Clark, *Drama in Gloucestershire* (1928), the theatre was also used as an Assembly Rooms. T F Dibdin remarked that the size was limited (*The History of Cheltenham and Account of its Environs*, Cheltenham, 1803) although the Cheltenham Master of Ceremonies, Simeon Moreau, commended the interior as 'neatly fitted up, and much frequented' (*A Tour of the Royal Spa at Cheltenham*, Bath, 1797). For a contemporary note on the theatre see the *Gloucester Echo*, 4 November 1989.

4 Detailed accounts of the Royal Family's visits to Cheltenham and Cirencester are given in both Goding's and Moreau's works. In David Williams' lampoon, *Royal Recollections. A Tour to Cheltenham* (1788), the visit is described as if written by George III. Fanny Burney (1752–1840) kept a detailed account of the Cheltenham visit too; see: Frances Burney, *Diary and Letters of Madam D'Arblay*, ed. Charlotte Barrett (1891). An account, together with the text of the address Charlton spoke on 15 August 1788 (the King's final attendance at the theatre during the visit), is to be found in *Gloucestershire Notes and Queries*, III (1885), 14–15.

John Boles Watson I's Headquarters at Cheltenham

The *Gloucester Journal*, 21 January 1787, mentions that prior to the royal visit Watson had enlarged the playhouse by the addition of a second tier of boxes and a description of the completed interior is given in the *Cheltenham Directory* of 1800. By the end of the century visiting celebrities at the theatre had included Sarah Siddons, Anna Maria Crouch, John Quick, John Bannister and Michael Kelly.

5   The layout of Cirencester Park is described by Samuel Rudder in *The History and Antiquities of Cirencester* (1780) and by C H Savory in *The History of Cirencester* (1858). A historical study of the gardens and of Alexander Pope's influence on their design is made by James Lees-Milne in *The Earls of Creation* (1962); see also: Peter Martin, *Pursuing Innocent Pleasures – The Gardening World of Alexander Pope* (Hamden, Conn., 1984).

6   The visit was made as a convalescence after the king's first attack of porphyria. Horace Walpole mentions the visit in his correspondence where it is suggested that the Cheltenham waters caused the king to have a relapse; see *The Yale Edition of the Correspondence of Horace Walpole*, ed. Wilmarth Sheldon Lewis, (1937–80). The *Morning Post*, 15 August 1788, makes mention of the end of the visit. Goding notes the address written by Watson.

7   The king and queen appear to have waited for the arrival of Dorothy Jordan (1761–1816) before attending the Theatre. Her repertoire consisted of *The Virgin Unmasked, The Sultan, The Country Girl* (David Garrick's version of *The Country Wife*), *The Maid of the Oakes* and *The Poor Soldier*, although in this last play Mrs Jordan played Kathleen rather than her usual transvestite role. Commenting on Mrs Jordan's popularity, the *Morning Post* remarked that 'next to the eagerness of the people to see the Royal Family has been their expectation of this comic heroine'. On leaving the spa the visitors presented to her a gold medal bearing on one side an engraving of the Comic Muse and on the verso, 'Presented to Mrs Jordan, Thalia's sweetest child'; see Brian Fothergill, *Mrs Jordan. Portrait of an Actress* (1965).

8   *The Chapter of Accidents* by Sophia Lee was first performed at the Haymarket Theatre in 1780. Shuter was believed to be the son of Edward Shuter (1728–76), the Covent Garden actor.

33

Chapter 3:
Watson's Temporary Theatre in Cirencester

Despite a hilly distance between Cheltenham and Cirencester, Watson determined that the latter town was good for business because of its larger population, numbering four thousand. Dissatisfied with the limited facilities afforded by the barn in the Three Cocks' Yard, no place for 'His Majesty's servants from the Theatre Royal, Cheltenham', and wishing to provide his Cirencester patrons with a more comfortable environment, the manager decided to open a new playhouse. The *Gloucester Journal* (31 October 1794) carried the following advertisement:

> THE THEATRE, CIRENCESTER
> will be opened next Wednesday, the 5th. inst. with
> THE JEW, a New Comedy
> now running with universal applause.
> To which will be added
> THE IRISHMAN IN LONDON
> On Friday Mrs. INCHBALD (late Miss Frodsham of the Theatre Royal,
> Haymarket) will appear in THE YOUNG QUAKER; after which, The
> popular new Farce, The Prize: or, 2,5,3,8.

Mr Watson respectfully announces to the town of Cirencester and its environs, that he has fitted up a Play-house in a warm and commodious manner, – although small, infinitely superior to that used heretofore. – All the fashionable new Pieces are ready, and in order to introduce every possible Novelty during the short period he has the honour to attend, None can be repeated; but a Play or Farce never performed here, (and sometimes both) will be given each night.

Such Ladies and Gentlemen, therefore, as may be partial to a particular entertainment will please to avail themselves accordingly and not to omit seeing it in expectation of its being acted again, which cannot take place in any instance.

Acting nights were Monday, Wednesday and Friday, Monday and Friday being market days in the town.

The first purpose-built theatre in Cirencester was opened in 1794. Its site is not now known, but it cannot have been far from the Market Place and parish church.

The opening piece was indeed new, for the highly successful comedy of *The Jew* by Richard Cumberland had been brought out at Drury Lane towards the end of the previous season. The play was noteworthy in that it presented the central figure in a manner far removed from the traditional Elizabethan conception of the Hebrew character. Introducing a new strain of sentimental humanism, Sheva the Jew is no brooding grizzle with a knife but something of a fairy godfather who smooths the troubled path to be trod by a pair of harassed lovers. The farce of *The Irishman in London* was a lively success that had held the boards for the two years since its

35

production at Covent Garden. It was the work of William M'Cready, an Irish-born actor-manager whose infant son was to become, not altogether willingly, a great tragic actor.

The house that opened on 5 November 1794 was small and warm.[1] Cirencester lacked a town hall other than the set of small rooms over the magnificent early sixteenth-century porch of the Parish Church, and the few rooms of any size at inns in the town were in regular use. But where the new theatre was situated is not known today and it is difficult for local historians to make a surmise.

In opening a new house Watson was out to attract a more elegant public to the play, the town's woolstaplers and yarn makers, the wine and cheese factors, the corn merchants and the edge tool manufacturers. The gentry, however, away on their estates were never likely to have been great patrons of the playhouse in Cirencester, seeking their pleasures sooner in Cheltenham and Bath.

The first season was a short one, lasting probably six weeks to finish in time for the Christmas celebrations.[2] The new house was filled with 'genteel and numerous audiences every night' so that a gratified Watson was moved to 'the warmest return of thanks for the extreme liberality and kind Patronage with which the Performances are honoured.'

Notes

1   The theatre historian Dr F T Wood states, without giving his source, that the 1794 theatre held 700 people. He agrees with Denning's three days of performance each week but substitutes Saturday for Friday. See: F T Wood, 'Notes on English Provincial Playhouses in the Eighteenth Century' in *Notes and Queries*, CLX (1931), 165.
2   In 1787 the Radnor Act was passed by Parliament allowing the manager of a provincial playhouse to apply for a sixty day licence. With only three nights of playing each week, it would have been possible for Watson to have stayed in Cirencester, had he wished, throughout the winter. If Anthony Denning is correct in assuming that the season finished prior to Christmas, then this may reflect the length of time the Cirencester audience could sustain a company.

Chapter 4:
The Theatre in Gloucester Street, Cirencester

William Fisher, a carpenter, occupied a small cottage in Gloucester Street, formerly St. Lawrence Street, Cirencester. The cottage was one of a group of ten, each having a patch of garden with a stable or outhouse and, judging by the restricted area of the site, the group must have been built along a narrow courtyard or passage, as was common in the town. The cottages and their outbuildings belonged to the Whatley family of attorneys, estate and insurance agents of Cirencester who had acquired them from John Arkill, a woolcomber. The townspeople called the cottages 'The Barracks', a name signifying small, lowly dwellings. They must have been minute indeed for ten to have occupied the site. Fisher proceeded to demolish the cottages behind those facing the street, together with the stable outbuildings, and shared privies. Of the three tiny dwellings in front he left the right hand one intact. The room over the other two he removed, gutted the interiors and knocked down the front rubble wall.

Utilising the back and side walls, which he increased in height, he built a new house facing Gloucester Street, giving it a handsome facade of dressed stone which he advanced two feet into the road to increase the living space inside. This house he divided into two dwellings by an entrance passage through the centre, four feet wide. The passage eventually led into a large new building twenty-four feet wide and fifty-two feet long with walls seventeen feet above ground. These he erected after making a six feet deep excavation. This was to be the shell of a new theatre. Natural lighting came from three semi-circular windows in the wall at the back of the stage. In the excavated area Fisher laid out the essential internal foundations to

37

support the wooden superstructure of the theatre. The stage contained three traps and the auditorium consisted of a pit below ground level and boxes and gallery above. The back wall of the house had been increased to a thickness of two feet, eight inches to bear the calculated weight of a full gallery.

Over the raked gallery there was a sloping ceiling which levelled and extended to the proscenium opening, probably leaving a circular ventilation hole above the pit.

Visitors to the theatre were to enter through the wide street door under its handsome fanlight. They would pay the cashier through a box-office locket in the wall of the entrance passage and proceed for the boxes straight ahead across a shallow lobby. For the pit they would have to negotiate the bend in the steps in the right hand corner of the lobby and pass along the pit passage under a row of side boxes. A stair to the left of the lobby led to the gallery. Extant walls and traces in old plaster still, or until recent years, visible in the parts of the building that remain suggest the constructional details.[1] The building had one defect. In 1780 the stream that ran as an open drain down Gloucester Street has been filled in. The pit was below the level of this and other water channels and consequently damp was experienced.

Fisher leased the completed building immediately to Watson 'together with all the seats, erections and fixtures' but he pointedly excluded from the contract the two dwellings at the front, each with one room up and one down, and also the garden at the back of the property. The rent was to be £10 a year plus a benefit night for William Fisher in each season, less £5 for Watson's house expenses. Fisher had to maintain the building, a responsibility usually incumbent on the lessee.[2] Repairs to the interior of a theatre would be a heavy drain on the annual rent. Redecoration, merely to cover grime from candles and smut from oil, was a costly business and, tax on candles apart, every increase in the price of candles and oil, as in 1781, meant the lessee used cheaper and fouler illuminants. Watson's parsimony was known throughout the profession. He was said to burn 'kitchen stuff in place of oil which is very offensive' to light the stage and on the plea of lighting the Cheltenham auditorium with wax he increased admission to the boxes by sixpence but 'after a very few nights the wax candles disappeared.'[3]

According to the contract Fisher could use the building for his own gain on any night Watson's company was not there, provided he gave Watson a month's notice in writing and did not present plays, shows or stage representations. Watson would brook no competition on his 'walk' and wanted ample notice should he need the usual three weeks in which to submit an application for a licence himself. Watson had no intention of tying his company to a regular season at the New Theatre. It was to be 'visited as may suit his convenience'. The contract to let was drawn up and signed in August 1799 but rent was due to Fisher from December of the previous year so Watson had been committed by word of mouth even before the cottages were pulled down. £10 a year was a small rent to ask but Fisher hoped for a full house for four hundred people and a generous return on benefit night, a carrot Watson dangled before anyone who did business with him. Fisher could expect perhaps £45 from a good benefit and even if he had only a single good one in a year of two seasons this would bring the sum up to a reasonable though not large return. Each cottage, before demolition had been worth £4 a year. Fisher had this much from the one cottage on the street which he left standing. He moved into one of the two dwellings in the new house.

Using ready-hewn material from older buildings, as was the practice, construction progressed rapidly that winter under Fisher's exertions and by 11 February 1799 Watson was able to make the following announcement in the *Gloucester Journal*:

NEW THEATRE – CIRENCESTER

J. B. Watson respectfully makes known to the Nobility and Gentry of Cirencester and its vicinity, that MR. WILLIAM FISHER, Carpenter, is by contract to have the produce of the First Night's Performance and he humbly flatters himself that he shall not be thought intruding when he hoped that he will meet with general patronage; having at the same time the pleasure to announce to his good and heretofore liberal patrons, that the Building is one of the neatest and most commodious for its size to be seen anywhere, and that Mr. Fisher appears to have used uncommon exertions, and spared no trouble or expense – for the accommodation of a Generous Public. Mr Watson will forebear promises of what shall be done towards the entertainment of the Public, while he has the honour of catering for them; he wishes but to be encouraged as his endeavours may be found deserving.

The House will open with one of the most fashionable and popular New Plays and Entertainments.

Places to be taken and Tickets to be had of William Fisher: Boxes 3s. Pit 2s. Gallery 1s.

Particulars in the hand bills of the exact day of opening, Ec.'

Whether Watson was honoured with Nobility and Gentry, as hoped, on the opening night must remain doubtful for the local historian, Samuel Rudder, averred that the surrounding gentry did not patronise the town, its markets and activities.[4] With the town's professional personalities in the boxes, general patronage, good and heretofore liberal, would amply fill the benches: the mercer and draper, the clothier, the hose manufacturer, the spinner of yarn, the brewer, the bookseller, the optician, the surveyor, the grocer, the ironmonger, the shoemaker, the mason, the baker, the tallow chandler, the boiler of soap, the candle maker, the maker of knives, scissors and razors, in short all those who made up the life of the busy town.[5]

The sight that greeted the possessor of a seat on the front bench in the gallery on opening night can readily be inferred from reports and reminiscences about the interior and the existence of a contemporary theatre of the same type at Richmond, Yorkshire, which still stands.[6] The gallery had room for half a dozen or more rows of fixed benches rising on a stepped floor. The side galleries, two benches wide, also stepped, ran along the walls to meet the proscenium. Underneath these, along the walls and facing the stage, was a series of so-called boxes, in truth a repetition of the galleries with the benches divided, at each post supporting the gallery, by a low, short partition rather after the manner of stabling for horses. The central box might, for a special occasion, have individual chairs. The orchestra pit was on the same level as the pit. Above it was a fore-stage with a proscenium door on either side. The cloth curtain covering the proscenium opening would be the universal deep olive colour; the box fronts with their posts and the gallery above would be in shades of matt sea-green. This traditional auditorium colouring tended to soften the light shed by the candles hung on the proscenium frontage and stuck in sconces above the boxes, all of which were left burning throughout the evening. This subdued auditorium colouring also gave an illusion of increased brilliance to the stage lighting. Brightly decorated costumes viewed against pastel scenery irradiated a borrowed splendour once the dark curtain had been drawn up.[7] The panels of the box fronts were usually decorated with painted swags, garlands or devices appropriate to the drama. For Cirencester Watson chose floral wreaths after the example of the box front decoration of Robert Adam's Theatre Royal, Drury Lane. On an earlier occasion Watson had described the contents of a playhouse:

> The various treasures of the Drama here
> You'll find in elegance of dress appear;
> Beauty and wit, combined with art, to please,
> And give instruction, at your ease.

Ease in a country theatre consisted largely in the difference between standing and being able to sit. In the centre gallery only those in the front row had a view of the actors when seated and the knee room in the side galleries, albeit alleviated by sitting sideways, was so constricted that those in the second row along the wall invariably stood up and, like their fellows facing the stage, often stood on the benches.

The side boxes underneath were, in addition, restricted in height, although the sloping ceiling attached to the beams supporting the stepped gallery floor afforded space in which to stand at the back if headgear was removed. The elongated shape of the side boxes, too, forced early comers, and people who did not want to be disturbed by every new arrival, into those seats with a side view of the actors on the proscenium, since box patrons had to enter from the lobby by the narrow door peculiar to each set of side boxes. Both sets were cut off by a complete partition from the boxes in the centre. With the prices the same for all box seats, admission to the centre boxes was obviously determined by social standing or the early crossing of the box-keeper's palm. A concession to the élite entering boxes took the form of hinges on part of the benches so that progress to the front seats might be made decorously, feathers nodding with grace rather than in convulsion. The boxes facing the stage were, however, only slightly roomier than at the side since the space under the gallery had to be shared by the centre boxes and the tiny, shallow lobby necessary to give access to the three box doors, the steps into the pit passage and the stair rising to the gallery. The noisy cheek by jowl pressure on good manners can readily be imagined but once everybody was settled a steaming conviviality would reign. Watson had every reason to be proud of the neat and commodious new theatre he had presented to the town without an outlay from his own pocket.

The first season in the new house probably opened in March because an advertisement, dated 13 May 1799, is for an actor's benefit and these usually came at the end of a stay. That would allow a season of the maximum permitted sixty days and a timely opening for the summer at Cheltenham. The performer seeking the favour of the public on 13 May was Mr Seward who had chosen a comedy and his usual role of Harlequin to entertain the house. Samuel Seward

Samuel Seward, a member of the Cirencester company at the new theatre from its opening in 1799, was an agile harlequin, who also ran a marionette theatre in Cheltenham, as shown here in a drawing by James Winston.

was a mime, comic actor and dancer, 'an ingenious man', who held a further useful string in working a marionette theatre. In his early days he operated at Bartholomew Fair, London, each August when the cloth, cattle, leather and pewter market at Smithfield drew vast crowds to London to see performers of all descriptions display their exhibitions and shows. It was one of the most popular concourses of people in the kingdom.

For his last appearance in Cirencester that season Seward was to act in *The Secret* by Edward Morris in which the old rogue Torrid cheats his ward, Rosa, of her fortune. A comic sub-plot is provided by Lizard and his numerous progeny who make life unbearable for the loathsome scoundrel, Torrid. Was Seward himself Lizard? He had a family which helped to operate his marionette theatre and the play offered great opportunity for numerous offspring to appear and so get a share of the evening's takings. This play, the last of Morris's three comedies, had only made its appearance at Drury Lane a short time before. Between pieces Seward danced a hornpipe and then 'added (for this Night only) a Compilation, from the most favourite PANTOMIMES at the Circus and royalty, where such entertainments are got up in the first Style'. *Harlequin's Best Fancy* was a *potpourri* of the most bespangled pantomime episodes in Seward's repertoire. It included the birth and death of Harlequin with the skeleton scene and Harlequin's 'renovation' after his demise.[8]

The evening came to an end on a festive note, arranged by Seward and accompanied by much rhythmic stamping in the audience. The stage was entirely filled 'with a COUNTRY DANCE by the characters, in a New Scene, representing a prospect from Oakley Wood painted expressly for the Night'. This was a singular compliment to the town as everybody, boxes and gallery alike, knew Oakley Wood, part of Lord Bathurt's great park, to which the public were admitted, abutting the busy streets of Cirencester. There people flocked for *al fresco* meals, round games and dancing at the height of every summer. In laying out the park Lord Bathurst had in 1721 built what he called 'my refuge in the wood', the Wood House, as it came to be known, and the spot was so idyllic that this small refuge, 'but a cottage, not a bit better than an Irish cabin', made way eleven years later for what appeared to be a magnificent ancestral ruin that gave the impression to one visitor of 'a venerable castle'. The baronial hall that was its central feature was constructed with genuinely old stone windows and doorways and was adjoined by artfully decayed and broken walls. The castellation was elaborated in the ensuing few years and fragments of other carved masonry erected opposite to complete the romantic setting of a green flanked by noble ruins and backed with dark trees. The whole was soon 'with thicket overgrown, grotesque and wild'.[9] As Watson's scene-painter Barrett, was at that time entirely engaged on backcloths in Gloucester for a sumptuous production of Sheridan's *Pizarro*, the drop of Oakley Wood would have come from the brush of Seward himself. He did the decorations for his marionette theatre and often painted full-size scenery for the Theatre Royal at Cheltenham. In any case the composition would have been based on well known prints representing the Wood House with the ruined castellation of King Alfred's Hall, as it was called, on the left of the green and fragmentary arches and other 'ancient' masonry to the right.[10]

Shakespeare's *Hamlet* was promised. There was an oral tradition that Watson's old friend John Philip Kemble once acted on the

J. Taylor sculp

Seward painted a backcloth for his Benefit depicting the Gothic folly in Cirencester Park, which was the subject of popular prints.

Cirencester boards and in the summer of 1799 he appeared as Hamlet at Cheltenham and Gloucester. Possibly he also visited Cirencester. To open the theatre for a single performance by a leading actor was common and a special licence may have been forthcoming to allow Cirencester to see Kemble's 'sensible, lonely' portrayal of Hamlet. The commonly used acting version was still Garrick's in which, amongst other alterations, the final scene was much simplified to lend prominence to the great actor's dying agonies. Kemble's own edition came out a few years later.[11]

Though the theatre was generally closed during the summer while the company acted at Cheltenham, the house was specially opened at least for one night, on Wednesday, 7 August, to take advantage of the presence in the district of Mrs Edwin of the Theatre Royal, Bath, who had appeared the night before at the spa town. She came over to Cirencester to ensure a packed house for her father, Mr Richards, a comic actor who was a member of Watson's company. She did this often wherever he happened to be to raise money for him, every time as the bills proclaimed, after he had 'prevailed upon her to perform'.[12]

Three pieces never before seen in the town were given, opening and ending with musical entertainment to show off Mrs Edwin's singing voice. She was a small, fair creature and a great favourite in comedy and farce due to her charm and vivacity and her lively, expressive face. She was also a living advertisement for the lessons in music, singing and dancing Mr Richards gave to genteel young persons.[13] The first piece was *Lock and Key*, a Prince Hoare farce with music by the Covent Garden house composer, William Shield. After a selection of songs *The Wedding Day* which followed was Elizabeth Inchbald's last comedy and perhaps her most diverting. It is full of bright dialogue in amusing situations which are thrown up by Sir Adam Contest marrying a country girl. Things become devilish complicated on the appearance of his first wife and the junketing gets quite out of hand when Sir Adam's son begins to feel amorously drawn towards the errant mother. Richards was the embarrassed Sir Adam and the audience would appreciate with zest Mrs Edwin's Gloucestershire accent as she took them into her confidence with the song, 'In the Dead of Night'. *The Sultan* which ended the evening was an established musical farce by Isaac

Bickerstaff that had held the boards for more than twenty years.[14]

While the audience was laughing at the conquests of Mrs Edwin, who seemed to vanquish even the heat of the summer's night, Fisher in his dwelling at the front of the building had to admit that month that he was still unable to pay the interest that had been due since May and that he was further in debt. Neither augured well for the benefit he had hoped to enjoy. He turned for help to the begetter of his misfortunes and Watson's hard business sense seized the opportunity for acquisition. He loaned the carpenter £150 to pay off the mortgage plus a further £100 on condition that the whole of the property be transferred to himself (Watson) as surety. The theatre, as well as the two dwellings and the garden which Fisher had wanted to keep as his own, thus slipped from his hands. Watson was an astute collector of bricks and mortar and he did not want to lose the theatre to Whatley, the attorney, who would never have agreed to £10 and a benefit each season for rent. Financially the year seems to have been a successful one for Watson, though the Pitt government must have put a strain on both his pocket and his patriotism by demanding two shillings in every pound he earned to finance the war against France.

By the opening of the winter season in 1801 Fisher's fortunes took an upward turn; on 16 November, he was again enjoying his right to a benefit. The advertisement in the *Gloucester Journal* described him still as 'Mr Fisher, carpenter, a Part of whose Contract at erecting the new Theatre was to have the first Night each Season' and the disadvantageous agreement of the summer before, though signed by both parties and formally sealed as a binding contract, has written across the outside, in pencil, the redeeming words, 'laid aside'.

A short season was announced for that winter. 'The Town and Neighbourhood will please to keep in Mind, that the Theatre will be open but seven weeks altogether', but it got off to a good start for Mr Fisher's benefit with a light bucolic programme of *Speed the Plough* and the farce *Fortune's Frolics*, interspersed as usual with songs by the members of the company. *Speed the Plough* was Thomas Morton's greatest success and though it had appeared at Covent Garden only the year before it was already a universal favourite with its striking assortment of well-drawn comic and serious characters whose several stories eventually prove to be inter-related. The farce of *Fortune's Frolics* continued the romp over the same stretch of country. It was a piece by John Till Allingham that had come out at Covent Garden three years before and, besides having had one of the new-fangled reaping machines in the harvest scene on the Birmingham stage, was noteworthy for its villain, Snacks by name, the hard, grasping steward of Lord Lackwit. Here in a farcical afterpiece was a type of jet-hearted villain who would shortly be appearing on many an evening when melodrama became all the rage.[15]

Notes

1   The house and theatre behind it still stand at 27 Gloucester Street, Cirencester.

Anthony Denning knew the theatre building for more than twenty years and had opportunities to inspect the structure. Many of the points he describes are based on his own observations. He also uses some material contained in the deeds, now in the possession of the present owners, and, too, a detailed knowledge of the similar Georgian Theatre in Richmond.

2   Some material relating to the Cirencester Theatre is to be found in the 1803 indenture, Watson to Ray and Gibbon, now in the Warwick County Record Office, Warwick (CR 1596, Box 93).

3   The information is taken from James Winston's manuscript notes, made in preparation for his publication *The Theatric Tourist* (1805), now in the Winston Collection, Birmingham Central Library.

4   Samuel Rudder, *The History and Antiquities of Cirencester* (Cirencester, 1780).

5   Such occupations as these are listed in the Cirencester pages of the *Universal British Directory of Trade and Commerce* by P Barfoot and J Wilkes (1790–8).

6   A description of this small working playhouse is given in *The Georgian Theatre, Richmond, Yorkshire* (Richmond, 1962) by Richard Southern and Ivor Brown. Its history is told by Sybil Rosenfeld in *The Georgian Theatre of Richmond, Yorkshire* (York, 1984).

7   It is open to question how bright the stage appeared to the audience, although there are indications that the English stage was more brightly lit than that of the Comédie Française, Paris; see an article in the *Public Advertiser*, 14 September 1765 and Gusta M Bergman, *Lighting in the Theatre* (Stockholm, 1977).

8   Samuel Seward (1731?–1810) was a native of Bristol. He played in the Cheltenham company during the summer seasons. His children helped him in mounting puppet performances at the Sadlers Wells Theatre, Cheltenham, which he managed. See: *Historic and Local Cheltenham Guide* (Bath [1805]); Seward's obituary in the *Gloucester Journal*, 23 July 1810; George Speaight, *The History of the English Puppet Theatre* (2nd ed. 1990); and the entry for Cheltenham in the Gazetteer in this volume.

9   Descriptions of Oakley Wood and the baronial hall, which became known as 'Alfred's Hall', appear in: Samuel Rudder, *A New History of Gloucestershire* (Cirencester, 1779); [W K Beecham], *The History and Antiquities of the Town of Cirencester* (Cirencester, [1842]); A B Bathurst, *History of the Apsley and Bathurst Families* (Cirencester, 1903); David Verey, *The Buildings of England; Gloucestershire. 1. The Cotswolds* (1970); Jean Welsford, *Cirencester. A History and Guide* (Gloucester, 1987).

10   In the Richard Percival Collection of material relating to Sadler's Wells Theatre (III) in the British Library (Crach 1 Tab 4 to 4), one Seaward [*sic*] is reported to be working at the Wells on scenery for *The Magician of the Rocks* in May, 1796. This person may possibly be the Gloucestershire actor, painter and puppeteer, Samuel Seward.

11   *Gloucester Journal*, 8 and 22 July 1799. A playbill for Kemble's visit to Cheltenham is on display in the Cheltenham Museum and Art Gallery.

The versions of Shakespeare's *Hamlet* Denning seems to have in mind are: *Hamlet, Prince of Denmark. A tragedy altered from Shakespeare by J P Kemble, Esq* (1796, with subsequent editions dated 1797, 1800, 1804, 1818); *Hamlet, Prince of Denmark. A Tragedy* (1763 with subsequent editions dated 1755, 1768); see also George Winchester Stone, junior, 'Garrick's Long Lost Alteration of *Hamlet*', *Papers of the Modern Language Association*, LXIX (1934), 890–905.

12   Elizabeth Rebecca Edwin (1771–1854) 'improved herself' in the provinces (*Thespian Dictionary*, 1805). In the past Watson had made a 'liberal offer' to her to join the Cheltenham company (William Oxberry, *Oxberry's Dramatic Biography and Histrionic Anecdotes*, 1826). She had visited Cheltenham with her husband John (1768–1803) earlier in 1797; see entry by Joseph Knight in the *Dictionary of National Biography* (1908).

13   Denning bases his description of Mrs Edwin on that given by Phylis Hartnoll in *The Oxford Companion to the Theatre* (1976). Fuller, but less complimentary, are Margaret Baron Wilson's remarks in *Our Actresses* (1844).

14   *Lock and Key* was first performed at Covent Garden in 1796.

Elizabeth Inchbald (1753–1821) was requested by Richard Brinsley Sheridan (1751–1816) to write *The Wedding Day* (Drury Lane, 1794) as a vehicle for Mrs Jordan (James Boaden, *Memoirs of Mrs Inchbald*, 1833); the similarity of the acting style of Mrs Edwin with that of Mrs Jordan is mentioned by Wilson.

The Sultan was first performed at Drury Lane in 1775.

15   Such demonstrations on stage of reaping machines were to become more common as time progressed. James Dobbs (d 1837) was an actor at Birmingham and Gloucester and demonstrated on the stage of the former in a performance of *A Bold Stoke for a Husband* (by Hannah Cowley, first performed at Covent Garden in 1783) a similar machine which he had invented. See: newspaper cutting in the Foley Scrapbook, IV, in the Worcestershire County Record Office, St Helen's, Worcester.

Chapter 5:
John Richer

Mr Watson respectfully addresses the Town and Neighbourhood; and is happy in offering for the Entertainment of his ever good and generous Patrons not only the late and best Productions of the London Theatres, got up in a superior stile, but also those Incomparable Exhibitions of the first Performer in the World in his Way, RICHER, whose elegance and wonderful Abilities have gained him the Admiration of the principal Courts abroad, and of their Majesties, the Royal Family, and all the Nobility, at the Queen's Fete at Windsor. Due notice will be given when his Apparatus, Ec. are ready.[1]

The new attraction will have been awaited with considerable interest in view of the royal patronage and particularly because of the Queen's individual recommendation. Queen Charlotte's fêtes at Windsor were a new rung on the social ladder deemed to be of great importance by those who could not aspire to the heights of a reception at court. The royal fêtes were comparatively small, informal gatherings at which Her Majesty offered her daughters, household friends, local tradespeople and others entertainment in the gardens she had created at Frogmore in Windsor Great Park, about half a mile from the Castle. There was music and amusement and the whole resembled a gilded village fair amidst a generally relaxed atmosphere in which court etiquette could be laid aside. The royal command for John Richer to appear formed the strongest of professional recommendations to the loyal Watson. For he was a fair judge of a performer's ability and dedication and his generous announcement of the young dancer was no mere publicity exercise in order to draw overflowing houses. He had a great admiration for

50

Richer and had taken a genuine liking to the young man. He obviously appreciated his superbly professional skill. Richer had for some time been drawing fashionable London out of town to Islington where the crowds at Sadler's Wells Theatre had on his first appearance dubbed the nineteen year old youth 'Charming Richer!' During his first season at the Islington summer theatre in 1793 he had created a sensation and in a house well used to rope dancing his pre-eminence was recognised from the start.[2] Watson had engaged some of the star performers at Sadler's Wells for his circuit as far back as 1785. Ten years later he was in London in the autumn and he must have been attracted to Sadler's Wells to see John Richer while he was the rage at the height of his initial success.

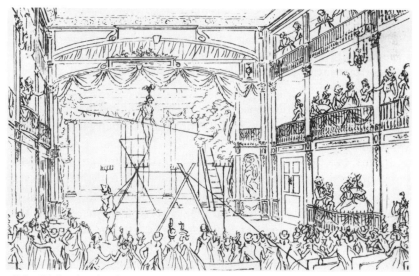

John Richer leaping from the tightrope at Sadler's Wells, as sketched by Anthony van Assen in 1795.

That year, 1795, an etching was on sale showing the interior of Sadler's Wells during the act of the most popular performer of the season. Anthony van Assen's sketch catches Richer at the apogee of his famous leap from the rope, the sort of feat that would determine Watson's showman heart to engage him at any price. Watson worked fast and succeeded in bringing Richer back to Gloucestershire with him, introducing the young man, aged twenty two, at

Tewkesbury in October. Richer stayed a month, taking a benefit in November, and was back in Gloucestershire the October of the following year. Watson cannily never stated in his bills what specific acts Richer would present. The seal of royal favour was recommendation enough!

Richer, at the age of twenty-seven, seems to have developed a physical appeal that made him desirable at closer quarters in drawing-room exchanges. It was at this stage in Richer's career that the critic and essayist, Hazlitt, saw him on the rope and was impressed by the dancer's superb performance so that he diversified his labours' by improvising a tight rope and trying to dance upon it'. When the essayist came to write 'The Indian Jugglers' in 1820 he could still say in abject admiration:

> It is a great many years since I saw Richer, the famous rope-dance, perform at Sadler's Wells. He was matchless in his art, and added to his extraordinary skill exquisite ease and unaffected natural grace.[3]

John Richer was still appearing at the Wells when Charles Dibdin jnr. took over management in 1800 but he left when Dibdin began swamping the programmes with the burlettas, pantomimes, operettas, farces, spectacles, musical entertainments, melodramas, burlesques and extravaganzas which the manager seemed to shake out of his sleeve. The London public wanted something new and the popularity of variety acts was on the wane. Richer was, in fact, the last rope dancer engaged at Sadler's Wells. He had already been trying in the provinces to find a new outlet for his masterly control of physical movement, probably with the encouragement of Watson who had obviously taken a lasting liking to the young man's qualities. Richer made his first appearance as a mime actor, under Watson's management, in December 1800 in the Grand Panto-mimical Drama, *Obi*, after the story of a negro robber, the terror of Jamaica who had finally been hunted down and killed in 1781. As soon as summer appearances at provincial theatres were over Richer was in Gloucestershire again and in October 1801 he appeared as Don Juan as well as the successful Three Fingered Jack.[4]

In January 1802 Richer announced his last appearance on the rope and failed to grace the opening of the redecorated Sadler's Wells when the theatre resumed under fresh management at Easter. He had been part of the entertainment there since childhood. Necessity had made Richer turn his back on London and seek a second career elsewhere but renunciation of his skill on the rope, flower of a lifetime of hard training, seemed incomprehensible. He was only twenty-nine.

Events in Cheltenham soon offered an explanation of this readiness, at the height of his power, to announce in the press an abrupt farewell to the international fame brought him by the danger every one saw in his extraordinary leaps. He and Louisa Watson, John Boles Watson's daughter, were married that spring. Was it to allay her fears that he agreed henceforth to be earth-bound? Watson forthwith incorporated his new son-in-law into his dynamic plan for his empire and made him manager for a season at Stroud which opened in April. Richer appeared as the leads in *Three Fingered Jack* and *Don Juan* and added a new pantomime ballet on a serious subject, *The Deserter* by Monsigny. He extended his repertoire with the evil Baron in *Alonso and Imogene*, the pageant in dumb show he produced based on the ballad by Monk Lewis, *Alonzo the Brave and the Fair Imogene*, and he went on to mime the dumb Francesco to Mrs Edwin's Selina in the melodrama, *A Tale of Mystery*.[5]

Notes

1 *Gloucester Journal*, 12 October and 9 November 1801.

2 Anthony Denning bases much of his information on Sadler's Wells and the young John Richer (b. 1773) on Richard Percival's collection of material relating to Sadler's Wells Theatre, vols II and III (British Library, Crach 1 Tab 4 b 4) and the second volume of H Barton Baker's work, *The London Stage* (1889). John Richer was the son of Jacques Richer, an acrobat and dancer who performed in Paris. There is further information in Thomas Frost, *Circus Life and Circus Celebrities* (1875) and George Speaight, *A History of the Circus* (1980).

3 William Hazlitt, *Table Talk* in *The Complete Works of William Hazlitt*, edited by P P Howe (1930–4), volume VIII. J P Malcolm described Richer in *Londinium Redivivium* (1802–07) as:

 . . . one of the handsomest and best made men in England. His skill . . . in dancing is aided by the most elegant motions, and his steps are infinitely more pleasing on the narrow diameter of a three inch rope, than nine tenths of our professed dancers on the stage. The wonderful leaps he takes, nearly his own height, terrifying those who see him for the first time. His correct manner of performing on the tambourine, when dancing, draws forth repeated plaudits.

John Richer is also mentioned in Charles Dibdin's *The Professional Life of Mr Dibdin written by Himself* (1803).

4   *Obi* by John Fawcett was first performed at the Haymarket Theatre in May 1800.

5   *A Tale of Mystery* by Thomas Holcroft, first performed at the Theatre Royal, Covent Garden, in November 1802 was said by John Genest (*An Account of the London Stage*, Bath, 1832, VII, 578) to be the first of the melodramas. The contention was based on Holcroft's subtle use of music as a commentary on the action. The role of Francisco was created by Charles Farley, not only an actor but also a highly experienced dancer responsible for the ballets at Covent Garden. Samuel de Wilde painted Farley in the part; the painting is now in the collection of the Royal National Theatre.

A bill for the Stratford Theatre (*A Tale of Mystery*, 16 March 1805) under Ray's management for the joint benefits of Mrs Barre and Mrs Keys indicates the heightened expectations which those who composed the copy aroused in their recounting of the plot of such melodramas.

Chapter 6:

The Winter Season of 1801–02

At the beginning of the nineteenth century the wage an actor received each week was variable and sometimes uncertain. It was said that Watson paid his actors one shilling in each pound of takings, plus the carrot of an occasional benefit, which amounted to between nine and fifteen shillings a week. A regular guinea was the wage he was prepared to pay those in his small band of leading permanent retainers. A beginner might expect five shillings for the first year and six and eight pence during a second. Five shillings a week was the wage paid to his farm labourers by Snacks, the hardhearted bailiff, in *Fortune's Frolics*.[1]

The man in charge of company discipline and the imposition of any necessary fines during the Cirencester 1801 winter season was William Buckle, stage manager, producer and prompter, one of Watson's steady retainers and already a veteran at the age of fortysix. He took on heavy roles himself while the lighter character parts in comedy and farce went to Robert Chamberlain whose eight years seniority and wide experience of the vagaries of theatrical life made him a reliable treasurer to the company. Chamberlain's memorable service to the theatre had been his kindly reception of the young John Philip Kemble when Mrs Siddons sent her brother to him with a recommendation, after she herself could find no opening for a raw recruit with her at Birmingham. Chamberlain took Kemble into his company during a season at Wolverhampton and gave him his professional debut in *Theodosius*, playing the title role, one that Cirencester had seen the young man's father act some twenty-five years earlier.[2] Although Buckle was accompanied by his wife who performed minor roles, Mrs Chamberlain is not mentioned and

Chamberlain was probably by this time a widower. His son, H by initial on the bills and Harry off stage, was juvenile lead and a dancer.

Of the other people in the company, the following are worthy of a mention. The principal dancer, as well as leading man and comic singer, was the versatile Field. Actor of all the chief comic roles was Richards, then in his fifty-sixth year. Miss Walton's father played a land-bound sailor amongst many small parts. A vocalist from Lichfield, in earlier days he had entertained visitors to Oakley Wood with his songs. Miss Weston's father bobbed incongruously from a lowly waiter in farce to young Captain Absolute in *The Rivals* while Miss Smith's father mimed and clowned his way through a variety of landlords and servants and her mother drew merriment from anything which was allotted to her. The leading lady of the company was the popular Mrs Carleton who with her husband had led the company in 1793 when they had acted Louis XVI and Marie Antoinette together. They had moved on to fresh fields after a benefit in April the following year and Mrs Carleton returned to the Watson company, this time alone, to lead the 1801 season.[3]

The only demand on Mrs Carleton's considerable powers one evening was to display anxiety and distress in the main offering of 'THE POINT OF HONOR, As done in three Acts at the Hay Market Theatre with the greatest possible Success and Approbation, from a German Original, and adapted to the English Stage, by Mr C Kemble', Charles, the youngest member of that theatrical family. The original was claimed by Watson as German, for everything German was then in fashion and everything French in bad odour because of the war; the original was, in fact, Mercier's *Le Deserteur*, a moving play based on a theme popular in the French theatre for the past thirty years. In *The Point of Honor* success was ultimately judged on the number of tradesmen's wives in the pit who fainted as the awaited hail of fatal shot was about to be fired. 'In Act III is introduced the very awful and impressive ceremony of shooting a Deserter' and to heighten the tension before the expected fusillade the scene was often 'provided with the necessary Military Parade' by borrowing trained soldiers from the local regiment of volunteers. On this occasion the 'Dead March and the ceremony used in Shooting a Deserter' had been presented in full and to the greatest effect for at the beginning of December 1801 Cirencester was fairly bristling with uniforms.

Ten days previously the North Gloucestershire Regiment had arrived in Cirencester with Colonel Kingscote of Kingscote at its head. He was a man known for his approval of theatricals. Smartness at drill had earned the regiment its entitlement to 'Royal' after George III had inspected the ranks on the downs beyond Weymouth in 1795. News of the impending arrival had prompted Watson to despatch from Cheltenham Buckle and Chamberlain to prepare at Cirencester a selection of suitable plays for a winter season to be graced by the troops.

Once the regiment had been billeted, Kingscote decided to bespeak a Saturday night performance for the entertainment of his men. The bill for 12 December 1801 was decorated with the royal arms and headed 'By Desire of Colonel KINGSCOTE and the OFFICERS of the ROYAL NORTH GLOUCESTER.'[4] The colonel's order for entertainment is the only recorded instance of a bespeak performance at the theatre in Cirencester. Theatrical performances were often given under the patronage of a corporation or club, the stewards of a race meeting, of a local personality, a lady of social distinction or a ranking officer, thus creating a fashionable night to which the gentry might be attracted. It was reassuring when taking tickets and places for a bespeak that the concourse of friends and acquaintances in the boxes would lend the evening the aura of a private party. One was certain of being seen in the right society and 'the best company would be surrounded by those they might be pleased to meet.' Bespeaks were for that reason frequent at nearby Cheltenham where the list of visitors to the spa was decorated with rank and title. The patron either guaranteed a certain number of guineas or bought a proportion of the better seats for distribution amongst friends, thereby gaining the privilege of choosing the entertainment for the evening. The services were always ready to sponsor a performance at the theatre. They were themselves keen amateur actors.

Colonel Kingscote's evening opened with military precision on the stroke of seven with Richards appearing before the curtain to recite an 'Ode on the Peace.' To start the entertainment proper the officers had chosen Mrs Hannah Cowley's popular comedy of

A bespeak performance at Cirencester in 1801 allows the regiment to take advantage of a brief pause in the Napoleonic Wars.

twenty years standing, *The Belle's Stratagem*, that paean to English beauty with its many lines and situations sure to draw approbation from the white gloves in the boxes at the slightest lead given by the gallant, fifty year old Colonel.[5] He was noted as a perfect and patriotic gentleman possessed of a truly British spirit of independence. It was well known locally that he had entered the Army early in life and served in Canada as a lieutenant until, at the age of twenty-two, he had inherited his uncle's estates in Gloucestershire where the family had lived since the twelfth century. After twenty years as respected magistrate and landlord at Kingscote the war with France had called him back to take up the colonelcy of the North Gloucestershire Regiment.[6] The hero on stage, Doricourt, just returned home from the grand tour, confidently throws off a weighted line, 'But I never found any man, whom I could cordially take to my heart, and call Friend, who was not born beneath a British sky and whose heart and manners were not truly English.' Rank and file would have agreed with this sentiment, perhaps vociferously, holding up Field's smiling Doricourt until he was permitted to resume after an obeisance. Letitia Hardy, the captivator of Doricourt's heart, was played by Mrs Charleton.

There followed a 'musical Entertainment, the Grand Dramatick Romance of *Blue Beard, or Female Curiosity!* with all the appropriate and characteristic Scenery'.[7] The curtain went up on

> a Turkish Village, a Romantick Mountainous Country behind it. Scene One displays the Procession of Blue Beard over the Mountains, with his Guards, Turkish Warriors and Attendants, Ec., being an exact Representation of Eastern Magnificence in Travelling . . . with a Stupendous Elephant, Bearing on his shoulders a Canopy, under which is seated the tyrannic Magician Blue Beard

followed by 'Horses, Camels, Palanquins, Banners, Ec.', this Procession over the Mountains paced to the beat of a Military March sounded on muted instruments as if from afar. All this splendour was achieved with perspective figures in the distance, reduced to appropriate size, cut out flat and painted in sumptuous colours, forming a procession almost as impressive as the parade of animals which had been made by Mr Johnston, the property master

59

at Drury Lane, out of pasteboard and papier mache in the London production of 1798. The equine grace he created had been considered 'surpassing admirable' even by the connoisseur of horseflesh and when the spectacle was revived at Drury Lane in 1811 memory claimed that Mr Johnston's quadrupeds had been far superior to the real menagerie animals that then made up the procession.

Second came

> a Grand Turkish Hall; afterwards the BLUE CHAMBER, Or, Cavern of Death with the shadows of Blue Beard's murdered Wives. Lastly the CASTLE from the top of which Irene perceives Selim at the Head of a Troop of Turkish Soldiers, who rescue Fatima and accomplish the Downfall of Blue Beard as he is about to slay her. Selim attacks him, and at the Instant, a SKELETON, striking the Tyrant with a Magic Dart, he is hurried away by FIENDS.

Long held single notes on a trombone had added a spine-chilling effect at Drury Lane.

Mrs Carleton obviously made a great impression with her Letitia Hardy in the earlier play *The Belle's Strategem*, for within a week, when she presented her Lady Townly in *The Provok'd Husband* at the combined benefit for Mr & Mrs Buckle and the two Messrs Chamberlain, the manager had to give out the old notice that 'Gentlemen are requested not to ask admission behind the scenes as all will be refused, that none may be offended'. Yet who the possessor of this magnetic personality was is not clear. Carleton, Carlton and Charlton, without first names, all occur in theatre companies during her lifetime and the variations in spelling appear to be used indiscriminately. Maybe the lady acquired her surname by marriage into the established Carleton company that toured the West Midlands successfully. She herself ventured into management a few years after her Cirencester appearances, taking a company of her own to Old Milford in January 1804. The choice of this small town at the south-west extremity of Wales was prompted by her confidence of success in entertaining service audiences. The natural roadstead of Milford Haven had sheltered a wartime government shipyard since 1790.[8]

Mindful of the pleasure on both sides of the footlights in having officers on stage, this resourceful actress laid plans with well weighted strategy for her forthcoming benefit night towards the end of the Cirencester season. The military appeared only too willing to be made captive by such a commander as Mrs Carleton, Colonel Kingscote readily gave permission for the whole Band of the Royal North Gloucesters to attend the New Theatre to shake the wooden structure with several Military Airs, while the young officers fell over one another to be rehearsed in their lines in order to appear with the lady in the farce. More ambitious volunteers came forward from their number to learn full parts and essay some heavy emotional acting opposite her in the serious play that was to open the evening. The benefit turned out to be something of a gala occasion for the boxes were (for that Night only) lined with carpet 'in order to render the House warm and comfortable'. Mrs Carleton may have approached Silk's Carpet Manufactory in Factory Yard further along in Gloucester Street and charmed, begged and borrowed odd strips and pieces with which to accommodate her Friends and the Public. This covering for floor and benches was the extent of the heating in the building despite the advanced winter, the presence of fires always being proudly announced on the bills lest they go unnoticed. Heating in public buildings was generally by open brazier. It had also been Mrs Carleton's intention to introduce burning coals into Cirencester New Theatre in some container or other to warm the response at her gala night, the lung-searing stench notwithstanding. In the event, the lady was able only in part to keep her promise that 'The Boxes will be lined with Carpeting, and Fires kept up during the whole Performance', which she had put out in her preliminary notice in the *Gloucester Journal* of the previous week. The promise of warmth was, in any case, an over-generous one and possibly made after the style of public relations used by Watson who at the same time announced a few nights at Gloucester where he begged 'to assure the Public, the House shall be made quite comfortable by constant Fires, Ec.Ec.' Managers usually committed themselves to no more than having the theatre 'well aired' which might entail little other than having had the stage fireplace in use during the morning's business of rehearsal. Fires or no fires, the pressing together into the confined space of a goodly crowd of excited bodies would have sufficed, without the addition of fumes from coke, to raise the temperature to a degree of warmth higher than most of the audience enjoyed in their homes or their places of work and higher by far than in any barrack room or private billet.

The winter that lay ahead was to be a hard one with its scarcity of grain and flour and the shortage of bread hardly less severe than in the previous winter of 1800–1801 when the poor man's standby of hasty pudding, flour boiled in milk, had started cold working days. During that winter a public subscription was raised in the town 'for the relief of the industrious Poor, amounting to nearly Six Hundred Pounds; and several weeks' distribution has already taken place, after the rate of the value of one shilling for every head of family, and sixpence each for every other member of it'. The enormous sum raised speaks loudly for the prosperity, wealth and generosity of the town's trading and professional classes, particularly since every purse had suffered attrition in the fifty per cent inflation in prices between 1799 and 1801.[9]

For her benefit night in the packed, 'warm and comfortable' theatre Mrs Carleton chose to show her powers as Calista in Nicholas Rowe's celebrated tragedy, *The Fair Penitent*. Richards was the proud Genoese nobleman, her father; Field was Horatio, the cause of the tragic outcome, and the 'haughty, gallant, gay Lothario' was played by one of the officers, all of whom, as amateurs, remained by custom un-named in the bill.[10]

Calista, the fierce, disdainful daughter of the princely Sciolto, is betrothed to Altomont (Buckle), a nobleman much in love with her strong and passionate temperament. He does not know that she had been seduced by the perfidious Lord Lothario and that Calista still dotes on her betrayer even though he has tired of her. On the appointed wedding day Horatio, brother-in-law and friend to Altomont, picks up a letter which shows where Calista's affections truly lie and Altomont himself witnesses confirmation of this in an exchange between Calista and Lothario. A duel ensues in which the nonchalant Lothario is run through. Old Sciolto is killed in the subsequent uproar and Calista, overwhelmed with grief at the loss of both the men she loved, stabs herself. The lurid story was borrowed, in outline at least, from Massinger and Field's post-Shakespearean tragedy, *The Fatal Dowry*, though the development of the characters was Rowe's own.

To stir other feelings after such ravishing of the emotions and to present happy hopes of immediate disbandment, Field appeared before a pictorial drop curtain and announced that it was his honour to recite an ode as spoken at the Bath Theatre by the celebrated Mr Elliston.[11] 'The Blessings of Peace and the Miseries of War' found ready response. Was it possible that the war with France that had strained the resources of the country for the past nine years could now be coming to an end? As Field recited, the drop, painted expressly for the occasion to depict destruction in war, was illuminated from behind and through its transparency there appeared as the footlights sank below stage level an allegorical picture painted on the reverse 'emblematic of Peace and Plenty'. It was the work of Barrett, the dancer, mime and scene-painter at Gloucester. Field continued to bear the brunt of the evening's entertainment, following on immediately with a selection of amusing songs, 'Jack at the Opera', 'The Chapter of Fashions' and 'The Origin of Old Bachelors', after which he was allowed to snatch a few minutes for quick change of coat whilst Miss Walton held the audience with a song un-named in the bill but alleged to be entirely new.

The after-piece of *Bon Ton* finished the evening.[12] In her part of Sir John's niece, ruined by town frippery, a transformed Mrs Carleton, Calista's pallor now banished with safflower powder, needed to establish her character on entry as the curtain rose for she had to let Lady Minikin (Miss Parsons) speak first. The means would be a gown so smart it could only have been provided by herself, her own latest and best, probably bought – or begged – from a grand lady at the end of that summer's Cheltenham season and bedecked with extra silk bows to point her frivolity and bear witness to her constant obeisance at the court of fashion. She could fairly sparkle as Lucretia Tittup the 'sweet', the 'heavenly', 'the finest lady in Europe', to her more intimate friends plain 'Titty'. Her Colonel Tivy, 'a bold young fellow and a soldier', younger brother of Sir Tan Tivy, was played by an officer of the regiment, as was Sir John's servant, Davy, who 'would turn rake and macaroni if he were to stay here in London a week longer'.[13] Besides wagering heavily amongst themselves about getting the parts they wanted, the officers had probably contributed handsomely to Mrs Carleton's benefit purse. The 'chaos' on stage was ultimately set right with the aid of a fire screen and opposing boudoir doors. The lines to draw the final curtain applause went to Sir John:

> I sally forth a knight-errant to rescue distressed damsels from these monsters, foreign vice and Bon Ton, as they call it; and I trust that every English hand and heart will assist me in so desperate an undertaking!

As was customary for a benefit night, Mrs Carleton had approached her friends and the leading townspeople personally and had had tickets and places in the boxes for sale from her lodgings, at Mrs Milton's in Dyer Street. Tickets for the pit and gallery could be had from the shop and office of Mr Turner, printer of the bills, in the Market Place next to the King's Head and from the bar-tenders at the principal inns. There was minimal control over the number of tickets on sale.

Another benefit, this time for Mr Knowles, box office keeper of the Cheltenham Company, also took place at Cirencester during the 1801–2 winter season. On this gentleman's services depended the asurance of a good place in the best part of the house. Admission to the theatre went nominally with possession of a token, though entry into the building might nevertheless have to be fought over, and in all parts of the house physical possession of a seat would prove nine tenths of the right to sit on it. For that reason servants were sent early to take possession of places in the boxes and the box doors were kept locked. To ensure that those taking box places would have somewhere to sit, spaces had to be allocated by the box office keeper. He was therefore a man of some account, for money achieved most things in all walks of life. The box office keeper needed to be experienced, discreet and reliable and as such could be a man of great consequence to frequenters of the theatre.

For his benefit night Knowles had brought a guest player, Stanley of the Theatres Royal, Edinburgh, York and Dublin, to draw the town in Sheridan's comedy, *The Rivals*. It was his first appearance in Cirencester and he had the task of presenting to a country audience Bob Acres, a country gentleman and would-be man of fashion, rival

64

of Captain Absolute (Weston) for the hand of the romantic young heiress, Lydia Languish (Mrs Carleton). Buckle played Faulkland, ever fretting over the whims and humours of Julia (Miss Parsons), ward of the testy old Sir Anthony Absolute (Chamberlain). The pronouncements of Lydia's aunt and guardian, Mrs Malaprop, 'as headstrong as an allegory on the banks of the Nile', were delivered by Mrs Smith.

Miss Weston and Miss Walton sang songs between the acts and the play was followed by the humorous interlude of *The Ghost*, a slight piece based on part of one of Mrs Centlivre's comedies. The amusement depended on the ability of the characters to get themselves out of embarrassing situations and tight corners, exercises that actors could readily elaborate upon with true comic business from personal experience. All of Mrs Centlivre's pieces were in due course brought to amuse the patrons at Cirencester and some were to hold the stage generally for as long as a hundred and fifty years. Mrs Centlivre would hardly have recognised *The Ghost* as presented at Cirencester, for only two characters remained from her success *The Man's Bewitched*. The light-hearted evening ended with the farce *My Grandmother* by Prince Hoare, a piece immensely popular for the opportunities it gave to the actors.[14]

Benefit bills, with their extra heading and name in large print at the top, long programme and occasional decorative edging in a wide border, were on larger sheets of paper than usual, eight by twelve inches as compared with six by ten. Playbills served as programmes at the theatre but were primarily intended to be distributed round the town as handbills and to be available at selected shops, the barber's and the main inns. Mr Watson always had his bills supplied locally wherever his company was acting but some companies printed their own bills on a small portable press which led a number of actors who left the stage to set up as general printer and booksellers in the hope of enjoying a steadier existence in the face of advancing age. Watson's habit of addressing his playbills to the vicinity as well as to the town was not empty form. His bills were carried afield until the population thinned, for at Gloucester in October 1790 there had been complaints of delay in bringing information of the renewed activity at the theatre. The most immediate method of publicity, however, was to have the offerings for the next night of acting announced from the stage at the end of the evening by the chief male actor in the main piece.

Some time during the last week of the season Watson himself came over to Cirencester, possibly from Gloucester where preparations for opening there could be left in the hands of Shuter or to son-in-law Richer who was getting ready a new production, 'with beautiful new Dresses and proper Scenery', of *Alonzo the Brave and the Fair Imogene.*

Watson probably had a manager's benefit and certainly appeared on stage to thank the Cirencester people for their patronage. He would collect the proceeds of the season from Chamberlain, the company's treasurer. When it came to giving out the next programme on the night of 4 January 1802 he dipped an indifferent quill pen and in the wide bottom margin of the bill for Knowles' benefit wrote a manager's request:

> 'Mr Buckle – I'll thank you to give out (after the 2nd piece) – as above
> 'With Good Emphasis and good discretion.'
> > > Shakespeare! – ahem![15]

This instruction, misquoted purposely from Polonius' praise of Hamlet's declamation when welcoming the players, is a jovial imitation of the manner of speech used by a tiresome, grandiloquent character in a play the company was giving that season. Dr Pangloss [All Voice], LLD, ASS, the tutor in Colman the Younger's *The Heir at Law* personifies the Englishman's favourite pastime of moralising. He quotes and misquotes from classical authors usually inappropriately, and after each display of faulty erudition pompously adjoins the name of the author, watching meanwhile for admiration mingled with awe from his listeners. Self-satisfied, he expresses feigned modesty and a loud 'hem!'. The faded note in browning ink at the foot of the playbill preserves the flowing hand and the lightness of temper that characterised John Boles Watson.

Notes

1   Leman Thomas Rede gives the salaries which the principal provincial managers paid later in the nineteenth century in *The Road to the Stage* (1827). Managers who bought some of the theatres of the circuit from Watson and his son are given here, together with the towns on their own circuit and the average weekly salary: J Bennett (Worcester, Wolverhampton, Loughborough, Ashby), 18/- (90p) to £1.5s (£1.25); Charles Crisp (Warwick, Hereford, Bridgenorth, Stourbridge, Carmarthen), £1.1s (£1.05) to £1.5s (£1.25); Jackman (Buckingham, Aylesbury, Bedford, Woburn, Wallingford, Woodstock, [Banbury]), £1; Charles Stanton (Stafford, Newcastle-under-Lyne, Drayton, Newport, Oswestry, Wrexham, Ashbourne, Burton-upon-Trent), £1.1s (£1.05).

2   *Theodosius* was written by Nathaniel Lee (1649?–1692), who in 1680 became mad and an inmate of Bedlam.

3   Much of the information here and later is taken from playbills of the Cirencester Theatre relating to performances at the turn of the century. There are collections of these in the Bingham Library, Cirencester; the Museum and Art Gallery, Cheltenham; and in the Gloucestershire Collection, Gloucester Public Library.

4   This playbill, giving a detailed summary of the play, is in the collection at the Cheltenham Museum and Art Gallery.

5   *The Belle's Strategem* was first staged in 1780 at Covent Garden.

6   The Gloucestershire branch of the Kingscote family lived at Kingscote Grange, Kingscote, near Tetbury, Gloucestershire, which house was sold in 1956. Many of Anthony Denning's remarks about Colonel Kingscote appear to be based on local knowledge of the family.

7   *Blue Beard* by George Colman the Younger (1762–1836) was first staged at Drury Lane on 16 January 1798. The original elaborate scenery which provincial theatres often emulated was designed by Thomas Greenwood the Younger (fl 1779–1822). In the London production the elephant was a mechanical one constructed by Alexander Johnston (d 1810), the Drury Lane machinist; he refused to hire a live beast from Pidcock's Menageria, claiming his own creation was preferable. See: *Memoirs of J Decastro*, edited by R Humphreys (1824) and Horace Foote, *A Companion to the Theatres* (1829).

8   See: the *Cambrian*, 1 January 1804. As Cecil Price points out in *The English Theatre in Wales* (Cardiff, 1948) small companies tended to come and go with great rapidity in South Wales.

Although Denning does not pursue the point, it is worth observing that Watson, according to the *Thespian Dictionary* (second edition, 1805), acted in Roger Kemble's company under the assumed name of Carleton. Was he in some way related to Mrs Carleton?

9   Some of the charities set up at the beginning of the nineteenth century are described by Jean Welsford in *Cirencester. A History and Guide* (Gloucester, 1987).

10   *The Fair Penitent* was first staged at Drury Lane almost one hundred years before this performance, in 1703. It is an example of a 'she-tragedy' with a heroine as the central character in place of the more usual hero.

11   Robert William Elliston (1774–1831), after touring the provinces, had made a successful debut at the Haymarket Theatre in 1796. He became one of the most popular actors of his day and eventually, in 1819, manager of Drury Lane. See: George Raymond, *The Life and Enterprises of Robert William Elliston* (1957) and Christopher Murray, *Robert William Elliston* (1975).

12   *Bon Ton* was written by David Garrick (1717–79) and first performed at Drury Lane on 18 March 1775, 'Bon ton' was a term synonymous with 'the height of fashion'.

13   A macaroni was an overdressed beau, sometimes posing as a versifier such as Sir Benjamin Backbite in *The School for Scandal* (first performed in 1777) by Richard Brinsley Sheridan. A selection of macaronic types are illustrated in *Comic Prints of Characters, Caricatures, Macaronis, etc.* (1776) by Mary Darly.

14   *The Rivals* by Richard Brinsley Sheridan was first staged at Covent Garden in 1775. Susannah Centlivre wrote *The Man's Bewitched* in 1709. *My Grandmother* by Prince Hoare was first staged at the Haymarket Theatre in 1793.

15   The bill is in the collection of the Bingham Library, Cirencester.

Chapter 7:

John Boles Watson II, William Hastings and James Winston

The *Heir at Law* was included in the 1802 repertoire in order to provide a congenial part for a lad of fifteen. John Boles Watson the Younger made his adult debut in that season as Zekiel Homespun, a warm-hearted, ingenuous farmer's son, protector of his older sister, with whom he has come up to the Metropolis to seek fame and fortune. The role of Cecily, his sister, was played by Mrs Carleton, just back from engagements at Brighton and Margate. She would shepherd him through the scenes they shared and for the rest Richards would keep the house happy with the Pangloss fatuities.[1]

For his benefit at Cheltenham on 11 October that year the young Watson essayed a very different role, trying his hand at the fiery, impulsive Belcour in Richard Cumberland's comedy *The West Indian*. As if doubting the lad's ability to carry the burden of the evening his father supported him by lavishing genuine native brogue on the Irish character part of Major Dennis O'Flaherty. William Hastings, a knowledgeable resident of Cheltenham experienced in theatrical affairs, after seeing the lad's attempt at the high-spirited Belcour declared quite bluntly, 'Jack will never be a Good Actor'. In the interval this young beneficiary was more at ease amusing his well-wishers with *The Cosmetic Doctor*, a skit on London fashionable quacks, fished from his father's ample rag-bag of songs. Coaching with singing possibly came from his musical mother. She may even have accompanied him on the pianoforte. *The Invasion* added a further topical touch to his solo offering. In two years he ploughed through an apprenticeship of no less than sixteen low comedy parts of blockheaded manservant and slow-witted country yokel. One of his best assumptions was the blundering manservant in a Colman piece, *The Review* and in this he appeared at a charity performance on the Bath stage in February 1804 when amateurs drew a large audience to augment the Bath and Bristol Theatrical Fund. This fund paid out support to actors who 'from age, infirmity or misfortune become incapable of exercising their profession' and besides the actors' own weekly subscriptions the public was asked to contribute through raised prices at an annual benefit. In this instance Watson Jnr. appeared under the wing of the recently widowed Mrs Edwin who was in the Bristol company and herself had the female comic lead in *The Review*. In April he again parcelled up his costume of green plus jacket, red waistcoat and buff breeches and journeyed to Bath to have his ears soundly boxed in *The Review* and the *Bath Chronicle* commented that he sustained the role 'with great characteristic simplicity and native humour' which can be taken as more than faint praise in a part which in London was entrusted to an experienced comedian, William Oxberry at Drury Lane and John Emery at Covent Garden.[2]

Of all the parts Jack Watson was to try, he discovered the line of business most congenial to him when he was only eighteen. Blackbeard the Pirate in the serious nautical spectacle of that name, as directed by Richer, allowed Jack Watson to expand as a married, faithless, lecherous and violent seducer. The Pirate's terrifying roar of 'Should the enemy prove victorious, Blow up the Ship!' would become something of a motto for the career into which the lad was feeling his way.[3] 'My dear son', as John Boles Watson fondly termed the youth, must have been proudly presented at about this time to the patrons at Cirencester but there is no news of a play in the Gloucester Street theatre at all during the five years that follow the close of the military winter season that ended in January 1802.

Most of Jack Watson's early attempts at adult roles were made in Warwick during the first season at Watson's New Theatre in Cocksparrow Lane which opened on 7 September 1802, despite the work that had to be carried out to finish the building. Richards was in charge of rehearsals and performances while the general direction of business was under Richer, now partner with his father-in-law in the theatrical enterprise. John Boles Watson was busy at Cheltenham bringing the summer season to a close and waiting for Jack Richer to return for a few nights to lend some distinction to the programmes at the depleted spa where business was poor.[4]

Obviously tired ('It is Twelve O'clock and I am almost Asleep.') and disgusted with the Watson benefit he had just sat through, Mr Hastings scribbled late on 5 August 1803 a hasty letter. It was a disgrace, he wrote, that Jack Watson's Belcour, with 'the old man' as Major O'Flaherty, should have filled the Theatre Royal Cheltenham to the tune of over £50 while the previous evening George Frederick Cooke (a great portrayer, particularly after drink, of the baser qualities in man and thus an electrifying Richard III) had harvested a meagre £25 for acting both in the play and the farce on his last night.[5] The Watsons must have been regarded with generous affection by their patrons to have reaped such a gratifying benefit because in the same season Mrs Siddons, then at the height of her fame, had been able to draw houses of only £65 as Mrs Haller in *The Stranger* and £70 as Mrs Beverley in *The Gamester*, despite double charges for admission to all parts of the house.[6] Commenting on the stock actors who brought entertainment to Cirencester, Hastings thought that 'on the Whole the Company is very indifferent' and having endured a farce, *Simple Simon*, he declared the author deserved a flogging, adding 'I am surprised the Manager can suffer such Nonsense to be performed'. He went on to relate that Macklin's satire, *The Man of the World*, was got up in so imperfect a state that Cooke declared next day that 'he would sooner be confined six months in the County Gaol than go over such another Night'.[7] Hastings was writing to James Winston, actor and newly part-owner of the Theatre, Plymouth, whom he had met the previous September while Winston was appearing with the Cheltenham company as a guest attraction.

Although Winston and his actress wife were presented as stars from London, the actor had come to Cheltenham with a flea in his ear. Only six weeks previously he had been so roundly hissed off the stage at Covent Garden in a comedy role that he appears never again to have graced the boards of a patent theatre in London. His usual haunt had been the summer season at the Haymarket where his line had been character comedy and farce, the mainstays of that theatre. At Cheltenham he finished his benefit night with the operatic farce, *Perseverance*, in which he played no less than five different characters, an amorous captain, a Frenchman, an idiot, a yokel and

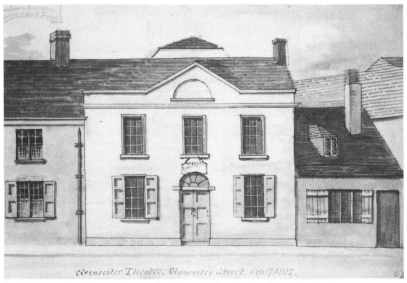

The Theatre in Cirencester, as in 1802. A drawing by James Winston.

an old woman. Though he laid no claim to it in the bill, the farce was from his own pen.[8] Winston was not, despite the self-confident five-part tour de force, a gifted actor and when he applied for a Cheltenham engagement the following year his services were not required. Success came to him in London subsequently as acting manager at the Haymarket, the Olympic and finally at Drury Lane.[9]

As theatrical chronicler and diarist and an avid collector of anything pertaining to theatrical life, Winston is now remembered; it was his intention to compile a record of every public place of entertainment in the British Isles with a list of all their known past performances. Whilst he was in Cirencester Winston drew, or obtained – it is unsigned though dated – a finished water colour view of the Gloucester Street front elevation of the Cirencester Theatre, which is now in the State Library of New South Wales, Sydney. This, as is the note at Harvard, is dated 17 September 1802. The drawing measured 7″ by 10½″ and shows the facade virtually as it still is today (1988) with its wide street door in the centre topped by a semi-circular fanlight and flanked by two sash windows of twelve small panes each. These three openings are matched above by three similar windows. The wooden shutters to the lower fenestration have gone

72

The theatre building as it is today.

as has a parapet at roof level which had at its centre a blind gable. The name of Weston, as nominal local manager, can be read on a board over the entrance, the full text of which ('Dealer in Tea and Coffee, Tobacco and Snuff') is given in a note pencilled in the margin, thus providing an indication of what might have been supplied in the intervals. The higher roof of the theatre proper rises behind the roof ridge of the dwelling house, as it does today. Next to the building on the right is a humble one-roomed cottage with an attic window in the roof giving a good idea of the tiny dwellings forming the Barracks, most of which were demolished to make way for the Theatre. This cottage left a trace of its roof-line where it joined the Theatre which can still be seen today. The cottage disappeared in 1808 when the town's Wesleyan Chapel was built. Unfortunately Winston recorded no details of the interior of the Theatre, not even its capacity. Presumably it was in its main features similar to any other playhouse in the provinces.

Winston's plan to issue a guide to the main provincial theatres of the British Isles in thirty parts led to the amassing of a vast amount of manuscript material through correspondents such as Hastings who supplied a drawing of the new Cheltenham Theatre made by a lad apprenticed to the builder. The first part of the guide, describing these theatres with a hand-coloured plate of the exterior of each, came out in March 1804 but the work failed to catch the interest of the public at large and, after the appearance of eight numbers, publication ceased. In an attempt to recoup some of his losses Winston had the unsold parts, plates and descriptions of twenty four theatres, bound together and issued as a book in 1805 under the title, *The Theatric Tourist.*

Winston did not have much good to say about the Watson company of actors, making the curious remark that the manager had several companies of which he retained the worst at Cheltenham where he depended for business on imported stars. In point of fact the company in which Winston acted Bob Acres at Cheltenham was exactly the same as had supported Stanley in the role at Cirencester and consisted of all Watson's leading players. The impression that Watson had several separate companies may have arisen from his letting his theatres and players off to his leading members, Buckle, Richards, Adamson, Chamberlain and Shuter, to try their luck at management on their own account in the hope of a good financial return. Winston did not enjoy the Spa and had nothing but contempt for the Cheltenham Theatre and all Watson's works. William Macready called Winston 'a miserable weasel creature' but Winston should rather be remembered as the industrious recorder of the theatres of his day. It is significant that he intended to include Cirencester in his list of noteworthy theatres in the British Isles.

Eventually Evangelism came to challenge the Cirencester drama on its very doorstep when in 1808 the Strict Wesleyans of the Old Persuasion built a substantial chapel, which still stands, adjoining the Theatre with similar gallery and exactly the same seating capacity. Something had to be done to halt the creeping erosion into theatrical business and Watson found it necessary to bring in entertainment more sensational than the old plays with their stock characters the public had grown used to over the past ten years.[10]

Notes

1   *The Heir at Law*, a comedy by George Colman the Younger, was given its first performance in 1797 at the Haymarket; it held the stage until 1906. Dr Pangloss, one of the farcical roles, is a greedy, pompous peasant.

2   *The Review, or The Wags of Windsor* by George Colman the Younger was first performed at the Haymarket Theatre in 1800; *Bath Chronicle*, 14 April 1804.

3   *Blackbeard the Pirate, or The Genoese Pirate* by J C Cross, first performed at the Royal Circus, 9 April 1798.

4   Prior to 1802 Watson has leased a building in Cocksparrow Street, Warwick. Wishing for improved premises, he attempted to negotiate a site in the Market Place but this arrangement fell through and he returned, presumably (accounts are not clear) to his original site and there rebuilt the playhouse.

5   The letter of William Hastings to James Winston (born James Bowes 1773 or 1779; died 1843) together with a bound copy of issues of *The Theatric Tourist* (1805) is in the Winston Collection in Birmingham Central Library. One of Winston's preparatory notebooks is also here and a further containing brief jottings about the Cirencester Theatre is in the Theatre Collection of Harvard University.

6   *The Stranger* was first performed at Drury Lane in 1798; it was a version by Benjamin Thompson of A F von Kotzebue's *Menschenhau und Reue*. *The Gamester*, a tragedy of some worth, was written by Edward Moore and first performed at Drury Lane in 1753.

7   G F Cooke (1756–1812) as Sir Pertinax McSycophant in Charles Macklin's play *The Man of the World* (first performed at Covent Garden in 1781) is considered in *G F Cooke, The Man and the Actor* by Arnold Hare (1980).

8   *Perseverance* by James Winston was first performed at the Haymarket in 1802.

9   See *Drury Lane Journal: Selections from James Winston's Diaries 1819–1827*, edited by Alfred L Nelson and Gilbert B Cross (1974).

10   The capacity of a theatre was usually expressed as the sum which would be taken at the box office on the night of a full house. I suspect that Denning has arrived at his estimate of the similar capacity of the two buildings by measuring the area of each which would be occupied by seating. It has to be remembered that in a theatre almost half of the ground area was taken by the proscenium, stage and dressing rooms.

Chapter 8:
A Relinquishment and a Return

Lengthy negotiations and the drawing up of innumerable draft leases resulted in the announcement by John Boles Watson that he had relinquished all business interest as a manager and handed over to Messrs. Ray and Gibbon who 'undertook the entire Management of the concern'. Edward Ray of Bethnal Green and George Collins Gibbon of Fenchurch Street, London, both actors, the latter said to be 'from the Theatre Royal, Covent Garden', acquired, for the sum of £1500 per annum, the use of the theatres at Cheltenham, Gloucester, Warwick, Stratford, Banbury, Walsall, Alcester, Tamworth, Evesham, Brecon, Stroud and finally of the theatre at Cirencester. Most of these houses had been little used in previous years.[1] In a separate agreement the new managers also acquired on lease for twenty-one years a theatre that Watson had begun to build in Cheltenham, the rent to be £200 per annum. This theatre was to open on the King's birthday, 4 June 1805.[2] By May 1803 Watson had abdicated from the running of all the theatres he possessed because of illness. He was fifty-five years of age. The nature of the illness is nowhere stated but is described as being 'occasional' and it did not prevent his appearing at the Cheltenham benefit for his son-in-law that autumn.

After lying sick for a short while at her father's house behind the Cheltenham Theatre, Mr Watson's daughter, Louisa Boles Richer, died unexpectedly on 17 July 1804.[3] Watson was shattered by the loss and expressed the wish, when he died, to be buried in the same grave as his much loved daughter. He had always evinced strong concern and affection for her and as her name never appeared on a theatre bill she may always have been of a delicate constitution, lacking the strength so abundantly radiated by her husband John Richer. The couple had been married just over two years. Louisa must have been in her early twenties and was especially dear to her father as the only child of his first wife, who had also died young. When he had married Henrietta Brown, a widow, as his second wife at Cheltenham by special licence on 18 October 1785 he was himself a widower, aged thirty-seven. Watson made a new will in which he bequeathed to his son-in-law, Richer, an annuity of £160, an indication that the latter's marriage had been a happy one.[4] This was an extraordinary gesture of affection towards Jack Richer. The bequest was similar in amount to the destined annuity for the support of Henrietta, his wife.

Difficulties in business and the effects of post-war inflation brought a final deterioration in the affairs of Mr Fisher, the builder of the Cirencester Theatre, during 1806. That September he was forced to sell not only the whole property in Gloucester Street (the dwelling house where he lived, the garden and also the Theatre) but also a house at the corner of Dollar Street and Thomas Street as well as two adjoining houses in the latter. The Theatre became the property of Joseph Pitt of Cirencester.[5]

When a short season opened with a Favourite Play and Entertainment at Cirencester on Monday, 11 May 1807, the managers, Ray and Gibbon, gave the first night as a benefit for Fisher, although he must have lost his right to that when he sold the theatre building. Ray and Gibbon were under no obligation to him and the prime mover behind the gesture may have been Watson. The state of Fisher's affairs were, however, not to be redeemed by the proceeds of one night. He left the town and moved to Cheltenham.

This benefit seems to have come at the end of what may have been a run of lean years in entertainment at Cirencester. Ray and Gibbon must have neglected the town, playing infrequently or at irregular intervals and to have allowed the fare offered to sink to a low standard for, after serious complaints, they issued the following on the day of the special benefit that opened the season:

The Town and Neighbourhood are respectfully informed that a few Evenings' Amusement will be presented previous to the Cheltenham Season; the Performers are selected from the first Provincial Stages, as every thing will be done to merit public favour, by due attention to regularity, and the production of proper and most popular New Pieces, the Managers hope to be honoured with encouragement and patronage.[6]

The days of playing were three a week as before and the visit seems to have been a trial run for new plays got up to amuse the visitors to the Spa, albeit without the London stars.

The announcement also bore the strongly worded ruling, 'No Admittance, on any account, behind the Scenes'. There are indications that the Theatre at Cirencester, in common with other provincial theatres of the time, afforded direct access from the pit passage to the dressing rooms under the stage and it sounds as if some patrons might have gone beyond directing their admiration across the footlights. Visitors behind the scenes were a nuisance even when they only stood in the wings on a benefit night, having contributed towards the benefit purse. At the time of his grand ballet pantomimes when his stages were crowded with dancers Watson had declared that 'The same attention and punctuality will be observed as in the London Houses; and no person whatsoever admitted behind the Scenes', to which he later added . . . 'or at Rehearsals'.[7]

At this low ebb after four years out of active management, Watson found it a ripe time to return to the running of the theatres he owned or rented. The new Theatre Royal at Cheltenham was now well established after initial financial troubles and he himself was apparently sufficiently restored in health to set about the revitalisation of theatrical life in Gloucestershire. To assist him, now that Richer had returned to touring, he made his old hand Buckle co-manager, possibly to supervise the theatres away from Cheltenham for Watson wished to avoid travelling and also to keep himself free to plan further expansion. He was first and foremost a man of business. His patrons' amusement was his pleasure.

The following announcement appeared in the *Gloucester Journal* (1 June 1807):

Mr. Watson respectfully makes known that, as he is again entering into the concern, he will, as he ever did, to the best of his power, cater with spirit and liberality for the entertainment of the Public. During the close of the London Houses, he has engaged a succession of the very first professional talents for Cheltenham; and, feeling it is his duty as well as his inclination to gratify his kind Patrons at Glocester [*sic*] and Cirencester, as occasion may offer, he has stipulated with Performers of eminence, to appear one night at least in each place.

On Tuesday, Thursday and Saturday the company would perform at Cheltenham. The night for Gloucester in these summer openings was to be Wednesday and Monday was reserved for Cirencester. The new leaf was not turned without some misgiving for Watson and Buckle hoped 'that Opening the Theatre one night a week in each town, and especially having to boast on that one night a Performer of superior note, will induce a general inclination to encourage the amusements of the Drama, and prevents the formation of Card Parties Ec.Ec. thereby enabling the Managers to support the Theatre with becoming propriety and effect'. The house needed to be full on such a night, as performers of superior note demanded a higher fee than they could command in London. Just a few weeks after the appearance of Watson's announcement Mrs Siddons, writing a letter from Liverpool noted:

> I can't expect to be followed like the great genius, Master Betty, you know; but I hope to put about £1000 into my pocket this summer. Tis better to work hard for a short time and have done with it.[8]

The first leading talent to appear was Mrs H Johnston, an actress with a handsome, amazon-like appearance who brought an evening of comedy though she was reckoned equally effective in tragedy and accounted a good Lady Macbeth. She came of a theatrical family and had met and married the actor, Henry Johnston, at an early age, appearing with him in Ireland and later in London where she played Ophelia to his Hamlet at the Haymarket in 1798. She was the original Miss Blandford in *Speed the Plough* when he was the original Bob Handy. There were six children of the marriage but she and her husband later became estranged. That lay in the future, however. When she came to Cirencester she was still only twenty-five.[9]

For her main offering she appeared as Letitia Hardy in *The Belle's*

Strategem, Mrs Carleton's role on the military bespeak evening in 1801. She also appeared as Nell, the cobbler's wife, in *The Devil to Pay*, a part which had brought fame and fortune to many a comedy actress.[10] Mrs Johnston returned for another appearance at Cirencester that season on 15 June, choosing to act Juliet in Shakespeare's tragedy and Roxalana in *The Sultan*, the part Mrs Edwin had performed some years before.[11]

29 June 1807 would have drawn all the town. William Henry West Betty was to appear. He was billed simply in the name he was universally known by, 'The Young Roscius', after the celebrated master actor of ancient Rome. Betty was now nearly sixteen and relying rather more on his true histrionic ability than when he had taken London by storm as a juvenile in the season of 1804–5. He had created a sensation then and had maintained his spell for one season more so that established players, notably Mrs Siddons, had stayed away from town, disgusted at the taste displayed by the public that clamoured after an inexperienced boy and declared him a Garrick reborn.[12] Eventually the public's revulsion at its own unbalanced taste caused it to decry the boy as wholeheartedly as it had fêted him earlier. Publicity played no small part in the creation of the original success and his father and his Irish instructor, William Hough, maintained a subtle barrage which left the tale that Prime Minister William Pitt adjourned Parliament to witness Betty's Hamlet.[13]

On Monday 17 August the Cirencester Theatre saw the most remarkable performance in its thirty years' existence. Sarah Siddons made a single appearance. At the age of fifty-two she felt that her health would not support an active career much longer and, declaring that she would soon retire, she went into the provinces that summer to make a farewell tour. Although she did not give up the stage entirely until 1812, she had already undertaken no new roles for five years. Cheltenham had been the scene of early success for her in Watson's former theatre and she made frequent return visits during his summer seasons. Now she was to make her first acquaintance with his new Theatre Royal there and had been engaged to appear on every acting night for a week, giving a selection of her greatest interpretations. She was advertised to play Zara, the Captive Queen, in Congreve's *The Mourning Bride*, which she repeated at Gloucester, then Margaret of Anjou in *The Earl of*

Warwick and finally, in Cheltenham, Euphrasia in Arthur Murphy's *The Grecian Daughter*. She was to have finished her visit with the performance at Cirencester but she was prevailed upon after this to return to Cheltenham, give her Elvira in Sheridan's *Pizarro*, go to Gloucester again to give Margaret of Anjou there and finally to make her farewell at Cheltenham in the greatest of all her roles, Lady Macbeth.[14]

Passing ready dressed in black along the pit passage on her way to the stage of the Cirencester theatre she may not have relished the smell of damp that assailed her nostrils but she can only have been pleased to look through the pit doorway up into the small, old-fashioned, rectangular auditorium and mark the intimacy of it. While the after-piece was being performed, Mrs Siddons was probably on her way again to Cheltenham by hired post-chaise. Little strength of imagination is needed to see her travelling back, glad that she had found time before the performance to visit Cirencester Parish Church where her parents had been married fifty years previous.

Notes

1   T F Dibdin mentions in *The History of Cheltenham and an Account of its Environs* (Cheltenham, 1803) that Ray and Gibson had become co-managers. The draft indenture of co-partnership is preserved in the Warwickshire Record Office, Warwick, CR 1596, Box 93. *Gloucester Journal*, 9 May 1803.

2   Watson bought a plot on Cambray Meadow, Cheltenham in 1805, inviting subscriptions at £100, later advertised as subscription shares with the right of free admission at 150 guineas. He built a new theatre in Bath Street, Cambray on the site of the Garrick Head at a reputed cost of £8000. A description of the Bath Street theatre and its opening is given in *The Historic and Local Cheltenham Guide* (Bath [1805]); see also: Theodore Hannam-Clark, *Drama in Gloucestershire* (1928).

3   *Gloucester Journal*, 23 July 1804.

4   Warwickshire Record Office, Warwick: drafts and wills of John Boles Watson dated 1800, 1802 and 1804. (Materials relating to Warwick Theatre, CR 1596, Box 93).

5   Joseph Pitt was Bailiff of the Borough; see: *Universal British Directory, Gloucestershire* (1791–8).

6   *Gloucester Journal*, 4 May 1807.

7   *Gloucester Journal*, 1 June 1789. The notice refers to the stage of the Booth Hall in Westgate Street, Gloucester, which Watson used throughout the 1789 season as his venue.

8   Cited by Thomas Campbell in *The Life of Mrs Siddons* (1834), II, 319–320.

9   Mrs Henry Erskine Johnston, née Parker (b 1782), made her first appearance at the Haymarket in the role of Ophelia, playing the same part a year later at Covent Garden. She was applauded in comedy. Dighton made an engraving of her on horseback in the role of Zorilda in *Timour the Tartar* by Matthew Gregory Lewis. See: *The Thespian Dictionary* (1805).

10   *The Devil to Pay* by C Coffey and J Motley, first performed in August 1731 at Drury Lane.

11   *The Sultan* by Isaac Bickerstaff was performed at Drury Lane in 1775.

12   A letter in the John Rylands Library, Manchester, from M Wilkinson to Mrs Thrale (5 October 1804) sums up Mrs Siddons' feelings about William Henry West Betty (1791–1874) in her reference to him as 'the puppet'. See: *The Letters of Sarah and William Siddons to Hester Lynch Piozzi*, ed. Kalman A Burnim (Manchester, 1969).

13   The career of Betty is given in the anonymous *The Life of William Henry West Betty* [1804], published by John Fairburn. His performances are studied in John Bisset's compilation *Critical Essays on the Dramatic Excellencies of the Young Roscius* (1804). See Giles Playfair, *The Prodigy, A Study of the Stage Life of Master Betty* (1967).

14   The roles Sarah Siddons undertook on this tour are described, as she played them at her last appearance in Dublin, in a series of letters 'from a lady of distinction, to her friend in the country' published as *The Beauties of Mrs Siddons* (1786).

Chapter 9:
Pageants and Celebrities

In September 1807 an elderly favourite of the public managed to cram an appearance into her crowded list of engagements: 'The Public are respectfully informed that previous to the opening of the Dublin Theatre, to which Mrs Edwin is hastening, after the conclusion of her engagement at Portsmouth, she will stop one night at Cirencester, Cheltenham and Gloucester'. Any programme headed by the warm hearted Mrs Edwin could easily fill the house to satisfaction. There was no need to announce the titles of the play and entertainment in which she would appear.

The season ran on until November 13th, the only other named programme being for Wednesday, 4th. On that night John Tobin's *The Curfew*, a new play from Drury Lane, was given. The piece, in the very latest romantic taste, was spoken in elaborate pseudo-Elizabethan language and had louring castles, dank caves and honest hovels as a background for the triumph of virtue and the defeat of base villainy. The music to this melodrama was by Thomas Attwood, son of a rich trumpet-playing coal-merchant who sent the lad from London to Vienna to become a pupil of Mozart. After developing into a prolific composer for the theatre in his early days, Attwood latterly devoted his talents to the church, eventually becoming organist at St Paul's Cathedral and music master to the royal family.

That evening ended with the famous *Shakespeare Jubilee*, a spectacular entertainment in two parts with dialogue, recitations, dances, songs, choruses and glees, which Garrick had devised and put on at Drury Lane in 1769 in order to recover the money he had lost in mounting the ambitious jubilee celebrations at Stratford-

A procession of characters from Shakespeare's plays had been planned as part of the Jubilee celebrations at Stratford-upon-Avon. It was staged by Garrick at Drury

upon-Avon in the September of that year. The jubilee (which, incidentally, marked the anniversary of no known point in the Bard's career) had been ruined by repeated and unprecedented downpours of rain during the major part of the three-day festival and a grand procession through the town of all Shakespeare's leading characters in magnificent costume had been cancelled.[1] It was claimed, extravagantly, that Garrick had expended £50,000 on the planned events. He had been made a freeman of the town in gratitude for his labours. On returning to London, Garrick wrote a stage show to make use of the cancelled procession, incorporating the songs he had specially written for the Stratford Jubilee and as the finale the cast re-enacted the crowning of Peter Scheemakers' statue of William Shakerspeare with a circlet of laurels as had happened in Stratford. There was something for every taste in the show, spectacle, farce and the music of Charles Dibdin, Thomas Arne and Thomas Attwood.[2] Its success was repeated at Drury Lane for almost one hundred nights.

The costumes in the original had been of the richest kinds of silk, satin and brocade decorated with galloon and ostrich feathers, all made to glitter out of the shadows with tinsel and applied pieces of coloured glass. How Mr Watson compressed so much splendour

Continuation of the Procession of Shakespears Characters.

Lane, and a version was mounted at Cirencester in 1807.

into the confines of the Cirencester Theatre is best left to his usual ingenuity and how he stretched his company to fill out the length of the procession defeats imagination unless he resorted to a common ruse whereby the patrons who bought tickets for the boxes could come round behind the scenes in the interval and be decked out with feathers, lengths of stuff, swords and head pieces and so swell the throng needed to parade across the footlights. It was often done when a masquerade or ball was called for in a play. A trifling extra fee from the box holders would be appropriate since as amateurs they would expect to pay for appearing on stage amongst the professional company. The gentry were incurably keen on amateur theatricals at the time.[3]

From 1807 to 1810 all news of the Cirencester Theatre lapses and it is likely that visits by the Cheltenham company were only sporadic. The country had other things to think about. The first half of 1807 was filled with news of widely dispersed disasters to British arms in the struggle against Napoleon. In July Buonaparte signed the Treaty of Tilsit with the Czar of Russia, thus isolating England and leaving her to carry on the struggle alone. July 1810 brought news of the death of Samuel Seward, the man who had endeared himself to the Cirencester public, firstly with his antics as Harlequin and secondly as painter of the Oakley Wood backdrop that graced the opening season of the new Theatre in 1799. At the age of 73 he had danced Harlequin 'with his usual activity' the night before he died. His puppet theatre at Sadler's Wells House in Cheltenham went, with considerable property in the town, to his son, Abraham, who also continued the business of painting scenery for the Watson company.[4]

Jack Watson, who had leased the Theatre Royal in New Street, Birmingham, was proving to be a chip of the old block in that he damaged the painted decorations of the auditorium of the Theatre Royal. Burning inferior oil and cheap tallow candles was an economy he had learnt from his father. The proprietors accordingly found him an unsatisfactory tenant but the Watsons seemed to have got away with a financial success by installing stoves in the theatre lobbies thereby giving Birmingham its first winter season of theatricals in the face of the bitter weather around the change of year 1808–09.[5]

Mrs Watson acted and sang in the early Birmingham performances and then her place was taken by Mrs J B Watson Jnr. This is the first mention of the valiant girl who took on the manager's son in matrimony and it is a matter for regret that nothing is known of her early life except that she had received the names Frances Margaret at

The Theatre Royal, Birmingham, which had been rebuilt in 1794, was rented for a time by John Boles Watson II in 1808 and later by John Watson III in 1831.

baptism. She played small roles, had a bent for comedy, could sing and she also played the piano.[6]

The engagement of leading star guests continued to bring in good money and on Wednesday, 10 October 1810 Cirencester acclaimed a famous one-man show at the Theatre that sold every seat in the house. Mr Bannister was making his last appearance in the Cotswolds before returning to London. John Bannister had devised a first edition of his solo entertainment, *The Budget*, in 1807 as a means of circumventing the old monopoly enjoyed by the patent theatres in London and he used it to support his large family in times of poor health and when he was without engagement, although he had had no real fear of penury from the time he ceased to be acting manager at Drury Lane. He had made his name as Walter, hero of *The Children in the Wood*, singing the interpolated songs splendidly.[7] He never learnt to read music, getting the tunes by ear from the Covent Garden pianist. He went on to become the best-loved comic actor on the English stage, famous for his sincerity and the heart he brought to his characterisations. He was even accepted socially for his solid virtue and unblemished reputation, which Charles Lamb referred to as 'his sweet good natured moral pretensions'.[8] The Princess Elizabeth, on hearing of his first selection, had arranged a party to entertain her parents and commanded him to court to give the original entertainment at the beginning of his first solo tour.

The entertainment offered at Cirencester was a new edition of *The Budget*, 'a vehicle for animated description, exhilarating monologue, song both unmixed and interspersed with prose, anecdotes serious and burlesque, sentiment and bagatelle, broad laughter, generous feeling, and moral instruction', in short, as Watson described it, 'that very agreeable melange'. Watson's bare announcement in the *Gloucester Journal* of 'a Miscellaneous Advertisement in Three Parts' was enough to draw the crowds but another advertisement for an earlier performance in May 1810 in a one night stand at the Bell Inn, Gloucester affords a fuller picture:

Patronised by their Majesties (before whom Mr. Bannister had the honour of performing the Divertisement, at the Queen's House, Frogmore) and which has been received with universal applause, by crowded audiences at Free Mason's Hall, the London Tavern, and the Theatre Royal, Haymarket.

The Public are most respectfully informed, that on Saturday next, 26th May 1810, at the Assembly Room, Bell Inn will be opened

Bannister's Budget;

Or, An Actor's Ways and Means, for 1810; being a Miscellaneous Divertisement, in Three Parts which will be spoken and sung by Mr. Bannister, late of the Theatre Royal, Drury Lane.

The above Divertisement is entirely new; the Prose and Verse which compose it, having been expressly written for the occasion by Messrs. Colman, Reynolds, Cherry, T. Dibdin, C. Dibdin Jnr. and others – The whole of the Entertainment has been revised, and arranged by Mr. Colman.

The songs are principally composed by Mr. Reeve, and will be accompanied by Mr. Reeve Jnr. on the Pianoforte.

Tickets at the Bar. Price of Admission Three Shillings.[9]

Such a performance at an assembly room provided 'drawing room' entertainment for large numbers of the public. The price was very reasonable for a London Celebrity. Admission to a ball at the King's Head in Cirencester that January (tea and coffee included) had been 4s.6d.

John Bannister, turned fifty when he brought his new programme to Cirencester, was son of a comic actor in Garrick's company who had also been an excellent bass singer and a good-natured, gifted mimic. John Bannister inherited his father's talents and had a voice of great compass which was capable of minute inflections and modulation. He was, like his father, a great mimic of other well-known actors. He had an expressive face in which the eyes were particularly striking, being endowed with softness as well as fire. He made an immediate impression on entry owing to his height and the elegance of bearing learnt from fencing and the dancing master. He called his entertainment *The Budget* because, like that of the Chancellor of the Exchequer, it was devised to bring in money.

Bannister, however, gave good value. His performance, with two intervals, lasted two and a half hours. His material provided by the leading stage writers of the day and the whole arranged and polished by George Colman the Younger, creator of Dr Pangloss and other favourite comic characters. One of Bannister's most popular pieces was a study of extreme old age which he called 'The Superannuated

Sexton'; another he himself no doubt enjoyed as a challenge to his powers was 'Two Ways of telling the same Story – by a Clergyman and a Boatswain'. Surely, too, he would not have missed the triumph of telling a tale in Gloucester dialect that no yokel in the gallery could have faulted. His father had been a Gloucestershire man, born at the ancient little township of Newland in the Forest of Dean. John Bannister's vivid imagery and pointed expression, divorced from the stilted declamatory style in a company, brought a foretaste of the 'natural manner' of acting. It established a close rapport between himself and his audiences which contributed largely to the great success of his solo presentations. Leigh Hunt called him 'the first low comedian on the stage'.[10]

This warm aura of intimacy that he could create in a small theatre with no other means than his own talent was, however, rudely disturbed during his evening at Cirencester. There was a fracas in the auditorium. The Second Royal East Gloucester Regiment of Local Militia was in the town at the time and the theatre was packed to suffocation by all ranks with as many bodies squashed along the benches as was possible. Lieut. James Reynell, resplendent in dress uniform, came to the theatre and demanded a seat in a box. He had no ticket, no reservation and no minion was keeping a place for him. Cutting short protestations and argument at the box office, he forced his way down the passage, crossed the foyer and stormed noisily into the front box. There was simply no room for him. In the melée that ensued the Captain of the Regiment, from his seat at the front of the box, tried to calm the arrogant Lieutenant but Reynell 'collared and struck' the Captain, as the charge relates, so that the Sergeant of the Regiment had to come to the Captain's aid. The Commanding Officer requested the Adjutant, Captain Edwards, to inform Lieut. Reynell to consider himself under arrest and to give up his sword. Reynell refused. An expectant silence must have seized the waiting audience. Disturbances in front of the curtain tended to inject unscheduled variety into the joys of theatre going. The upshot was a court martial at Bristol and Lieut. Reynell was ignominiously dismissed the Regiment for conduct unbecoming to an officer.[11]

Glimpses into the pleasures of the 1811 summer season are provided by the preservation in fortuitous ways of three bills from the August of that year. Two of these are held in the USA by the

Theatre Collection of the University of Harvard. They are the earliest to bear the name of Watkins as printer, a prosperous and respected bookseller, stationer, vendor of patent medicines and holder of a stamp office. He, his wife, Jane, their six children and five relatives, with their complement of six servants, occupied nineteen marked places in the Parish Church pews on Sunday.[12] Amongst them sat Philip Watkins' shopman and it was this trusty retainer who a few years later took over the issue of tickets for reserved box places at the Theatre and produced to patrons, over the counter of the stationer's shop in the Market Place next to the King's Head, the plan of the box seating.

On Monday, 26 August, to open the last week of acting until October, Watson the Younger thanked the patrons of Cirencester and introduced from Cheltenham, for one evening's performance Palmer of the Theatre Royal, Drury Lane Company, in the arduous and popular character of Falstaff.[13] The same inexhaustible little band finished the evening with *Blue Beard*, that spectacular entertainment which had brought Colonel Kingscote's programme to an end ten years earlier. The scenery and oriental properties had worn well, for the *Cheltenham Chronicle* (3 June 1811) had been able to say, despite the long years of use, that 'the style in which this romantic spectacle was produced, acquired, and richly deserved, the applause of a numerous and respectable audience'. The magical effects employed to create the requisite weird atmosphere were obviously still chilling the blood of willing audiences.

Another bill from 1811, that for Wednesday, 28 August, now lost, came into the hands of 'Rambler' of the *Wilts. and Gloucestershire Standard*, Cirencester's weekly newspaper, in 1906 and he, providentially, printed the full text in his column of gossip and comment on 8 September. For this last night of the summer season Jack Watson had come over to present 'one of Shakespeare's best Tragedies, Macbeth' with Alexander Pope, late of Drury Lane and Covent Garden, in the title role.[14] 'This very superior Tragedian, who has, for many years, stood in high Estimation with the Admirers of the legitimate Drama', was the celebrated Irish actor from Cork, and Cirencester had the good fortune to see him, aged forty-eight, still at the height of his powers. He was on the point of returning to the London stage which he had deserted after a dispute with the Covent Garden management three years earlier. He had for a while been in financial straits but at this point in his career he must have cost Watson a high fee for 11 April he had netted £700 at a benefit at the King's Theatre, ample proof of the opinion London still held of him. In his prime he had no rivals but the Kembles. His chief attraction, indeed Leigh Hunt said it was his only asset, was a fine, mellow and powerful voice. Most people, except Leigh Hunt, said he also used his strong and well formed body with dignity and grace. His face showed harmony of feature but was not endowed with any great range of expression, which may account for his abject adulation of the mercurial Kean, to whose Richard III he often played Richmond. It was his voice that produced his aura of deep pathos but in the main Leigh Hunt found him bombastic and ridiculous. In the company supporting the visitor, young Watson was Lennox and Shuter did service as a Bleeding Captain though he doubtless got more fun out of being a Witch, of which there were more than three, their weird company being separated into the speaking and the singing kind. Young Watson's wife, the two Misses Waldron and Mrs Bennett augmented the brew and Hecate was chanted by a man, Mr Comer. The incantations may have been helped out by Bennett as well, as he was only required for Duncan, the old King. Certainly Miss F Waldron was worked to the full. Under her witch's rags she was ready, letter stowed in bosom, to make a grand entrance a few shakes later as a majestical Lady Macbeth.

Notes

1   In 1760 some discussion had taken place about celebrating the bicentenary of the birth of William Shakespeare (1564–1616) but, with David Garrick abroad, no one had been found to organise this. The new town hall in Stratford by Robert Newcombe of Whittingdon in Gloucestershire, intended to be named 'Shakespeare's Hall', was completed in 1769. Garrick was requested to sit for his portrait to be painted by Thomas Gainsborough (1727–88) and hung within. Completed, it showed the actor in a grove leaning against a bust of Shakespeare. Garrick, in turn, promised to provide the town with a portrait of Shakespeare; that of the playwright sitting in his study by Benjamin Wilson (1721–88) materialised as did

Garrick's additional gift of the splendid copy in lead of the statue of Shakespeare by Peter Scheemakers (1691–1781) which was placed on an exterior wall looking down Chapel Street. This presentation of works of art grew into the Shakespeare Jubilee. See: Robert Bearman, *Stratford-Upon-Avon. A History of its Streets and Buildings* (Nelson, 1988); Joanne Stochholm, *Garrick's Folly* (1964); J C Trewin, *The Story of Stratford upon Avon* (1950).

2   Charles Dibdin (1745–1814) was a prolific composer of light operas and musical plays in addition to his work as a singer and a manager of the Royal Circus, later the Surrey Theatre. See: W Kitchiner, *A Brief Memoir of Charles Dibdin* (1984), and Robert Fabruer, *The Theatre Career of Charles Dibdin the Elder (1745–1814)* (New York, 1989).

Thomas Arne (1710–1778) composed music for the stage, including Shakespeare's plays, oratorios and ballad operas. He set to music parts of Garrick's 'Ode upon Dedicating a Building and Erecting a Statue to Shakespeare'. See: B H Horner, *The Life and Work of Dr Arne* (1893).

Thomas Attwood (1765–1838) was organist of St Paul's Cathedral, composer to the Chapel Royal and one of the first professors of the Royal Academy of Music; he is now remembered principally for his church music.

3   This enthusiasm for dramatics is reflected in the number of private theatres which existed in large country houses. An account of these is given in *Temples of Thespis* by Sybil Rosenfeld (1978).

4   *Gloucester Journal*, 3 July 1810.

5   According to the Minute Book of the Proprietors of the Theatre Royal, Birmingham (Birmingham Public Library, Archives, Lee 387) the Theatre Royal was let to Jack Watson for twelve months from November 1808 at a rent of 800 guineas together with an undertaking to give one night's takings towards the recent costs of redecoration (memorandum, 13 October 1808). M'Cready, one of the proprietors, complained that Watson used scenes and properties without permission (memorandum, 23 March 1809); it is also claimed in the minute book that Watson attempted to evade the Lamp and Scavenger Levy (memorandum, 25 July 1809). Later the proprietors recorded that Watson had used candles (presumably tallow) which had injured the new paintwork (memorandum, 26 September 1809). Nevertheless, the proprietors were willing to let the theatre to Watson for a further annual term at the same rate but, after consultation with his father, he declined to take it on (memoranda, 16 and 17 October 1809).

6   The Local Studies and History Department in Birmingham Central Library has a collection of the Theatre Royal, Birmingham, playbills covering this season. Frances Margaret Watson's name later crops up in a letter (now in the Gloucestershire Records Office, Gloucester) dated 22

January 1838 to Rowland Paul of Cheltenham about her son's imprisonment for debt in Warwick Gaol.

7   *The Children in the Wood* by Thomas Morton, first given at the Haymarket on 1 October 1793.

8   John (Jack) Bannister (1760–1836) is mentioned in Charles Lamb's essay 'On Some of the Old Actors' in *Essays of Elia* (1832). According to John Adolphus in *Memoirs of John Bannister, Comedian* (1839) *The Budget* was given at Hereford and Gloucester in 1809 and at Southampton in 1810 before Bannister appeared in Cirencester.

9   *Gloucester Journal*, 21 May 1810.

10   Leigh Hunt, 'Mr Bannister' in *Critical Essays on the Performers of the London Stage* (1807).

11   Richard Barry O'Brien, 'A Memorable Night at Cirencester Theatre – 150 Years Ago, Tonight', *Wiltshire Herald and Advertiser*, 14 December 1941; Ernest Whatley, 'A Stage Story', *Wilts and Gloucestershire Standard*, 26 January 1876.

12   The pew rent books for the Church of St John the Baptist, Cirencester, are preserved at the Gloucestershire Record Office, Gloucester.

13   This actor may have been Robert L Palmer (1757–1817), a dancer, actor and singer, painted by Samuel de Wilde. When young he played jockeys and similar nimble men but he coarsened and thickened with age.

14   Alexander Pope (1762–1835) was for several years leading tragedian at Covent Garden and also performed at Drury Lane. He was a skilful portrait painter. In Leigh Hunt's *Dramatic Essays*, ed William Archer and Robert W Lowe (1824), 'Mr Pope', Hunt writes:

> Mr Pope has not one requisite to an actor but a good voice, and this he uses so unmercifully on all occasions that its value is lost and he contrives to turn it into a defect . . . In short, when Shakespeare wrote his description of 'a robustious fellow, who tears a passion to tatters', one would suppose that he had been shown, by some supernatural means, the future race of actors, as Macbeth had a prophetic view of Banquo's race, and that the robustious phantom was Mr Pope.

Chapter 10:
The Death of John Boles Watson I

John Boles Watson was no longer active and had for some time been ailing. On 19 September 1811, he summoned three men from the theatre he could respect, J D Adamson who had handled tickets and booking office for years, Robert Chamberlain, the actor and trusted Treasurer who had grown old in the company, and the fellow Irishman and eminent tragedian, Alexander Pope, recently Macbeth at Cirencester. Declaring that he felt unwell though of sound mind, Watson filled two sheets of post paper with a 'rude sketch of my wishes and meaning, desiring it may be considered my sole Will and Testament in every point'. At the foot he added, 'I have scribbled the foregoing rather on the spur of the moment'.[1] But the end he so confidently expected did not come at that time and he lived on, in failing heath, for another year and a half at his cottage, cared for by his second wife, Henrietta. He had relinquished direction of his theatrical empire to his son who was already spoken of as 'the Manager'.

There was a fair stock of scenery and costumes, well worn over the years, though the true state of affairs may have been indicated by Winston who in his prejudiced venom had said that only one pair of wings could be found at Cheltenham.[2] The acting was still carried by the reliable few Watson had recruited and the enterprise continued to run on the lines he had established, relying heavily on visiting performers to bring in real profit. He no doubt read in the local paper of declining standards of presentation, powerless to reverse the regrettable trend. Watson himself, independent of the theatre, had a comfortable income from property, mortgages and investments.

94

John Boles Watson I (1748–1813) first ventured into theatrical management in about 1779 and created a dynasty that lasted for some fifty years.

John Boles Watson died during the evening of Wednesday, 18
March 1813,

> the much respected Manager of our Theatre. He has for a number of
> years been affected with gout, which terminated his existence by an
> attack on the vitals.

The *Gloucester Journal* had this to say:

> Endowed with strong natural abilities, he was an accurate observer of
> the human character; and his talents, added to the facilities presented
> by the peculiar sphere in which he moved, rendered him at all times a
> pleasing and entertaining companion, replete with anecdote, and
> happy in the means of giving its effect. He likewise possessed a turn
> for poetry; and both in this department and in the lighter topics of
> prosaic composition evinced unusual celerity and spirit. If, owing to
> the situation he filled in life, he acquired a levity of manners, and a
> singularity of exterior, which the more grave or demure would
> sometimes pronounce exceptionable, yet, on the other hand, he was
> frank, sincere and benevolent, loyal to his King and zealously
> devoted to the best interests of his country. In his profession, he was
> vigilant and active, and very desirous, as well from natural
> inclination, as the more powerful operation of gratitude, to please
> and delight that public which never fails to encourage and reward
> personal merit. His errors were venal – his virtues many and solid:
> and it is with extreme anguish of mind that the writer of this article
> who knew him well has attempted to give this faint sketch of his
> character. The effort, in justice to the deceased, should have been
> made by a better and more skilful hand.[3]

His true memorial, however, is to be found in the pages of *The
Itinerant* by Samuel Ryley, where he appears in Volume IV, Chapter
VIII, as the bubbling manager of the Theatre Royal at the spa of
Lax-Water (Cheltenham), ninety miles from London.[4] Tom Gag, as
Ryley dubs him, has journeyed up to London to engage new actors
at the tavern known as the 'Opposite Prompt and Prompt Side',
situated in Russell Court, Covent Garden, which served as a
rendezvous for the profession and an employment exchange or
hiring fair for acting engagements in the provinces:

The Death of John Boles Watson I

One evening I sauntered into a room at the O.P. and P.S. their usual rendezvous, where I met with a motley group of at least fifty of both descriptions, and a curious assemblage it was. There were managers of first, second and third rates; first, those dignified personages who govern theatres royal; next, those who preside over theatres by licence; and lastly the humble purveyors for public amusement whose ambition soars not beyond that appendage to agriculture – *a Barn*. The actors were not less diversified than the managers. Some were dressed in the first stile of fashion; others barely clean and decent; and a third class neither one nor the other . . .

I had not long been seated, when a tall good-looking, but shabbily dressed man, in years, came hobbling up, in the room, and bowing to each box, seemed perfectly acquainted with the company. He smiled, snapped his fingers, and with much vivacity exclaimed, "Well, here I am, gentlemen, come to see you once more. Tom Gag's true to his time you see, though the gout has nearly laid me up, I was determined to come. Must have some of you – smacking salaries, and overflowing benefits – now's your time – Tom Gag's your man – shan't live to come another year – go out, some of these days, like the snuff of a candle – no matter. Finch, bring a bottle of wine – stop – that smells too much of the pocket – a glass of brandy and water will do."

Having settled, Gag (Watson) is overheard trying out on an eager, penniless young actor, anxious for an engagement, his way of recruiting. Bursting into an immoderate fit of laughter and throwing half a guinea on to the table, Gag exclaims,

"There, my fine fellow, that will keep you in *bub* and *grub* till you reach Lax-Water. Let me see – we open on Monday, to-day is only Thursday; you'll walk it in three days easily; thirty miles a day is nothing to a young man like you; I'll meet you there – you shall have a pet part to open with – *eighteen* hog a week – and a benefit, which never fails. The natives will fill your Pit and Gallery; the visitors your Boxes; and, at the end of the campaign, you'll have money in [the] bank, or say Tom Gag's no conjurer. Come my service to you, and success to your benefit."

To gain some information of this strange personage, the Old World Actor addressed himself to an intelligent-looking man who sat next to him:

97

"What, Sir!" he replied, "don't you know Tom Gag? I thought every theatrical person had either seen or heard of him! He is manager of the theatre royal at Lax-Water: has accumulated a fortune by care and perseverance; and though never a performer of any eminence himself, is a tolerably good judge of acting, and collects a company every summer, capable of entertaining one of the most fashionable audiences out of London. He is a very clever fellow, and has the gift of wheedling and talking the folks into anything . . ."

These Irish powers of persuasion resulted in a fine, vividly lifelike portrait-miniature now in an ivory case at the Cheltenham Museum and Art Gallery. John Boles Watson is seen, his jovial days almost over, the features pale and ashen and drawn with marks of care and pain. Only the eyes retain their penetrating sparkle. The portrait may have been painted by the actor–miniaturist and fellow Irishman, Alexander Pope, and started in the autumn of 1811, around the time of the signing of the will. The *verso* of the miniature bears an inscription in brown and faded ink:

Mr Watson
Manager of Cheltenham Theatre
1812
D[ate] of D[eath] 1813

Notes

1 John Boles Watson's will is in the Public Record Office (PROB 11/1544, 226, folios 65–6).
2 Birmingham Central Library: Winston Collection, manuscript notes by James Winston in preparation for the publication of *The Theatric Tourist* (1805).
3 *Gloucester Journal*, 22 March 1813.
4 Samuel William Ryley (1759–1837) was an itinerant provincial actor whose adventures are recorded in the nine volume work *The Itinerant, or Memoirs of an Actor* (1808–17). This passage is quoted in Pierce Egan, *The Life of an Actor* (1825), on which see George Speaight, *Collecting Theatre Memorabilia* (1988) p. 87.

Chapter 11:
John Boles Watson II's New Management

At the end of May 1813 Jack Watson presented himself as sole proprietor and manager of the Cirencester Theatre with thanks for 'that liberal support and most flattering encouragement his late Father experienced during a succession of nearly forty seasons'.[1] He had a new set of stock scenery painted and continued his father's money-spinning policy of bringing brighter talents from London to liven the favourite old pieces in which 'minor roles were savagely cut and actors left the star to carry the performance', as had been noted in the *Cheltenham Chronicle* (3 June 1811). After seeing *The Exile* by Frederick Reynolds in November 1812 the *Cheltenham Chronicle* offered

> one hint to the Manager and we will exile the subject. The throne on which Elizabeth sat, we conceive, must have been dragged from the tomb of some fallen Czar, for Time had devoured its drapery and left it unadorned with anything but native timber; and the 'peopled court', so much talked of, was dispossessed of a single personage to give it brilliancy. Perhaps the Poet did not intend his ideas should be embodied on the stage; good care was exercised in this particular. And then the soldiers, or body-guard, of the Empress were disgraceful. Had not the author kindly told us they were warriors, their dress, movement and discipline would never have convinced us they were the sons of Mars.[2]

Obloquy fell from the same height on Watson's wife in November 1812.

> We were sorry to observe Mrs. J. Watson's Ninette [in *The Young*

Hussar] dressed so adverse to the author's meaning: he evidently intended the character as a decrepit piece of antiquity, but the above lady threw into her countenance the rose of youth and whilst complaining of her *old* bones displayed all the agility of sixteen. Her costume was characteristically erroneous and the part misconceived.[3]

Not that Jack Watson would have prevailed much against Frances Margaret, the wife he took while he was still nineteen, for she was a capable woman with a mind of her own and possessed of an astute business sense lacked by Jack.

There were, however, other departments where he could vent any remaining zeal. In June 1811 it had been remarked that 'The revenue of the Prompter, if his salary be adequate to his labour, must be princely indeed'.[4] Not only did the actors pay scant respect to their lines but it had also become

painful to witness the absurd and unpardonable errors of the scene shifters who, unheedful of their duty, wantonly sacrifice dramatic chastity: they sometimes leave an uninscribed marble pillar in the midst of a grove as a monument of their ignorance; or a cluster of trees 'thick with leavy honours' as an empowering shade in a lady's bedchamber; and to crown the whole, they suffer the moving grove to luxuriate midway in the apartment of a country-inn.

The great rejoicing at the abdication of Napoleon that took place in Cirencester in May 1814 must have veiled many an imperfection at the theatre, however. Townsmen decorated the streets and touched off illuminations for two days of feasting and pleasure. Despite the unfavourable weather the buildings were decked with lights in coloured glasses to unprecedented and brilliant effect, laurel and artificial flowers strung up spangled with tiny lamps, and triumphal arches erected and hung with the ensigns of England and royalist France. On the second evening one of the triumphal arches was splendidly illuminated with four hundred lights and an exhibition given of transparent paintings, 'designed by the finest artists for the present glorious occasion' such as could be hired from London. Later that night a boat, to honour the marine contribution to success, richly illuminated and decorated with suitable inscription was drawn through the streets. The bells of the parish church rang out over the heads of the crowd, bands played, fireworks were let off and there were dinners for every rank of society. An ox was roasted whole in the Market Place.[5]

On 20 February 1815 Jack Watson announced his plans for the season at the three Cotswold Theatres:

> Theatres Gloucester, Cheltenham and Cirencester
> Mr Watson, Proprietor and Manager, impressed with the liveliest sense of Gratitude for the very distinguished and liberal Patronage he has so frequently been honoured with, respectfully announces the commencement of the present Season; and having engaged many of the most popular performers from the Metropolitan Theatres to occasionally appear on these boards, (as Circumstances may permit) he trusts he shall merit a continuance of that liberal Support he had hitherto experienced from the Nobility, Gentry and Public at large.[6]

The news just a week later that Napoleon had escaped from Elba and was already at Cannes improved the prospect of a good season since travel on the continent, previously prevented by the revolution and subsequent wars, would still be out of the question and, in spite of the demands of the increased number of visitors to the Spa and the larger population of Gloucester, a season was maintained at Cirencester throughout that momentous summer with the nights of acting again restored to Mondays, Wednesday and Fridays. Mrs Bennett, who had performed in Liverpool, Edinburgh and Dublin was engaged as the leading lady. Crook arrived from Drury Lane. Quadrille, a character actor who also happened to be useful backstage, brought his daughter to augment the corps-de-ballet. Addison, the box office keeper, continued in that office, as well as acting on occasion. Lastly, the indispensable Shuter continued to serve, along with his family.

William Betty, now just short of his twenty-fourth birthday, was the illustrious visitor during the summer, still in his roles in old plays that had made his name as a boy. Watson found it necessary to remind the public, indeed a new generation of playgoers, that Betty's youthful genius and ability was the astonishment of the theatrical world and then had to go on to make the worn announcement that this celebrity could be seen on Wednesday, 5 July as Young Norval in the Tragedy of *Douglas*. Betty was, however, still impressive.[7]

Shuter's old role of the Shepherd who brought up Young Norval went to one of the new players, Jones, whose wife was also in the company and another newcomer, the second dramatic actress, Miss Moody, was Lady Randolph, Norval's mother. Shuter was there as a mere officer and while the stage was being made ready for the farce he sang a comic song and his daughter followed with a dance.

Two of the plays presented with great éclat in that same season were *The Castle Spectre* by Matthew Gregory Lewis and the last play that Sheridan wrote, his only tragedy, *Pizarro*.[8] Towards the end of

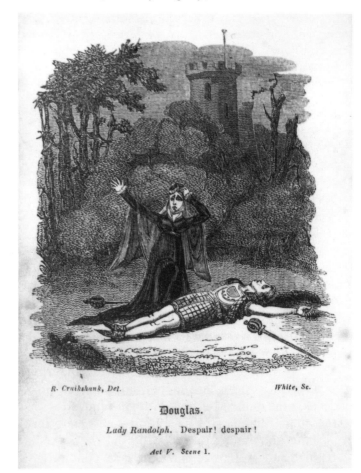

R. *Cruikshank, Del.*   *White, Sc.*

Douglas.

Lady Randolph. Despair! despair!

Act V. Scene 1.

Master Betty, the child actor, was still starring as Young Norval in *Douglas* when he visited Cirencester at the age of nearly 25.

102

this play, as the body of the native warrior-chieftain was carried to its burial, many must have thought of the seven thousand British dead who lay on the field of Waterloo. Every Sunday collections at church doors were made 'for the purpose of affording relief to the widows and orphans of those brave countrymen who fell, and for those wounded' at the battle leading to a victorious outcome. Enthusiasm for a celebration was not as strong in Cirencester as it had been the previous year when Napoleon laid aside his crown.

R. Cruikshank, Del.   *White, Sc.*

The Castle Spectre.

Angela sinks upon her knees, with her eyes rivetted upon the figure, which for some moments remain motionless.

Act IV. Sc. II.

'Monk' Lewis's *The Castle Spectre* was typical of the strong melodramatic fare that John Boles Watson II was offering in 1815.

103

Notes

1   *Gloucester Journal*, 7 May 1813.

2   *The Exile*, written by Frederick Reynolds and with music by Joseph Mazzinghi (1765–1844) was first performed at Covent Garden in November 1808.

3   *Cheltenham Chronicle*, 5 November 1812. *The Young Hussar* by William Dimond with music by Michael Kelly was first performed in 1807.

4   *Cheltenham Chronicle*, 20 June 1811.

5   *Gloucester Journal*, 2 May 1814.

6   *Gloucester Journal*, 20 February 1815.

7   Newspaper puffs still praised the actor. The painter Benjamin Robert Haydon (1786–1846) in 1815, however, found Betty a sad fellow:

> He talked of his past blaze with a melancholy sigh, and drowned recollections as they crowded into his mind, and flushed his cheek, with a sort of gasp that allowed the wine to rush down his throat as he put the glass to his mouth to drink it.

See: entry for 30 May 1815 in Benjamin Robert Haydon, *Diaries*, edited by Willard Bissell Pope (Cambridge, Mass., 1960).

8   *The Castle Spectre* was first staged in 1797 and *Pizarro* in 1799 both at the Theatre Royal, Drury Lane.

Chapter 12:
Fenton's Strolling Players

T S Porter, the Cirencester printer and stationer, launched a weekly magazine for 1816 which he named the *Gleaner* since it was to contain a selection of articles.[1] Contributions were invited, but Porter forewarned that 'Indelicacy, Immorality or Sedition' in the content would cause rejection. Fortunately Porter did not consider that theatricals held any tendency towards immorality and the pages of the *Gleaner* show a lively and continuous interest in theatrical events in the metropolis, giving news of Edmund Kean, noting the death of Dorothea Jordan in France and providing a full account in July of the death in squalor and the funeral in Westminster Abbey of Richard Brinsley Sheridan, with Lord Bathurst heading the list of mourners behind Sheridan's son and members of the family.

The Theatre in Gloucester Street remained silent all through 1816 but there was, after a depressing spring of snow, rain and high winds and a very wet early summer, a short season of theatricals by a strolling company which set up its stage in the Assembly Room at the King's Head.[2]

A notice in the *Gleaner* read:

This theatre was opened on Monday Evening 22 July. The decorations are generally light and simple, and although much allowance ought to be made for the very short time in which it has been prepared for the Public, there is a great display of taste, and above all that ingenuity which produces great effect from very slender means – a painted Scroll Work in imitation of low relief ornaments the Frize [sic] of the Proscenium; in the centre of the Frize is a circular blank space, left, we suppose, for the Head of Comus or

105

Thespis . . . we must observe that the dead yellow ground gives a washy appearance to the whole of the interior of the Theatre, which is however much relieved by a warmer tint of orange on the sides of the Proscenium on which a variety of tasteful moulding appears – The Drop Scene represents in the Foreground, the ruins of a Roman Temple, through the remaining Pillars of which, you see in the distance a similar Edifice, upon which the revages of time have made less impression . . . There are minor Drop Scenes well executed, and all pleasing except one, which we were told was intended for a street in Warwick; it may be very like, but has a dark, narrow and smoaky appearance and looks as though threatened with impending storm . . .

The same judicious principle has obtained in disposing of the lights; as while they shed over the Pit and Boxes a sort of soft and yellow moonlight, they glare on the Stage and Proscenium with the splendour of a Mid-Day Sun. Of the Orchestra we can say but little, as the leader of the band appeared rather indisposed; arising perhaps from the grand novelty of his situation, or rather, as we supposed, suffering under the reaction produced by great previous excitation.

Of the Performers we defer at present a detailed opinion: suffice it to say, that in the *Tragedy of King Richard* and the Afterpiece of *The Prize*, Mr. Fenton, junior, reminded us . . . of Cook's [*sic*] Duke of Gloucester in the heat of Bosworth Field when Richard and Richmond 'Amazed the Welkin with their broken Staves' the assistance of the Uproarious Gods had great effect and in a comic Song of Mr. Charles, the overflowing of their jocund hearts in the Chorus was truly electrifying. The Pit and Boxes were not so much crowded as we might expect on the opening of a New House, owing, we hope, to the unfavourable state of the weather.

This new theatre at the King's Head opened with some of the best scenes from *Richard III*. The newspaper account continued:

Mr. J Fenton's Richard was a very respectable attempt, he dressed and look'd the part well, the misshapen leg and lordly load upon his shoulders were not forgotten; . . . his action indeed is generally good, as is his voice, but, by mouthing rapid utterance he is often quite unintelligible: he has a fault common to most young Tragic Actors, he overdoes his part . . . We would remind him that deep and strong passion is not always loud . . . His Faults are, however, corrigible, and we doubt not he will improve.

J. Fenton's rendering of Richard III at the King's Head in 1816 seems to have been based upon that of David Garrick, here painted in that role by William Hogarth.

The tent scene in Bosworth Field was well got up. As Richard is half reclining on his couch, and courting that repose which flies the guilty mind, he is reproached in the most sepulchral tones by the Ghosts of those he has murdered; his agitation becomes excessive . . .[3] Lady Anne was well filled by Mrs. Fenton, though tragedy is not her fort [*sic*]. In *en bon point* she resembles Mrs. Watson, of the old Theatre; in genteel Comedy she is very superior to her, but in the lower casts of character she is not equal.

Mr. Fenton, the older, is a very good actor in his particular line, his range is not so wide as the Son's, but he is more easy, more natural . . . Mr. Rowland, as an old man in a grey wig, fine embroidered satin waistcoat, and light drab coat, when he has little to do, and less to say, is tolerable; in other characters he is a mere thing.

Mr. Hamilton dresses himself well as a would-be buck and lounger, and endeavours to please, but we think he has mistaken his calling.

Mr. Charles is a handsome youth and a promising actor, but he has much to learn, and Mr. Williams still more.

It has really surprised us to see how this small company, in so small a house, has been able to get up several pieces, which depend so much on spectacle and decoration. *Timour the Tartar* (bating the lack of

107

cavalry) was noisy, bustling and grand; the effect of the battering ram against the massy walls of the turret soon succeeded, and it was amusing to see the people within assisting the besiegers to enlarge the embrasure.

The Castle Spectre too has been very well managed. The silence and gestures of the ghost had a very forcible effect on the audience; the thunder and lightning was well introduced; the latter seen through a large Gothick window of coloured glass at some distance had an excellent effect. The tortures of guilt we never saw better displayed than by young Fenton in Osmond. One circumstance diverted us much, just before the storm began we saw a shabby urchin pass slowly through the house, and across the stage to the back scenes, with the thunder under his arm, in the shape of a large sheet of copper; a Promethean offence which we expected would have called down immediate vengeance from the Gods, but it passed unpunished . . .

The writer of this account simply signed his piece 'M.M.'

On Monday, 2 September 1817, came 'M.M.'s last report:

This little theatre closes this Evening with a Variety of Entertainments, Tragedy, Comedy, History, Pastoral, Pastoral–Comical, Historical–Pastoral, Scene individable and Poem unlimited. All for the benefit of the elder Mr. Fenton, and we hope as a good Actor and Father of a respectable Itinerant Company he will have a very crowded House.

Of *Othello*, on Wednesday, we saw only part, but enough to confirm our former opinion of Mr. J. Fenton's acting; and, if he be as young as we take him to be, under able tuition he may become 'if not the first, in the very first line'.

Miss Moody, of whom we have not spoken before (although last not least) was much above a mediocrity in Desdemona; as an Actress she has self possession with diffidence; and as a Woman, though not pretty, she is what we still admire, gentle, unobtrusive, retiring. – In the After Piece *Of Age Tomorrow* we were sorry to see Mr. Charles as Haas Holchus, it was Mr. Fenton's character to a T. The former, as Cassio, was quite in his place . . .

In a Pantomime called *The Algerine Pirates* on Monday Evening, one occurrence highly delighted us; the thing was well got upon, and the subject at this juncture interesting; but the critical situation to which we allude and the effects on the audience, was worth all the Plays we have seen. After the wreck of the English vessel the Captain is invited to the house of the Pirate Captain, is refreshed with wine and is shown with great seeming kindness and hospitality to his bed room; he discovered, however, too late, that the civilities of his Host are not sincere; and still further, that he proposes to murder him in his sleep; he is alone, not within hail of his crew, he is in the hands of a murderous ruffian; in this dilemma he looks first for the means of escape – this is impossible; his next resource, the natural impulse of a gallant officer was his sword, and clasping his hand on it with confidence he is about to lay himself down, but he thinks for a moment, and under a true feeling of his defenceless state he come forward from his couch, and in an attitude of prayer throws himself upon the holy keeping of his God. It was an admirable scene, and although it was in him not only an act of duty, the burst of approbation from the whole house, was a public acknowledgement of principle most truly gratifying to us . . .[4]

The leaders of the troupe were no strangers to Jack Watson's company for young Fenton – he could have been little more than nineteen – had been one of the Princes in the Tower when Jack Watson put on *Richard III* at Warwick in November 1806. His brother had shared his fate, the senior Fenton had been lieutenant of the Tower of London and Mrs Fenton, Duchess of York. The drop intended for a street in Warwick had the very hallmark of Watson management in its sooty appearance, a truly Watsonian canvas pickled in his special brand of fumes from tallow and cheap oil. Business was bad in 1816 and Jack Watson possibly let the Fentons have the scene when he could offer them no employment himself. Young Fenton may have borne out 'M.M.'s' prognostication because on 23 December 1829 a Mr Fenton played Gratiano at Drury Lane in *The Merchant of Venice* when the Shylock was Edmund Kean.

'M.M.' appears to have been a frequenter of the Theatre in Gloucester Street in its earlier days for old Mrs Watson had not acted there for many years. He cannot have been to the Theatre of late or he would not have called the King's Head theatre 'so small a house' since with its floor of 66 feet by 26 feet and its height of 21 feet it was roomier that the Theatre which disposed of only 52 feet by 24 and a height of about 17 feet. He was doubtless looking back to the days when a Theatre crowded with Nobility and Gentry appeared to hold a vast number of people in contrast to the sparsely filled pit and boxes at the King's Head and was fondly remembering the time when the building of a permanent playhouse in the town had raised hope of frequent and regular theatrical entertainment. 'M.M.', with his knowledge of London performers, may have been the Editor, Mr T S Porter himself.

The orange fronted stage hastily erected in July 1816 would have been the Fenton's own collapsible platform with which they travelled. Whether they brought with them gallery and boxes is open to doubt. Such complete travelling theatres did exist and the Assembly Room at the King's Head could easily have housed the structure but an *ad hoc* strolling company is hardly likely to have such grandeur at its disposal. The terms, boxes, pit and gallery, often denoted no more than the prices charged for the divisions of a flat floor in an existing hall, nearer or further from the footlights according to price and rank of society.

The Assembly Room was again the scene of theatricals in 1819 when on 14 May an extra performance was given by Mr Gyngell's company in a 'Variety of new Entertainments' for the benefit of Claud Blundell. The bill survives only as a fragment but Monsieur René Colombier walked the Tight Rope laden with paper flowers and the whole came to a climax in 'Fireworks of a most innocent Nature' which did not extend to the auditorium. At the end there were some surprising Transformations, these last doubtless at the hand of Gyngell himself who, the name not being a common one, is likely to have been the conjurer who ran a troupe of variety artists, equilibrists and jugglers in the early part of the nineteenth century, as mentioned in the *Era Almanack* of 1868.[5] Inflation killed the *Gleaner*. The price had to be raised from 3d. to 4d. in July and the magazine closed at the end of its first year. Porter had, however, to wait only a few years to see a permanent company of actors in Cirencester.

The return to England of the 200,000 war-time soldiers and sailors led to unemployment and widespread distress. 'I should like to see meetings called to provide either a depot of fuel, or a magazine of potatoes, or a supply of blankets to be sold at a cheap price, as was done in your benevolent town some years ago', wrote one correspondent and in February, amidst snow, rain and high winds, there was a distribution of coals to the poor. One in eight were on parochial aid. 'The war is now at an end and many thousands of labourers are returned to their homes who can be hired at reasonable wages', so Lord Bathurst laid out a new road to Stroud round the boundary of Cirencester Park to replace the one which ran through his domain, thereby providing work for 'the lamentable number of labourers now out of employment for whom farmers have no business in the present depressed state of agriculture'. In June 'the inhabitants of the town were most plentifully regaled with excellent old strong beer, at the seat of Earl Bathurst, during which the bells rang out a merry peal' to mark the first anniversary of the Waterloo victory but such manifestation of traditional Georgian paternal bounty could not allay the spreading social agitation and unrest, even in a rural district. 'At a time when the distress of the country has drawn the attention of the people to the subject of economy it may be proper to draw attention to the fact that Earl Bathurst receives £7,320 plus £6,000 as Secretary of State,' cried one voice.

In 1815 Henry Ryder, Bishop of Gloucester, took his seat in the House of Lords. The following year he journeyed to Cirencester to confirm no fewer than 456 young persons in the Parish Church on one day. The flapping tails of the fox-hunting parson had long since disappeared over the frosty horizon. The close alliance between squire and rector loosened as the Church carried its mission beyond the bounds set by lay patronage. The century that had done its best to enjoy itself had made revelry the eighth deadly sin. The assembly for the country gentry with its sorbets, ices, jellies and dancing to follow lost its glitter. Clothes became discreet and dark in colour. The place for entertainment was the home. Deprived of the robustness in their traditional open-air jollifications such as harvest feasts and mop fairs, the lower echelons of society found that the theatre was a sanctuary within which they could regain something of their lost excitements. Former colourful, eccentric characters, old ways and discredited customs could be seen in old plays and after-pieces; actors were there for the baiting; bottles of drink could be smuggled in; loose women arrived after second price. From being a fashionable venue for all ranks of society, the theatre became an unchanging shrine for devotion to old, comfortable familiars and heroes. To hold a mirror up to nature was no longer desirable. It

111

presented too dull a picture. So known and trusted stage characters, both comic and serious, were repeated over and over again under little varying guises in play after play until they flattened into hack writers' types.

Notes

1   Porter's premises were situated on the north side of the Market Place in Cirencester. The *Gleaner* first appeared on 8 January 1816.

2   According to the present (1992) Managing Director of the King's Head Hotel, the Assembly Room was divided into bedrooms in 1938. The hotel is situated on the western side of the Market Place.

3   The description sounds as if Fenton may have modelled his attitude on that of David Garrick in the same role, preserved in William Hogarth's oil painting.

4   The various members of the Fenton family are difficult to identify and would in themselves make an interesting study. Fentons were playing at the Warwick Theatre in 1806 and the following year in Tamworth. Mostly the roles were light and augmented by singing comic songs. The name then occurs in Wales where a Fenton was manager of a small professional company which from 1808 until 1811 helped annually with the summer private theatricals at Tremadoc. Fenton, probably the manager cropping up in Cirencester in 1819, was advertised as manager of the Evesham Theatre in 1817. A bill for the Daventry Theatre (*Love in a Village*, 20 October 1837) informs that Mr Fenton played the minor role of a footman and Mr and Mrs H Fenton took the romantic leads. South Wales theatres at Neath and Tenby were taken over by a Mr H Fenton, an actor from the Liverpool, Birmingham and Swansea theatres, in 1843, without financial success. The *Era Almanac* (1878), p 68, mentions the death of two Fentons: Charles in February 1877 and James Gill in August 1877. The former was a scenic artist as well as an expert Harlequin; he played such roles as Dromio and Nym during the 1850s at Sadler's Wells Theatre and then became a burlesque player at the Strand Theatre in the 1860s. See: W Davenport Adams, *A Dictionary of the Drama* (1904); Cecil Price, *The English Theatre in Wales* (Cardiff, 1948).

The Pirates by James Cobb was first staged at the Haymarket Theatre in 1792.

Of Age Tomorrow by Thomas John Dibdin was first performed at Drury Lane, 1 February 1800.

5   An anonymous coloured woodcut of a conjurer named Gyngell is in the Theatre Collection of Harvard University. The subject is shown three-quarter length, standing behind a table with a wand in his right hand and a bottle in the left with a bird just above it. See: Lillian Arvilla Hall, *Catalogue of Dramatic Portraits in the Theatre Collection of Harvard College Library* (Cambridge, Mass., 1931). Information on Gyngell will be found in Thomas Frost, *The Lives of the Conjurors* (1874) and in Edwin A. Dawes, *The Great Illusionists* (1979); he was also a puppet showman, on which see Speaight, *The History of the English Puppet Theatre* (1990).

Chapter 13:
George Shuter's Benefits

The summer season of 1817 came to an end with the company benefits. A bill remains for the night 22 September when George Shuter did his best to draw a full house by appearing in three of his favourite pieces.[1] He carefully chose new and old roles which would not over-tax him. A Shuter benefit had to be a romp and this one started with a musical entertainment in two acts, *The Maid and the Magpie*, which had opened the season at Gloucester as a new production in February 1816. This affecting story is based on fact. Shuter played the role of Blaisot a young lad (youthful roles did not daunt the aged actor) who discovers that a magpie had taken a silver spoon which Annette has been accused of stealing. She is imprisoned in the Town Hall (a building still standing in Palaiseau, the play's location) awaiting execution but luckily is finally saved by Blaisot's perspicacity.

By the time Jack Watson had got scenery painted and obtained the mechanical magpie there were no less than three English versions of this French story. He produced the first that had appeared at the Lyceum in London, a musical version, at least true to the highly effective original *melodrame historique*. Samuel Arnold, the future manager of Drury Lane, freely translated the original three acts into two and added songs and ensembles with music composed and selected by Henry Smart. The characters, under varying names, became so popular that burlesques of the tale and the many versions began to appear. *Another Maid and Another Magpie* poked fun at them and the joke quickly degenerated into *The Man and the Monkey, or Who stole the Partridge?*. As a melodrama the piece retained its popularity for years and innocence delivered was still

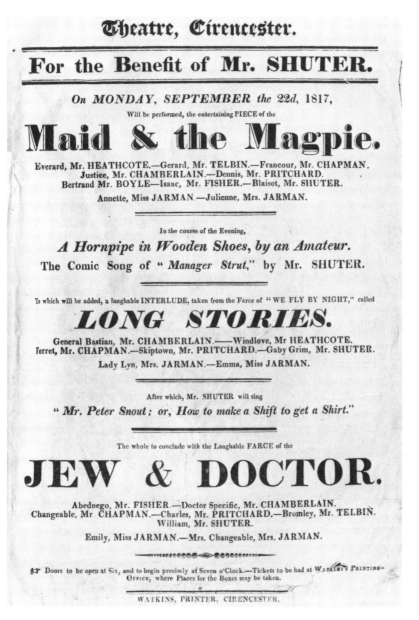

Theatre, Cirencester.

For the Benefit of Mr. SHUTER.

On MONDAY, SEPTEMBER the 22d, 1817,

Will be performed, the entertaining PIECE of the

Maid & the Magpie.

Everard, Mr. HEATHCOTE.—Gerard, Mr. TELBIN.—Francour, Mr. CHAPMAN.
Justice, Mr. CHAMBERLAIN.—Dennis, Mr. PRITCHARD.
Bertrand Mr. BOYLE—Isaac, Mr. FISHER.—Blaisot, Mr. SHUTER.

Annette, Miss JARMAN.—Julienne, Mrs. JARMAN.

In the course of the Evening,

A Hornpipe in Wooden Shoes, by an Amateur.

The Comic Song of " *Manager Strut,*" by Mr. SHUTER.

To which will be added, a laughable INTERLUDE, taken from the Farce of " WE FLY BY NIGHT," called

LONG STORIES.

General Bastian, Mr. CHAMBERLAIN.——Windlove, Mr HEATHCOTE.
Ferret, Mr. CHAPMAN.—Skiptown, Mr. PRITCHARD.—Gaby Grim, Mr. SHUTER.

Lady Lyn, Mrs. JARMAN.—Emma, Miss JARMAN.

After which, Mr. SHUTER will sing

" *Mr. Peter Snout; or, How to make a Shift to get a Shirt.*"

The whole to conclude with the Laughable FARCE of the

JEW & DOCTOR.

Abednego, Mr. FISHER.—Doctor Specific, Mr. CHAMBERLAIN.
Changeable, Mr. CHAPMAN.—Charles, Mr. PRITCHARD.—Bromley, Mr. TELBIN.
William, Mr. SHUTER.

Emily, Miss JARMAN.—Mrs. Changeable, Mrs. JARMAN.

Doors to be open at Six, and to begin precisely at Seven o'Clock.—Tickets to be had at WATKINS'S PRINTING-
OFFICE, where Places for the Boxes may be taken.

WATKINS, PRINTER, CIRENCESTER.

George Shuter was a popular member of Watson's company for more than forty years with his broad humour and hornpipe dancing.

bringing tears of relief in 1858 when Henry James Byron, who had entered the Middle Temple as a barrister, wrote the spiciest take-off in his burlesque *The Maid and the Magpie, or The Fatal Spoon*. With that jibe the triumphal career of the play came to an end but, perpetuating itself as it died, it bequeathed its most engaging character to the care of the British theatre-going public at large. Two years after 'The Fatal Spoon' Blaisot, the eternal adolescent, was reborn on Boxing Day 1860 as Buttons, the same, light-hearted, lover–friend as had delighted the generation of playgoers in *The Maid* during their youth. J H Bryon introduced Buttons in hs Burlesque Extravaganza, *Cinderella*.

Actors augmented their salaries by giving lessons in manners, deportment and elocution; Shuter might well have had a dancing pupil in Cirencester who was pushed before the footlights at this point to take advantage of the good humour infecting the house. An amateur clomped on to perform Shuter's hornpipe in wooden shoes in his stead and the elderly actor undoubtedly clapped him heartily as he himself followed to give his action song called 'The Manager's Strut'. As a comic vocalist he was irreplaceable. The evening continued immediately with a laughable interlude, *Long Stories*, George Colman the Younger's operatic farce *We Fly by Night* bereft of the musical numbers, so that Shuter could delight his friends with a glimpse again of that favourite character, Gaby Grim.

On completion of this to satisfaction, Shuter stepped before the curtain with the character song, 'Mr Peter Snout', and the evening concluded with the laughable farce of *The Jew and the Doctor* with Shuter distracting attention from the main business of the play with his antics in the minor role of the servant, William, dancing attendance on the old miser, Bromley (Telbin). Here was a Thomas Dibdin farce that had been delighting audiences for the past thirty years, Cirencester having first seen it when it was new during the opening season at the Theatre in Gloucester Street in 1799.[2]

Another success by Thomas Dibdin from the Theatre's first season was chosen by Shuter when he was back in Cirencester the following year leading an entirely new troupe of nine players. 9 February 1818 saw him again in all three pieces of a light-hearted programme. The main offering this time was Dibdin's 'admired Comedy in Three Acts' *The Birthday*, one of the charms of which was the setting of naval jargon against country dialect. For good reasons, Shuter played the less sympathetic of two brothers, a gouty, old naval officer retired to the country, by name Captain Bertram.[3] The piece opens in the garden of the cottage where Mr Bertram, the Captain's twin brother, is being helped from the door by Emma his daughter and the sprightly young maid, Anna. It is his first venture into the air after a long illness and he has come to sit outside to celebrate his sixty-third birthday. The occasion is saddened by new recriminations in a law suit against his twin over a garden not worth £100. A young man has come to ogle Emma, with whom he is greatly in love. He is in fact Harry, the Captain's son, secretly working for a reconciliation between the estranged brothers and knowing full well that there is only hope of his marrying Emma when his father and his uncle have concluded a lasting peace. Completely in agreement with him and doing everything to abet his cause is Jack Junk, a jolly tar with salt still on his bell bottoms despite long years ashore as Captain Bertram's manservant. Nothing can rob him of his boatswain's habits and galley language. Mr Bertram readily promises his daughter's hand to the young man and to complete the happiness of her father's birthday Emma goes to call on her uncle, the Captain. The tetchy old sea-captain softens and gives his niece his purse. He regrets the ancient quarrel as well as the £500 it has cost him in legal fees. Emily leaves, overjoyed, for home.

Lawyer Circuit is about to arrive and Jack Junk wheels the Captain into a closet and leaves him there to overhear the machinations of Mrs Moral, the housekeeper and the lawyer, who is enraged at the news of Emma's visit. He has been preventing any conclusion of the law suit in order to extract as much money as possible from the Captain before the rogue and Mrs Moral carry out their long planned intention to marry. The last scene represents the disputed garden, a pavilion on either side with a ship carved on the door of one. The well worn canvas strikes a familiar note. Is not this the same garden with two pavilions painted for the last scene in *The Midnight Hour* in 1787 and still doing good service?[4] The two invalids totter in from opposite sides. They have not met for fifteen years, since the dispute that broke out in this very garden. Emma joins the twin brothers' hands and Mr Bertram learns that Harry is his nephew. Jack Junk holds a little hand-joining ceremony of his own with Anna, the maid.

In the next piece Shuter appeared as Sancho, the valet. The piece needed the like of Shuter for *Lovers' Quarrels* was otherwise a great bore although of noble descent. Moliére wrote *Le Depit amoureux* and from part of it, with an admixture from Dryden's *An Evening's Love*, Vanbrugh made *The Mistake*. From this came *Lovers' Quarrels* and these quarrels begat, in 1816, *Lovers' Quarrels, or Like Master, like Man*, by which time the original Restoration wit had evaporated to leave a tiresome show of pouting and posturing.[5]

In this most patrons would have looked for Shuter under the bowed grizzlings of Mr Meagrim (migraine) but instead he shed another score of years and finished the evening as James, a young French waiter, the juvenile lead in *Blue Devils*.[6] This is George Colman the Younger's version of Parat's *L'Anglais*, a skit on the English character. It had held the stage for the past thirty years and tells of a rich Englishman, out of humour with the world in general and himself in particular, languishing in a French hotel, unable to make up his mind on the finality of suicide. He has found Russia too cold, Italy too hot, Holland too dull and now France too depressingly gay. A bullet will put an end to the intolerable boredom of having nothing to do on a full stomach. To shoot himself on foreign soil however might give the impression he was fleeing a halter in his own country. For the honour of England and as a warning to those coming after him he would write his memoirs. He rings for the landlord, whereupon promptly enters the nervous, exhausted Monsieur Dennison; the name is a bare-faced country refusal to attempt the French 'Demisou'. Meagrim finds he is not the only mortal with problems. The landlord is obviously at his wits' end and rushes away. James and Annette, Demisou's daughter, whirl in clutching one another, totally absorbed in themselves alone, and settle down at one of the small tables. Demisou has not only refused all idea of their marrying but has summarily sacked the penniless James after only three months' service. Annette, eighteen, must marry a man with money. James thinks he should seek his fortune on the high seas but Annette cannot bear the thought of parting, let alone the danger, so they begin to contemplate suicide together. Meagrim fancies he has found a pair of companions for his last journey and through the subsequent cross-talk supposes that

Annette might be willing, as an alternative to suicide, to find the necessary rich husband in himself. His interest in life revives and even when disabused by the young lady, he promises to help the lovers. To make James a qualified suitor Meagrim presents him with two hundred louis d'or and goes off to obtain Demisou's consent to the marriage. The Bailiff arrives to declare Demisou bankrupt and is turned away by James flourishing his new purse. Meagrim, regretful though he is at seeing Annette securely in the waiter's arms, leaves his sheets of paper blank exclaiming:

> I have hithertoo been sick of life because I experienced nothing but its disgusts. You have taught me to relish its pleasures. I now discover that a rich man's greatest and purest joy lies in assisting his poorer fellow creatures.

The banter and cross-talk in this little piece, just forty minutes long, calls for speed and adept timing. The laughter it set off was heightened by the satire in the French popular image of an Englishman over-ready to contemplate suicide. Shuter must have added greatly to the merriment by giving a caricature of the Romeo he might have attempted in his youth.

This is the last recorded performance Shuter gave in Cirencester and in view of the turn of events the following year he is unlikely to have given many more for in 1818 the lease of the Cirencester Theatre John Boles Watson had signed in 1799 expired. Shuter was in Tewkesbury towards the end of 1818 when he arranged a new ballet and took a benefit in November. In 1819 he was still singing his comic songs though his daughter undertook the dancing of his famous hornpipe for him. At Cheltenham he appeared occasionally in farce and comedy playing old men such as Sir Lucius O'Trigger (*The Rivals*) and Sir Peter Teazle (*The School for Scandal*) until the last notice tells of him bringing out a new medley of comic songs, no doubt the old, tired favourites still, for the visitors to the Spa in July 1821, by which time miscellaneous performances or bills of variety had become popular.

Shuter had been with the company for no less than forty-two years, having been one of John Boles Watson's earliest recruits. What he had done prior to 1779 is nowhere recorded yet expertise in the execution of the rigging for Captain Cook's ship drill at Monmouth in 1790, his ordering of the drill on that occasion and his life-long desire to delight his friends and patrons with his dancing of the hornpipe may point to a few early years of life in the navy. Did he choose the unsympathetic role of Captain Bertram in 1818 in order to enjoy the pleasure of doing full main-deck justice to the Captain's rolling naval oaths? George Shuter had been dancer, ballet master, singer and competent actor in every type of play. In selecting the actor for his company Watson had been a good judge of ability as well as of character. Shuter's happy relationship with the public had been supported by his wife, his two boys and his daughters. Master George appeared at Cheltenham as a boy of seven to augment his father's benefit return, singing a comic song his father had taught him. The following year the boy learnt how draughty stages were when he appeared as Cupid. For a benefit with his mother in 1793, at the age of ten, he was joined in a dance by the elder of his two sisters. He also sang a patriotic song and the next year Edward, aged five, joined his siblings in a dance to swell their father's benefit at Cheltenham. In July 1796 Master George enjoyed a benefit entirely on his own owing to a misfortune he had met with and from which he was then happily recovering. The girls, as Miss Shuter and Miss E Shuter, did not stray far from the company but the boys joined companies at Chester, Cork and Dublin. Both were comedians after the style of their father. George achieved the distinction of appearing at Drury Lane. Mrs Shuter continued at Cheltenham as countess, baroness, empress and other weighty ladies until in 1823 a benefit was given for her alone. Travelling in all weather had for several years been out of the question for her husband and eventually he was not able to appear, even in his own town. His name does not figure on Cheltenham bills in subsequent years and little short of death would have kept him from the footlights.

George Shuter had enjoyed a special position in the company, as the large number of benefit nights he and his family were given by the Watsons, father and son, shows. The public were benevolent, not to say indulgent during the latter years, towards him and his shuffle of a hornpipe. He must have had an open, engaging stage personality and he undoubtedly always gave of the utmost of his powers. His record is remarkable in the face of the public's usual tendency to demand novelty at all costs. The engagement of visiting attractions from London was becoming a need in order to draw crowds to the box-office.

Notes

1   *The Thespian Dictionary* (1805) contains a brief entry for Shuter giving him as the son of Edward (the original Squire Hardcastle in *She Stoops to Conquer*) and mentions that he was a great favourite at the Wolverhampton Theatre. If this rapport was maintained, it was possible it prompted one of the Shuter family to take on the managership there in 1820 in which task the aspirant unfortunately proved a failure and retired in 1822. See: newspaper cuttings by J B Hardcastle, 'Old Wolverhampton Sixty Years Ago', in the Archives of the Central Library, Wolverhampton.

  The playbill for this benefit night is in the Gloucestershire Collection, Gloucester Central Library. RX 79.3.

2   *The Jew and the Doctor* by T J Dibdin was first staged at Covent Garden in 1798.

3   *The Birthday* was first staged at Covent Garden, 29 January 1797.

4   *The Midnight Hour* by Elizabeth Inchbald was first staged at Covent Garden, 22 May 1787.

5   *Lover's Quarrels* by Thomas King was first performed at Covent Garden, 11 February 1790.

6   *Blue Devils* was first staged at Covent Garden in 1798.

Chapter 14:
John Boles Watson II's Farewell

John Richer had remarried with Catherine Long in 1817, he forty-four and she thirty-seven. They were living in a fine house, standing in its own orchard, at Swindon, a village, two miles out of Cheltenham. Surrounding them were the books, paintings, silver and handsome china that witnessed Catherine's taste and education and the trophies and curiosities John had collected in the days of his European fame. She was of independent means, owning land nearby at Prestbury, and had income from rents and interest. Richer, despite his illustrious past, possessed little money. In September 1811 the elderly Watson was aware that his son-in-law had 'tradesmen and other present embarrassments' and in his will left him £400 from the £2000 assured money due from the Westminster Office, £200 within three months of the old man's death and £200 a twelvemonth later. John Richer had, however, always had an assurance roof over his head. His father-in-law had ordered in his will that £17 plus all taxes should be paid annually to the owner as rent for the cottage in Constitution Place where Richard and David Withington, Watson's aged brother-in-law, lived. This cottage, which Richer had improved and made pleasant by adding a garden, was the home created when he married Watson's beloved daughter, Louisa. Richer had doubtless made a good husband for Watson to remain as favourable towards him even though Richer had reverted to his career of eminent rope-dancer while international acclaim was still there for the seeking instead of settling down as joint manager and showing himself a steadier and shrewder support than the old man expected his own son to become.

Watson could not have objected to John Richer's remarriage.

Henrietta was Watson's second wife. She had been a widow and he a widower when they were married at Cheltenham in 1785. The marriage had brought him the desired son and heir. John Richer's new marriage brought him comfort but no children. On his remarriage Richer's interest in half the cottage was turned into an annuity, probably of £50 a year. Provisions and bequests of this type were a millstone round Jack Watson's neck. His father had directed that £20 be sent to William Watson, his brother, each year. To his wife, Henrietta, he left for life 120 guineas a year and, free of all rent and taxes, the cottage near the Cheltenham Theatre where they had lived together.

With the family cottage and the cottage in Constitution Place on his charge but occupied, Jack Watson rented a further cottage and premises near the Cheltenham Theatre with ground enough to house a large aviary. The cottage was small and eventually the building material obtained in dismantling the aviary was used to add a scullery to the cottage. The rent was £20 a year but from 1817 onwards Jack Watson neglected the formality of paying this. The furniture and contents were his property but they were soon signed away as part of a security to his Cheltenham solicitors. His affairs were a labyrinth of legal complication which he was neither diligent nor practical enough to comprehend. Despite the £1600 in life insurance inherited from his father after the bequest made to Richer, Jack Watson could find no alternative to his cash problems in 1816 but to turn to old Robert Chamberlain, the thrifty Treasurer of the Cheltenham company, in order to borrow £200. Though he thought 10% interest high he needed the cash so pressingly that he not only agreed to it but borrowed a further £200 from the same source two months later. Chamberlain appears to have done well out of the company as John Boles Watson had himself once raised a loan of £500 from him, offering the land on which the Hereford Theatre stood as surety.[1] Watson senior had also raised a loan of £85 from William Buckle, an old and reliable member of the company, in order to buy a house in Cheltenham. Buckle was still receiving £15 a year interest from Jack Watson in 1821. It is amazing that the astute John Boles Watson had borrowed money at 18% and left the burden to be carried on by his son. The father was, however, a man of devious ways and this arrangement may have been some form of pension to William Buckle while the capital value of the house in Watson's hands rose steadily in value during the prevailing wartime inflation. George Shuter nowhere figures in the Watson financial entanglements. He seems to have made provision for him out of his many benefit nights.

From property in Cheltenham, including the shop under the colonnade of the Theatre Royal, occupied for years by a John Shuter, Jack Watson received an income of some £260 but this was swallowed up in a huge annuity payable to a colonel and his wife who must have secured it by surrendering an amount of capital to Watson senior years before.[2] The unfortunate part of this arrangement was that the colonel and his wife lived to an extreme old age, too long for the deal to be a joy to the Watsons. There remained, of course, the bricks and mortar of the theatres at Cheltenham and Gloucester, both bringing in a declining return even when in use, as well as the other theatres his father had built at Warwick, Hereford, Tamworth, Walsall and Stourbridge.[3] Watson's theatres were in a deplorable condition. In the decline of theatrical business after the war the theatres at Warwick, Tamworth and Walsall had been let to the Widow Nunns of Birmingham. These according to the contract, should have brought in £269 but because of their state they were worth no more than £150 a year, even if the widow was able to pay. These leases ran out in 1818 and the former theatrical empire rapidly became a liability.[4]

Cash was Jack Watson's problem. Income was mortgaged before it came in. Some of his embarrassment was due to the complicated dealings his father throve on during the former era of general expansion, especially extensive building, although much of his trouble was generated by what his solicitors deemed 'the very imperfect will of the late Mr Watson'. To add to the tangle Jack Watson had little sense of the value of money and no notion of restraint. His easy and indulgent youth had also made him impractical. After the removal of his father's pressure to settle debts promptly, he was inclined to leave bills unpaid on all sides. This extended to his theatrical business. By 1818 the musicians in the company had not been paid 'for a long time' and at the Gloucester Theatre James Tanner had not been paid his two shillings per attendance at the Box Door for so long that he claimed he was owed

£11.10.0. Jack Watson fobbed him off with £3, no doubt quite sure that Tanner had had his free hand well silvered when opening the box door to the prosperous of Gloucester. William Parke, the oboist, related how, during a visit to Cheltenham in 1800, he was introduced by John Boles Watson to one of the minor actors with 'This is Mr D----y: he is the best-dressed man in my company, though he has one of the smallest salaries – but his wife takes the money at the pit door!'[5] In Cirencester Jack Watson owed the large sum of £51 to Search, the ironmonger. Pitt, the carpenter and bricklayer, was waiting for £15 and Bruerton had never been paid for nails and the mending of the dressing room floor and for new hinges to the seats in the boxes. Philip Watkins was owed over £5 for printing Watson's last bills in Cirencester. £2 odd was owing to William Miller for candles and last, but not least, there was due to Robert Havilland, liquor merchant, no less than £21.16.3, equivalent to a year's rent for a modest dwelling.

Jack's private life was in a similar state of irregularity. He relished the social turmoil of Cheltenham Spa with its promenade lined with fine shops as well as enjoying the rural sports the surrounding countryside had to offer. He liked to go shooting on the Brecon, riding and coursing. He bought a new whip and a pair of dog couples and had them added to his will at William Newman's in Cheltenham to bring his debt up to £16.13.6d., never intending to pay. He ran up almost £2 for a Superfine Hat at Shipton's, the hatters, in Cheltenham in June 1817 and bought another one of the same fine quality for the summer of the following year. Both were added to the bill, as well as two boys' hats at two shillings each.

Jack Watson had two sons and two, possibly three, daughters. His solicitors always avoided stating the number of his children since the total was unknown, all of them being illegitimate. Yet he assumed responsibility for them and they bear the family names of Boles and Watson. It says much for Jack Watson's regard for his children that he did not repudiate the younger boy, who was mentally retarded and had for some time to be boarded out with a farmer, Matthews, at Redford near Gloucester at a weekly cost of eight shillings. The boy ran through clothes and shoes quickly and his health occasionally incurred a doctor's bill, all of which Redford paid and charged, hopefully, to Watson. The father taught the restless, garrulous boy to recite Norval's entrance speech as Master Betty had delivered it in the tragedy, *Douglas*. The boy was also taught to recite passages from the Bible.[6] John, 'my eldest son', was the infant who had appeared as Cora's child in *Pizarro* during the Watson season at Birmingham in the winter of 1808–9.[7] The boy grew up to make his own way as actor and manager and when theatrical business began to decline worked with his father in running the minor Watson theatres. Henrietta, referred to as the youngest girl, was brought up by Mrs Watson who treated her as her own daughter. She became an actress in the company. An elder daughter was christened Louisa, after Jack Watson's sister who died as the first Mrs Richer. This daughter, like her namesake, did not go on the stage. Jack Watson also made reference to a daughter, Clara Boles Watson, and if she is not identical with Louisa this must be his third.

The pressing need to fill the benches increased Jack Watson's reliance on cunning and bluff in business, resulting in promises that went beyond the bounds of showmanship. An expedient to raise ready money was to declare a benefit night for his wife at Gloucester, where the family still enjoyed some personal popularity, and it was at one of these in May 1817 that he announced he would henceforth be devoting his whole time to the theatres at Gloucester and Cheltenham.[8] This did not mean that Cirencester would be excluded from a celebrity visitation. With the chance of a good return Kean, for instance, was brought over only a fortnight after the announcement was made but, in general, Jack Watson must have realised that his stock as well as his credit were exhausted. Retrenchment would have to be the order of the day.

At this low ebb in his affairs, only a month later, towards the end of June 1817, the Bristol newspapers carried an advertisement informing that the Bristol Theatre Royal was to let. It had been empty for years as the Bristol and Bath theatres were run as a single company. Jack Watson applied for the Bristol lease. The proprietor accepted his offer rather than that of Robert William Elliston, soon to be manager of Drury Lane, and Jack Watson shouldered the liability of a rent for theatre and dwelling house of £450 a year, plus attendant rates and taxes. Furthermore he promised to make improvements in the theatre for the greater comfort of the patrons to the tune of £500 confidently forecasting that 'under his unremitting exertions, the Drama will assume a style of propriety, correctness and elegance which will at once both merit and receive the approbation of those who may honour it with their patronage'.

On 18 August it was made known in Cheltenham that Watson had taken the Bristol Theatre Royal 'for a term of years' and, indeed, he was ready to open in Bristol ten days later with the Gloucester company led by a series of celebrities from London, headed by Eliza O'Neill and Maria Foote. Bristol soon discovered the quality of Jack Watson's management. The auditorium had been given a partial redecoration in fairground pink and green but scenery was sparse and left in the usual Watsonian gloom. Eventually a new act drop made its appearance accompanied by some scenes new to Bristol painted by Seward and probably brought from Gloucester.

It is likely that Jack Watson travelled from Bristol through the rigours of January 1818 in order to see his mother. She died and was buried in February, thus breaking the last personal link that connected him with Cheltenham and what he might have regarded as the 'good old days'. The company came to Gloucester to take advantage of the crowds in the city for Assize Week and then returned to Bristol at the end of March to catch the Easter holiday public. Here the proprietors of the Theatre Royal reiterated their demands for the rent which so far Jack Watson had not been able to include in his transactions of business.

In May the Bristol proprietors decided to have done with Watson's peregrinations and procrastination and, in the continued absence of rent, put a distraint on his scenery and costumes and all that he had in the Theatre. In the face of this Watson took an ill-considered step. To stave off the insistent demands for rent he issued two cheques on Fisher and Ashmore's Bank in Cheltenham to the value of £100, with no assurance that the money was available. A representative of the Bristol proprietors later made the journey to Cheltenham but to no avail and, after talks with the bank and Watson and his solicitors, returned with the knowledge that the rent was likely never to be paid. Jack Watson, as no doubt his solicitors pointed out to him, had brought himself within the meaning of the term 'practical insolvency', a matter which the law made its concern. Watson had the effrontery to ask for postponement of payment until Christmas (eighteen months without the payment of rent would have passed) and the proprietors proceeded to seek powers from the magistrates to clear the manager out of their theatre.

The quality of Jack Watson's effects is indicated by the result of the sale which then took place. Removable goods brought in a mere £48. The auctioneer's expenses amounted to £43. No one wanted the scenery and the proprietors took it over at a generous £250. This left Watson owing £200 still for his twelvemonth fiasco. It was hoped Watson would eventually redeem his scenery and pay the debt but prolonged negotiations came to nothing. The proprietors could easily have ruined him by making him bankrupt. For some reason they refrained from so doing. In the circumstances it is not surprising that there is no sign of entertainment at the Cirencester Theatre after Shuter's benefit evening in February 1818.[9]

In the October of that year Jack Watson announced that the Gloucester Theatre would shortly be brilliantly lighted with gas though, again not surprisingly, nothing materialised and by the end of the year it was learnt that he was to relinquish the management of the Gloucester and Cheltenham theatres. He had let them to Crisp, the energetic manager at Worcester and Chester, the agreed annual rent being £546. This move staved off eventual collapse but it could not save Watson's reputation.[10]

The *Cheltenham Chronicle* (15 April 1819) was particularly outspoken. The paper wished

to congratulate our Townsmen on the reform that seems likely to restore this department of our amusements to the standard of classical taste and dramatic excellence. We are now about to part with Mr. Watson, and we will not, by one unkind retrospection, embitter the circumstances which may have induced him to withdraw his name from the Establishment. Satisfied, as we are, that nothing less than a total and sweeping change of system could have promised him the least prospect of ultimate success, in retaining the management; we are convinced that he will feel a vast pressure of care and anxiety removed from his mind by disposing of it as he has done.

We are prepared to co-operate with Mr. Crisp's efforts to rescue the Drama from prostration and give a stimulus to the exertions of histrionic talents, seeing that the reproof of just criticism is not less useful in abashing the dull, self opinionated pretender than the voice of praise is delightful in cheering and supporting the modesty of merit.

We now have the prospect of seeing the Drama restored to the place it should hold in mental amusement and rational estimation. We wish to see the Legitimate Drama revived, and modern madness and maudlin melo-drama for ever condemned to that oblivion to which they are assuredly hastening.

The counter-blast came from Gloucester like a shot: 'Mr. Watson, without hesitation, pronounces it to be a Falsehood to the uttermost – an idea only created in malice and baneful in publicity'.

The *Cheltenham Chronicle* termed this 'so intemperate, so uncandid, and so indecent a calumny' and at the opening of the Cheltenham theatrical season in May, when a new gas chandelier gave the auditorium 'an air of neatness, cleanliness and good order', the paper shot its final, parting arrow with, 'In short it looks as if we have some one concerned in its direction who understands the business, who knows how things should be done and does them accordingly'.[11]

Notes

1　There are limited reference to these financial affairs in the papers relating to the theatre in the Warwickshire Record Office, Warwick. However, Anthony Denning uses sources here which I have not discovered.

The Hereford Theatre, built by John Boles Watson 1786, was situated in Broad Street. The three Crisp brothers succeeded Watson in management. The building was very small, its takings amounting to only £40, although on popular benefit nights they could exceed £60. See: *Hereford Journal*, 26 October 1786; W J Rees, *The Hereford Guide* (Hereford, 1827); *Notes and Queries*, I (1868) 141–2 and CLX (1931) 301.

2　*Harper's Cheltenham Street Directory* of 1844 details the shops which stood under the portico of the theatre at 9 Bath Street: at the time of publication a shoe-maker, cabinet-maker, and tailor did business there.

3　At Tamworth the Town Hall, built by Thomas Guy in 1701, was used as the theatre; later John Boles Watson replaced this with a large purpose built playhouse. See: C F Palmer, *The History of the Town and Castle of Tamworth* (Tamworth, 1845); H Charles Mitchell, *Tamworth Town and Tower* (Tamworth, 1936) and Henry Wood, *Borough by Prescription* (Tamworth, 1958).

The site of the Walsall Theatre, also purpose-built, was in Old Square. This was erected in 1803, built by subscription in shares of £50. Each subscriber received interest and a 'silver ticket', a transferable admission token. See: Thomas Pearce, *The History and Directory of Walsall* (Birmingham, 1813).

In 1793 John Boles Watson built his Stourbridge Theatre adjacent to the Talbot Hotel, itself sometimes a temporary playhouse. See: H E Palfrey *Some Account of the Old Theatres at Stourbridge* (Stourbridge, 1936); information has also been supplied by Susan Rachel Wallin of Stourbridge.

4 Pearce, in his book noted above, states that Mrs Elizabeth Nunns had in 1813 rented the Walsall Theatre from Watson and that she was the daughter of Samuel Stanton who had often visited the town with his company.

5 William Parke, *Musical Memoirs* (1830), I, 285.

6 It was rumoured that the mentally afflicted boy was drowned in the River Wye and his body discovered at Ross where, ironically, John Boles Watson I had set up a theatre.

7 Birmingham Central Library: Collection of playbills of the Theatre Royal, Birmingham.

8 *Gloucester Journal*, 26 May 1817.

9 For further details of Watson's Bristol interlude see: G Rennie Powell, *The Bristol Stage* (Bristol, 1919); Kathleen M D Barker, 'The Theatre Proprietor's Story' in *Theatre Notebook*, XVIII (1963/4), 79–91; Kathleen M D Barker, *The Theatre Royal, Bristol. The First Seventy Years* (Bristol, 1961).

10 The city authorities invited tenders in the *Gloucester Journal* (26 October 1818) from firms to light the city by gas, and possibly Watson claimed that as soon as this was available he would light the theatre by it.

John Crisp leased the Gloucester Theatre from 1 May 1819 for seven years at an annual rent of £545 which included the garden and cottage (occupied) at Cheltenham. A tenement at the south end of the theatre in Cheltenham was rented at £20 per annum (Gloucester Record Office, Gloucester, D2025, Box 73).

11 *Cheltenham Chronicle*, 8, 15 and 22 April 1819.

Chapter 15:
Samples of the Repertoire during John Boles Watson I's Management

The repertoire which John Boles Watson's company performed at the Cirencester Theatre resembled that of many other provincial companies. Experimentation with dance and documentary were rare generally and instances of Watson's engagement in these are given in this chapter. The manager, too, was bold enough to stage new writing and this too is exemplified. The date spread of the plays considered here is from 1787, through the years of the French Revolution until 1801.

The manager entrusted a grand spectacle to the dancing members of the company, the serious ballet of *Don Juan*. Work began on this in 1787. The English *Don Juan* differed considerably from the original Viennese ballet of thirty years before and though Gluck's instrumental music of the original was used, William Reeve added a number of songs, duets and choruses in the English style. The character of the Don, as well as the course of his exploits, followed Thomas Shadwell's Restoration play *The Libertine*, rather than Molière or Corneille. Unbeknown, Watson had started to announce his forthcoming production as the final rehearsals were taking place in Prague for the first performance of Mozart's new opera on the subject. Watson's production ran into difficulties 'on account of the multiplicity of stage business, different displays of scenery, machinery, Ec.' and the public did not see his Tragic Pantomimical Entertainment until January 1788.[1] It was first performed at Gloucester with the scenery, machinery, devices and transparencies by the painter and machinist at the Royalty Theatre, in London, Cornelius Dixon, one of the most competent scene painters active at the time. The proscenium at the Royalty was twenty-eight feet across and Dixon made copies of the *Don Juan* scenery about half as big as his originals suited to the size of the theatres at Cheltenham, Hereford and Brecon. Watson reminded his patrons in the *Gloucester Journal* that the entertainment had been got up 'at great expense, no attention, cost or labour being spared, to render the whole compleat, and superior to anything of the kind exhibited in the country'.[2]

The London revival had been under Carlo Delpini, an Italian dancer and mime Garrick had brought to England and who had made himself famous as Clown in the generation before Grimaldi.[3] As a producer of ballets he often arranged entertainments for the Prince Regent at the private theatre in the Royal Pavilion in Brighton. Delpini had himself danced Scaramouch, the braggart Commedia dell'Arte character which was utilised as Don Juan's comic servant, a part affording opportunities to Joseph Grimaldi's inventiveness when his turn came to step into vacant shoes. Watson wrote a prologue to the entertainment which he spoke before the curtain and from which these lines are excerpted:

> The Stage, from earliest time, has been a school
> To teach fond morals by the golden rule;
> A mirror clear, in which mankind may view
> Virtue and vice in colours warm and true.
> The precept given, example marks it strong,
> Points out the line that severs right from wrong,
> Imprinting what is good upon the mind that's young,
> Shews manhood how to steer a happy mean
> And warns old age of the conclusive scene.
> These general purposes the drama claims
> And variously your suffrages obtains.

The piece had the patrons entralled and quite oblivious of any intended moral:

The Murder by the Libertine of the Lover who is his rival in the affections of Donna Anna, the cool premeditation with which he takes the life of the Commandant, Don Guzman, Donna Anna's father, are objects which sufficiently mark the depravity of the Heart. Alarmed by the Pursuit of the officers of Justice he flies to the Sea

Shore and solicits some sailors to take him on board their Vessel to avoid falling into the hands of the law – That prevailing Argument, Gold, being applied, he at length puts to sea, but even here Divine Vengeance still pursues him, and, a violent Storm arising, his devoted Bark is wrecked and himself thrown on Shore. Scaramouch is saved on the back of a Dolphin and lands to read the catalogue of the Don's loves to the Fisherwomen. Their Pity being excited by his Distress they give him relief, but his prevailing Vice seeks to repay their kindness with an attempt upon their Virtue. Their Unhappy Father, interposing, is shot by the Libertine with his own Gun. The Second Part opens with an Equestrian Statue erected to the memory of the Commandant, which Don Juan views with the greatest unconcern, nor can the Appearance of the bloody letters on the pedestal give his heart one Pang of Remorse:

> By Thee I fell.
> Thy Fate's Decreed;
> Heaven will Revenge
> The Bloody Deed.

In seeming disdain, he challenges the Statue to give him a meeting at a banquet, where he next appears in a Scene of Dissipation and Riot. Dreadful and uncommon Noises surround the tavern. The Statue entering beckons Don Juan after him, who is led into a Dismal Subterraneous Cavern filled with bones . . . Sudden flames . . . Fiends, Furies . . . Fear and Remorse seize him and the Libertine is destroyed amidst a Shower of Fire.'[4]

The 'proper Scenery and Machinery for the View of the Ocean, Ship boarded by Don Juan, putting to Sea, afterwards wrecked' well justified the expense and the initial performance went off 'with continued Applause, from beginning to end, to an overflowing audience, as genteel as numerous'. Watson's production long remained in the repertoire to preach on the just wages of sin. It was this mimed entertainment that gave Byron the title for his narrative poem:

> I'll therefore take our ancient friend Don Juan –
> We have all seen him, in the pantomime,
> Sent to the Devil somewhat ere his time.[5]

133

We move forward to 1789, the year of the French Revolution. Watson was quick in staging a new show, *Uproar in Paris*, three months after the events depicted in it. This was a dumb show, enlivened with much shot and gunpowder, first given in Gloucester as 'a splendid pantomimical Entertainment in Two Acts'. To show the public how vividly true to fact the whole representation of the French uprising was he gambled for a full house by staking nearly a whole column of advertisement in the *Gloucester Journal.* He claimed his show displayed

> one of the grandest and most extraordinary spectacles that ever engaged the feelings of mankind, grounded on authentic facts, prepared and conducted under the direction of Mr. West, as it is now performing in London with the most universal applause. Amongst a variety of other striking matters incidental to the event will be a real representation of the whole plan of of attack, storming, capture and demolition of that horrid sepulchre of a people, the BASTILLE; the assault, and dreadful massacre of the citizens that first passed the draw-bridge; the execution of the Governor and Deputy Governor; the several military engagements, and procession on that and other occasions; together with the proceedings that gave freedom to France.[6]
>
> The new scenes painted by Mr. Whitmore, Particularly an external perspective view of the BASTILLE and the draw-bridge, both of which will be stormed, taken and destroyed by the military and citizens. Also a picturesque view and affecting representation of the internal Part of the Bastille, a View of the Subterranean Dungeons in that once terrific prison. Lord Masserene will be discovered, with the other prisoners, as found in their state of confinement; with the various instruments of torture, the different gratings, dungeons, cells and particularly the famous Iron Cage.[7]

The description and detail suggest how closely Watson copied the production of much the same name then running at the Royal Circus. He brought down West, the famous clown and mime pupil of Grimaldi, to direct the action of the show. Two new scenes, an exterior and an interior view of the Bastille, were probably painted by Mr Whitmore who possibly worked later at Covent Garden on the spectacular productions of John Philip Kemble. Whitmore may have carried out the work for Watson at Gloucester as he was present on the first night to take the part of the Marquis de la Fayette. Carleton was hero of the piece, the leader of the attacking troops, Henry du Bois, and Withington was the hated Governor of the Bastille. Watson urged his patrons to take seats early:

> The overflow of company at the Royal Circus, Astley's and Sadler's Wells, every night to see this most interesting entertainment is such, that even Ladies and Gentlemen of title and distinction cannot obtain seats after the doors open, and the performances of the horses are obliged to be omitted, to admit spectators into the ride.

The highly dramatic version copied by Watson had been staged originally by Philip Astley, competing with two dialogue versions at the Royal Circus and Sadler's Wells. Astley later elaborated his show to include severed heads in wax of the Governor and de Flesselles which he had obtained from his neighbouring showman in Paris, Dr Curtius. The Doctor's cabinet of waxworks stood next to Astley's Paris establishment on the Boulevard du Temple.[8] Curtius was preceptor and 'uncle', possibly father, of Marie Tussaud. In the year Watson opened his new playhouse and was presenting *Jacobin Cruelty* she fashioned the severed head of Robespierre with which she would one day in her turn horrify Cirencester. The head was consummately realised so that it appeared warm, with the bruise still growing from the shot that had shattered the jaw in Robespierre's bungled attempt to cheat the guillotine.

It is of interest to note that in the rival piece at the Royal Circus called *The Triumph of Liberty* the creator of Henry du Bois was Miell. This actor subsequently went into provincial management and in the year before Watson's venture at Cirencester Miell took over Worcester and Shrewsbury, previously leased by Watson. The arrangement between the two managers was termed 'a coalition of both companies to bring forward the representation of the favourite new pieces in truly respectable style.' Business, however, does not appear to have flourished under Miell, for in less than a year he was acting in the Cheltenham Company, billed as 'formerly manager at Worcester and Wolverhampton'.[9]

There is another curious footnote to Watson's *Uproar in Paris*. He drew his patrons' attention to the fact that the entertainment was not wholly grim:

After the release of the prisoners from the Bastille the Procession for
the Execution of the Governor and his Party ends the first act, which
is the finishing of the sublime part of the entertainment. The second
act commences with the COMIC and PANTOMIMICAL BUSINESS

in which the principal characters were transformed into Harlequin,
Columbine, Clown and Pantaloon to introduce excerpts from a
variety of London pantomimical performances!

The Children in the Wood staged in 1794 during the opening season
of the newly built theatre in Gloucester Street was a short piece by
Thomas Morton based on the Norfolk crime universally known
through ballad and chapbook. It was a contrast to the previously
presented horrors of the French Revolution. Morton omitted the
compassionate robin and made the outcome of the story a happy
one. Far from being 'an opera in two acts', it was more a play with
music by Samuel Arnold, one time organist at Westminster Abbey
and known locally for his work at the Three Choirs Festival. The
piece was popular everywhere and could easily be put on using the
stock scenery of baronial hall and cottage interior with a wood
placed behind to show off the full depth of the stage. Morton later
wrote the sentimental comedy of *Speed the Plough* which became a
hardy favourite at Cirencester.[10]

*Jacobin Cruelty, or Louis the Unfortunate, a New Tragedy in Five
Acts* also had a third title, *Democratic Rage, that much talked of and
truly affecting play which has been brought out and performed an
unusual number of nights since the lamentable Fall of the French King.*
This type of entertainment staged on the same evening as *The
Children in the Wood*, the dramatic documentation of well-known
events reported in the newspapers, drew audiences in hordes.
Gripping topicality allowed them in this case to relive the widespread fear aroused in England by events across the Channel just a
year earlier. Most of the plays of this writer, William Preston, were
inspired by historical events. Watson puffed overmuch in advertising
the excellencies of his production. His claim of 'a correct copy being
obtained from the Theatre Royal, Crow Street' was true but
misleading as the published text could be had for the ordering from
Dublin where it had run into a second edition since the play's first
night there in June.[11] The claim that 'attention is paid to prepare

proper dresses and the necessary apparatus for this extremely interesting and awful performance', was borne out when Shuter came before the curtain to recite a prologue specially written by Watson. The events were then unfolded by Shuter as the man of fashion, Robespierre, and Mr and Mrs Carleton as Louis XVI and Marie Antoinette. Simmons played Marat and Villiers, deputy manager and player of heavy roles, the Duke of Orleans; the Dauphin was played by Shuter's elder boy, George, aged ten, and Watson's brother-in-law was found a part as La Mignon. There is little doubt which of the events most fully satisfied public interest. Within a short time the last act had taken on a separate existence in Watson's repertoire under the title, *The Guillotine, or The Death of Louis XVI.*

A popular play, staged in 1794 at Cirencester, was *Wild Oats* by John O'Keeffe about which Watson pronounced, 'No play since *The School for Scandal* has received such universal applause or drawn so many brilliant audiences in the time'.[12] Certainly it engendered a great sense of pleasantry throughout, had lively, pointed dialogue, a plot with movement and new characters. Central to the meetings and misapprehensions is Jack Rover, a profane, happy-go-lucky strolling player with a quotation from his roles in a wide range of tragedy and comedy to suit every turn of events. The play occupies itself at great speed with the winning of a rich wife, finding long lost parents and discovering that a best friend is in fact a brother. There is time on the road to learn something first-hand of travelling actors' usage. The manager of a company of comedians, Lamp, keeps himself warm with a blanket and is a miserable figure against the all powerful Trap, prompter and Treasurer to the company. He engages the actors, distributes the bills and collects stage properties, keeps the box book, issues tickets on the night and prompts the play. He also has a book in which he writes up the cast lists, recording who acts what. Rover refuses twelve guineas for six nights despite it being a liberal offer and holds out for £20, which he gets. He supplies his own tragedy costume, which is with him in his trunk. To bring down the curtain Rover takes a step forward from the assembled characters:

But now for *As You Like It.* I shall ever love a play. A spark from Shakespeare's Muse of Fire was the star that guided me through my desolate and bewildered maze of life and brought me to these unexpected blessings.

> To merit friends so good, so sweet a wife,
> The Tender Husband be my part for life;
> My Wild Oats sown, let candid Thespian laws
> Decree that glorious harvest – your applause.

A popular afterpiece, also presented in 1794, was *The Midnight Hour*, the sinister sound of which is dispelled by the second title, *The Battle of Wits*. This was one of Mrs Inchbald's popular comedies. Many of her plots derived from French and German originals, this piece coming from a play by Dumaniant.[13] Set in Spain, it consists of a variety of tricks and contrivances verging upon improbability in so far as the hero is a brand of harmless Don Juan determined to gain access to Julia, niece of the general, Don Guzman. Julia is in raptures at the thought of being wooed by force. The hero begins, unsuccessfully, in wig and cloak and eventually gets within kissing distance of his quarry by hiding in a sea chest that is brought into the general's house. The favourite last act consists of a game of hide and seek to defeat padlocked doors, with the heroine finally whisked away by her hero just as the church bell strikes midnight. The triumph of love is abetted by the opening instruction, *Stage dark*. The scenery for this last act Watson had had painted in 1787 by Dixon of the Royalty Theatre and it was doubtless showing signs of wear after seven years of constant travel, but it never failed to enchant with its moonlit vista into an English–Spanish–French–Italian garden, the foreground flanked on either side by quaint pavilions. Mrs Inchbald's plays were liked for the kindly, humanitarian view they took of man's foibles and little weaknesses.

Another stirring French Revolution play was *The Tragedy of the Maid of Normandy*.[14] In 1789, when euphoria over the fall of the Bastille set up cries of 'Liberty!' in England, the French royal family had been in considerable odium because of their support of the colonists against Britain in the American War of Independence and their reception of an embassy from the Sultan of Mysore seeking to stir up hostilities against England. In 1794, with England in arms

138

against regicide France, public feeling had veered dramatically. Any trace of *Uproar in Paris* had to be expunged from memory and Watson recommended this piece most warmly to his patrons as 'the celebrated new and very affecting Tragedy' and 'a most pathetic and interesting new play, showing Jacobin Cruelty and French Principles in their true Colours'.

To restate the manager's unshakable loyalty to the Crown, Watson had again written an original prologue which closed, amidst universal applause, with the words:

> May all Republicans with envy see
> A Monarch happy, and his Subjects free;
> May Peace extend her Olive-branching wings,
> And Freedom smile beneath the Reign of Kings.

These fervent sentiments were spoken before the curtain by Shuter. It was the Queen's role (played by Mrs Carleton) that brought the play provincial success. Its premiere was given at Wolverhampton earlier that year under Miell's management and it was due to the coalition between Watson and Miell that Cirencester was privileged to see the original production. Miell had chosen the play for his benefit at Gloucester where it was advertised as 'never performed here, and licensed by the Lord Chamberlain of His Majesty's Household'. To attract a bumper house on that occasion Miell had brought to Gloucester to act an unspecified character, for that one night only, the author of the play whom he proudly announced as John Edmund Eyre of Pembroke College, Oxford.[15]

In the winter of 1801 Watson staged a newly written comedy, *Speed the Plough* by Thomas Morton who wrote *The Children in the Wood* considered earlier in this chapter.[16] The central figure is the tender-hearted Farmer Ashfield, homely and generous, yet, at a turn, hot tempered as well, a John Bull character of appeal to the whole house. The old man dotes on his daughter, Susan, who is in love with Bob, son of Sir Abel and the late Lady Handy, though the young man himself is at the moment hopelessly smitten by the charms of Miss Blandford, daughter of Sir Philip, a dark character said to have killed his erring brother years before and to have done away with the brother's little son. While Bob Handy sighs between

Sir Philip's daughter and Susan Ashfield, the audience is kept amused by exchanges between Farmer Ashfield and his wife and Sir Abel and his new Lady. This over-dressed comedienne was formerly a servant in the Ashfield's farmhouse and to the unending mortification of poor Sir Abel her acquired gentility is constantly being puckered by the tickle from her hayrick origins. The erring brother, supposedly dead, turns up to clear Sir Philip's name and to discover that his presumed lost son is no other than Henry, the boy brought up on the farm as the Ashfield's own. Henry is promptly affianced to his cousin, Miss Blandford, and Bob Handy quickly decides in favour of Susan before she can refuse him. As the curtain is about to fall a man arrives who proves to be Lady Handy's supposedly long dead husband and amidst the resulting consternation a relieved Sir Abel gently but firmly places his Lady into the newcomer's arms.

Farmer Ashfield may be forgotten now but one of the characters lives on, though she never appears on stage. The farmer's wife is so concerned with what their neighbour will think of the goings-on at the farm that the good man is driven to exclaim in exasperation:

> Be quiet, wull ye! Always ding, dinging Dame Grundy into me ears –
> what will Mrs. Grundy say? What will Mrs. Grundy think?

As a symbol for censorious, strait-laced neighbour, Old Mother Grundy outlived the play and Grundyism became synonymous with narrow-minded respectability.

This representative selection of plays is a reminder of the importance of comedy in the provincial theatre. In addition to those mentioned here the witty plays of Richard Sheridan maintained their popularity to the end of the eighteenth century, together with the light, sentimental pieces of Richard Cumberland and George Colman the Younger. Several of the gothic heroic melodramas and the tragedies of the day are considered in the next chapter.

Notes

1 *The Libertine* by Thomas Shadwell was first staged in 1675 at the Dorset Gardens Theatre. William Reeve (1757–1815) was an actor, organist and composer. In the latter capacity he was engaged at Astley's Hippodrome and later composed music for the pantomimes at Sadler's Wells Theatre of which he was part proprietor. See: Eric Blom, ed., *Groves Dictionary of Music and Musicians* (1954).

2 *Gloucester Journal*, 21 and 28 January and 4 February 1788.

Cornelius Dixon (fl 1783–1821) was engaged by John Palmer (1742–98) on the opening of the Royalty Theatre, Wellclose Square in 1787. The fare at the Royalty consisted mainly of burlettas and pantomimes and it was for these that Dixon was the designer. From 1812 he was engaged at Drury Lane.

Watson built the Brecon Theatre in 1787 (*Gloucester Journal*, 21 January 1787). *Don Juan* was staged there in 1790; a playbill for this piece is held in the National Library of Wales and the text is given in 'Eighteenth Century Playbills of the English Theatre in Wales' by Cecil Price in the *Journal of the National Library of Wales*, VI (1949–50), 270–1. The Hereford Theatre, also built by Watson, was described in the *Hereford Journal* (21 September 1786, the year of its opening) as 'very handsome'.

3 Biographical details of Carlo Antonio Delpini (1740–1828) are to be found in his obituaries in the *Gentleman's Magazine* and the *New Monthly Magazine* (1828). He often worked in private, aristocratic theatres: for example, at Wargrave, Berkshire, he not only designed and directed productions for the Earl of Barrymore (1769–1793) but also designed his theatre for him. See: John Williams, *The Life of the Late Earl of Barrymore* (1793); E Beresford Chancellor, *Old Q and Barrymore* (1925).

4 *Gloucester Journal*, 21 January 1788.

5 *Don Juan*, canto 1, verse 1. Byron may have seen a pantomime such as Thomas Shadwell's *The Libertine* which prompted him to write *Don Juan* but the poem is more likely to have had its origin in the Italian burlesque; see T G Steffan's introduction to *The English Poets, Lord Byron, Don Juan* (1982).

6 For many Englishmen the Bastille, a fourteenth-century Parisian fort converted into a state prison, was the symbol of inhumane immurement, although at the time of its fall on 14 July 1789 only seven prisoners were found to be confined there. Lawrence Sterne in his book *A Sentimental Journey through France and Italy* (1768) expends a chapter on his horror at the sight of one of the Bastille's long term prisoners.

Gloucester Journal, 21 and 28 September 1789.

7   This Whitmore is difficult to identify. Samuel Whitmore, assisted by several of his sons, was actively engaged in scene painting for fifty years from the mid 1770s, for the last twenty years of his life working at Covent Garden. In his possible link with Watson the 'Irish connection' may be at work for in his younger days Samuel Whitmore painted in Dublin and Kilkenny. According to Lord William Pitt Lennox the latter town was strong in private theatricals in the eighteenth century. It also possessed a public theatre.

8   Allardyce Nicoll mentions three versions of this entertainment. In 1789 *The Bastille* was in rehearsal at Covent Garden. *The Triumph of Liberty, or The Destruction of the Bastille* was put on at the Royal Circus and there was *Paris in an Uproar, or The Destruction of the Bastille* at the Royal Grove Theatre. Both pieces were presented in 1789, neither is credited by Nicoll with an author; presumably the shows were evolved as a kind of historical spectacle. See: Allardyce Nicoll, *A History of English Drama, 1660–1900* (Cambridge, 1955) and A H Saxon, 'Capon, the Royal Circus, and The Destruction of the Bastille', *Theatre Notebook* XXVIII (1974). The West, described as a 'famous clown' is difficult to identify. James West was a circus proprietor from about 1810 and was involved with the Royal Circus in 1816.

9   Of William Miell (d 1797), the *Thespian Dictionary* (1805) notes that he was born in England, established as a comedian and then, before entering theatrical management, was superintendent of a circus. In 1784 he was deputy manager of the Chapel Street Theatre in Dublin.

10   *The Children in the Wood* was first performed in 1793 at the Haymarket Theatre. *Speed the Plough* was first given in 1800 at Covent Garden.

11   The play received its first production, as the text implies, at the theatre in Crow Street, Dublin, in 1793. With remarkable speed it crossed the Atlantic and was given at Charleston, South Carolina, in 1795.

12   *Wild Oats*, written by John O'Keeffe, received its first production at Covent Garden in 1791.

13   The original play was *Guerre Ouverte* by Dumaniant, the *nom-de-plume* of A J Bourlin. Elizabeth Inchbald was commissioned by Thomas Harris, manager of Covent Garden, to prepare an English translation which was first staged in 1787.

14   *The Tragedy of the Maid of Normandy* by Edmund John Eyre (1767–1816) received its first night at the Wolverhampton Theatre in January 1794. Although licensed for performance in the Midlands, the Lord Chambelain refused, for political reasons, to licence the play for presentation at Bath.

15   According to Isaac Reed in the *Biographia Dramatica* (1812) Edmund

John Eyre was a student at the Cambridge Pembroke College which, before graduating, he left to become an actor. Initially Eyre joined a theatre company near Windsor, playing Joseph Surface as his first role. In 1791, during the management of Miell, Eyre joined the Wolverhampton company and the following year, on his benefit night, he spoke an occasional address of his own composition. In it he bemoans his 'adverse fortune' and lack of fame. The address appears in his *Poetic Essays and The Fatal Sisters* (1797). Fame did not by-pass him altogether as in 1806 he appeared as Jacques (*As You Like It*) at Drury Lane. See: John Genest, *Some Account of the English Stage* (Bath, 1832); *Notes and Queries*, VI (1858), 414.

For the notice of Miell's benefit see the *Gloucester Journal*, 5 May 1794.
16   *Speed the Plough* was first given at Covent Garden in 1800.

Chapter 16:
Selections from the Repertoire during John Boles Watson II's Management

On looking at the plays in Jack Watson's repertoire we realise at once that a change of management has taken place. No longer is the willingness to experiment in evidence; nor, with a few exceptions, do we find so rapid a following up of the successes of the London patent houses. Revivals of works established for some years form the safe fare which Jack Watson offered to his patrons. In order to illustrate a range of work the plays in this chapter are those presented in the Gloucestershire section of the circuit, rather than solely in Cirencester. It is possible however that, although unadvertised as such, they may all have been staged in the bijou theatre in Gloucester Street.

Mrs Siddons visited Cirencester in August 1807, appearing as Mrs Beverley in *The Gamester* by Edward Moore. According to a report in the *Gloucester Journal* the actress had appeared in the part at Cheltenham previous to the advertised programme and had been received by a most brilliant circle with rapturous applause, some of the first nobility in the land gracing the boxes. The paper added that the audience had repeatedly been in floods of tears.[1] There is no doubt that Mrs Siddons found the role congenial in that it reflected much in her own character, especially the strain of melancholy which increased with the sadness of her own personal and private life. Writing from Cheltenham in August 1798, the year she lost her daughter, Maria, she had said,

> I must go dress for Mrs Beverley – my soul is well tuned for scenes of woe, and it is sometimes a great relief from the struggle. I am continually making to wear a face of cheerfulness at home, that I can

GAMESTER.

Mrs SIDDONS as Mrs BEVERLEY.

Act V. Scene 4. Bev. O! for a few short. Moments! to tell you
how my Heart bleeds for you. —

As Mrs Beverley in *The Gamester* Mrs Siddons reduced her audiences to floods of tears.

145

at least upon the stage give a full vent to the heart which, in spite of my best endeavours, swells with its weight almost to bursting; and then I pour it all out upon my innocent auditors.[2]

Since writing that letter she had lost another daughter, Sarah.

Mrs Beverley is the first to enter after the rise of the curtain and the applause of welcome that greeted her must have made it demanding to establish the gloomy mood of both character and play. Sunken and spiritless from the start, Mrs Beverley had moved into a lodging house with her husband after he had gambled away all her fortune. Their furniture and belongings have just been sold but with great resignation in poverty she will not reproach him as long as she has his love. She is only disturbed that Beverley has not spent the night with her, the first time since their marriage. Charlotte, her sister, whose chances of marrying Lewson are now reduced, urges her to take action with the erring husband. He is at heart a kindly man and devoted to her but Mrs Beverley should seek to separate him from Stukely, an early suitor of Mrs Beverely years before her marriage and a self-styled friend to Beverley. Stukely's plan is to ruin the husband while pretending to help him and so win the wife for himself. Charlotte asks Mr Beverley for the return of money he has in his safe keeping for her but he prevaricates, having gambled it away. Stukely instructs him to take Mrs Beverley's jewels in an attempt to win money enough at the gaming tables to repay Charlotte. The man tells Mrs Beverely that her husband has given her jewel case to a mistress and, pressing his advances on her, declares his undying love: 'I will make a widow of you and court you honourably'. She forcefully repulses him. Realising that Lewson is aware of his true character, Stukely hires a ruffian to do away with him. Mr Beverley quarrels with Lewson in the street in front of others for meddling in his private affairs. The hired murderer falsely reports that he has stabbed Lewson to death and Stukely sees to it that Beverley, recently clapped in gaol for debt, is charged with the murder on the strength of the dispute with Lewson that took place in public.

Mrs Beverley, Charlotte and Lewson, who have bought off the man sent to murder him, come to Beverley in prison with the news that an uncle has died and left him a fortune but, already broken by debt, conscience and accusations, Beverley has taken poison:

Lend me your hand, love – so – raise me – no – 'twill not be – my life is finished – O! for a few short moments, to tell you how my heart bleeds for you – that even now, thus dying, dubious and fearful of hereafter, my bosom pang is for your miseries. Support her, Heaven! – and now I go – O! Mercy! Mercy!

William Macready acting alongside Siddons at the end of her career wrote of Mrs Siddons' reaction to her stage-husband's death:

Her glaring eyes were fixed in stony blankness on his face; the powers of life seemed suspended in her; her sister and Lewson gently raised her, and slowly led her unresisting from the body, her gaze never for an instant averted from it; when they reached the prison door she stopped, as if awakened from a trance, uttered a shriek of agony that would have pierced the hardest heart, and, rushing from them, flung herself, as if for union in death, on the prostrate form before her . . .[3]

A play which also offered audiences a fill of horrors was *Blue Beard* by George Colman the Younger.[4] In 1801 Colonel Kingscote and his officers had requested the melodrama. Ten years later it was again given in Cirencester possibly with the same elaborate scenery which added to the terrors of the action. Chief of the horrific delights was still the Blue Chamber, or Cavern of Death. Above the entrance to this is a life size painting. Blue Beard is discovered showing his latest wife a picture of himself in amorous supplication to a beautiful woman. The wife will not be denied a sight of what lies beyond and as the key he has handed her is inserted into the lock the door sinks into the floor and the revealed chamber now shows walls of blue streaked with streams of blood running over tombs of white marble. On the central sarcophagus reclines a skeleton, a dagger clutched in its grip.

The picture over the doorway has miraculously changed and now shows Blue Beard beheading the beauteous creature he at first adored. Gradually can be discerned written in blood on the sarcophagus (and lit from within), the words 'The Punishment of Curiosity'. The shades of Blue Beard's slaughtered wives pass in warning. Fatima, the latest, is seized to undergo the ordeal. She attempts to defend herself against the monster and moves to snatch the dagger from the grip of the skeleton but the heap of bones rises erect, holding the weapon beyond the reach of her panic-stricken gropings.

Swiftly the reeking atmosphere is slashed by the flash of a scimitar. Her rescuer, Selim, brandishes his drawn blade as he rushes in. A fight to the death ensues, the blaspheming Blue Beard retreating against the central tomb until he is overthrown. Thereupon the arm of the skeleton falls as if the dagger in the rattling hand were of lead, plunging the blade deep into Blue Beard's heart. Blue Beard dies raging, and corpse and avenging bones sink into the grave-trap amidst leaping tongues of red fire. The Magic Cavern changes suddenly into a Garden festooned with fairy lights waiting the arrival of Fatima and Selim.

In 1814 *The Miller and his Men* had been twice advertised as in rehearsal. Both postponement and rehearsals were possible ruses on the part of the manager to whet interest in a play known by name from its phenomenal success as an afterpiece in London in October 1813. The morning after the premiere *The Times* had said the piece called forth 'peals of approbation; and *The Miller and his Men* was given out for a second representation amidst great applause'. The *Morning Post* found this melodrama yielded 'considerable amusement' and that 'an agreeable bustle is kept up from the beginning of the piece to its end'.[5] Jack Watson had shown business acumen comparable with that of his father in obtaining this 'new and very interesting piece', as he described it, as soon as approbation by London public and critics prompted its publication. He put the piece into rehearsal so that he could have it ready for the spring season of 1814 at his Gloucester Theatre which he had had redecorated by Seward during the winter. Seward also painted the splendid scenery for the new piece though Jack Watson misinformed the public by advertising the text as copied from that 'in use at the Theatre Royal, Drury Lane'. The piece had come out at Covent Garden. The manner in which Watson produced it 'gave universal satisfaction, as was fully proved by the reiterated plaudits with which it was received'.

The author was Isaac Pocock, then at the beginning of a long list of melodramas, notably adaptations, many from the novels of Sir Walter Scott. *The Miller and his Men* may not have been entirely his own invention. It is said that a hack writer by the name of Lyons sent the Covent Garden management a play called *The Robbers of the Rhine* and had it rejected only to find his plot used in Pocock's melodrama. The piece owes something to Schiller, whose brand of robber had by 1813, however, fallen from Robin Hood glory and to Pixerécourt, a man formed by the violence and idealism of the French Revolution, whose own words, 'I write for those who cannot read', would serve as motto. Not for nothing was Pocock son of a marine painter at Bristol, where he was born, and a pupil of Romney in the portraitist's later phase as an historical painter. Pocock had his 'Murder of Thomas à Becket' exhibited at the Royal Academy in 1807 and *The Miller and his Men* opened with one of the most celebrated of picturesque settings ever to appear on the English stage. On a rocky eminence stood the play's centre of interest, a windmill with it sails turning. At the end of the piece the mill is blown off the face of the earth, accompanied by red flashes of fire behind a transparency of the mill rising in flame-girt smithereens, a rain of shivered timbers and flying limbs. Mr Quantrill received due acknowledgement in the *Gloucester Journal* for the effective execution.[6]

Moving back to Cirencester two highly successful plays, written at the end of the previous century, were presented in 1815. These were *The Castle Spectre* and *Pizarro*. The first play, a dramatic romance, was a staggering pastiche of Gothic horror put together by Matthew Gregory Lewis, generally known to his audiences as 'Monk' Lewis, from the title of his first novel. Notwithstanding obvious poaching from German and English sources, this piece, rigged out with grand costumes and spectacular scenery and robustly acted to a background of music garnered by Michael Kelly, never failed to sweep audiences into waves of excitement and enthusiasm. They were quite oblivious of the bombast in the acting and the playing for effect at every turn and acclaimed each succeeding scene with delight.[7]

As the Town had expressed a wish to see William Betty again, he appeared the week after *The Castle Spectre* as Rolla, the celebrated figure in the much admired tragedy *Pizarro*, with Mrs Waring, the previous week playing the innocent heroine Angela, as Elvira the soldiers' trull.[8] Special scenery was brought from Cheltenham showing a view of Pizarro's Tent, the Temple of the Sun, a

Subterranean Cavern in the Rocks and the Bridge over which Rolla makes his Escape. The manager was particularly anxious that the list of scenery should not be omitted when the *Pizarro* bill was read out from the stage. He was eager that the public's appetite for more spectacle should be thoroughly whetted and a full house ensured. He marked the bill specially because he could no longer charge double prices for a boy wonder as his father had.[9]

Jack Watson came over to Cirencester himself to supervise the performance and to take the part of Alonzo, Rolla's friend. The house was doubtless full soon after the doors opened since the play was one of the few successful late eighteenth-century tragedies and every leading actor aspired to displaying the range of his voice, nobility of demeanour and the classical line of his physique, all of which were required to make a truly noble savage of the Peruvian leader.

The colourful background to the story and the telling dramatic situations had encouraged August Friedrich von Kotzebue's German play, *Die Spanier in Peru*, to be translated into English twice before Sheridan adapted it for the London stage. The literary élite preferred reading the sublimities of Schiller to watching Kotzebue's mastery of theatrical effect – George III, a great playgoer, thought it a very poor piece – but the dramatic spectacle drew crowds from the public in general wherever it was performed. Sheridan had a great gift for gauging the current taste of the theatre-going public and would have enjoyed the heightened effect contemporary events could give his words sixteen years after the premiere.[10]

The play was presented at the Cirencester Theatre on 10 July 1815 by which time news had reached the town that the Allies had entered Paris. A highlight of the play was the call to arms made by Rolla (William Betty) in the Temple of the Sun. The setting showed the place of Peruvian worship, with a transparent Sun and a miraculous descent of fire upon the Altar. Arms and banners were paraded and ceremonially blessed to a military march and though Betty may have felt that much of the pomp of Drury Lane was missing, any lack of tinsel will have spurred him on to use his voice the more deliberately in Rolla's rousing speech to the nation:

150

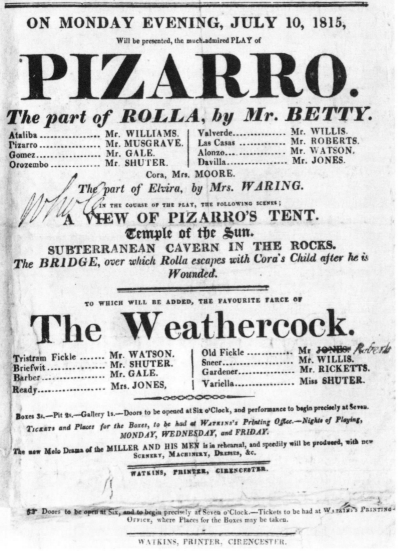

THEATRE, CIRENCESTER.

As it seems a general wish of the Ladies and Gentlemen of the Town and Neighbourhood to see Mr. BETTY perform again, the Manager, ever studious of adding as far as possible to the entertainment of the Public, has the pleasure to inform them, that on MONDAY next, he will appear in the Character of ROLLA.

ON MONDAY EVENING, JULY 10, 1815,

Will be presented, the much-admired PLAY of

PIZARRO.

The part of ROLLA, by Mr. BETTY.

Ataliba	Mr. WILLIAMS.	Valverde	Mr. WILLIS.
Pizarro	Mr. MUSGRAVE.	Las Casas	Mr. ROBERTS.
Gomez	Mr. GALE.	Alonzo	Mr. WATSON.
Orozembo	Mr. SHUTER.	Davilla	Mr. JONES.

Cora, Mrs. MOORE.

The part of Elvira, by Mrs. WARING.

IN THE COURSE OF THE PLAY, THE FOLLOWING SCENES;

A VIEW OF PIZARRO'S TENT.

Temple of the Sun.

SUBTERRANEAN CAVERN IN THE ROCKS.

The BRIDGE, over which Rolla escapes with Cora's Child after he is Wounded.

TO WHICH WILL BE ADDED, THE FAVOURITE FARCE OF

The Weathercock.

Tristram Fickle	Mr. WATSON.	Old Fickle	Mr. JONES Roberts
Briefwit	Mr. SHUTER.	Sneer	Mr. WILLIS.
Barber	Mr. GALE.	Gardener	Mr. RICKETTS.
Ready	Mrs. JONES,	Variella	Miss SHUTER.

Boxes 3s.—Pit 2s.—Gallery 1s.—Doors to be opened at Six o'Clock, and performance to begin precisely at Seven.
TICKETS and Places for the Boxes, to be had at WATKINS's *Printing Office.—Nights of Playing*, MONDAY, WEDNESDAY, and FRIDAY.
The new Melo Drama of the MILLER AND HIS MEN is in rehearsal, and speedily will be produced, with new SCENERY, MACHINERY, DRESSES, &c.

WATKINS, PRINTER, CIRENCESTER.

☞ Doors to be open at Six, and to begin precisely at Seven o'Clock.—Tickets to be had at WATKINS's PRINTING-OFFICE, where Places for the Boxes may be taken.

WATKINS, PRINTER, CIRENCESTER.

The recent defeat of Napoleon lent a new significance to the patriotic speeches of Rolla in Sheridan's drama of *Pizarro*.

151

My brave associates – partners of my toil, my feelings, and my fame! –
can Rolla's words add vigour to the virtuous energies which inspire
your hearts? . . . These bold invaders, by a strange frenzy driven,
fight for power, for plunder, and extended rule; we, for our country,
our altars, and our homes. They follow an adventurer whom they
fear: we serve a monarch whom we love – a God whom we
adore . . . The throne we honour is the people's choice; the laws we
reverence our brave fathers' legacy. . . . Tell your invaders this, and
tell them, too, we seek no change: and, least of all, such change as they
would bring us.

The house rose immediately in shouts of approval. The words
expressed exactly the fear and pride in every heart.[11]

The final words given to Elvira (Mrs Waring), as if addressing the
French, sadly intoned:

Spaniards, return to your native home, assure your rulers they
mistake the road to glory. Tell them the pursuits of avarice, conquest
and ambition never yet made people happy, or nation great.

The audience was still as she moved across the stage to make her exit,
passing the body of the tyrant Pizarro on which she cast a look of
agony, betraying that she still loved the man. The play came to an
end with the Peruvians intoning a Solemn Dirge while the dead
Rolla was raised on a bier and, flanked, by Alonzo and Cora with the
child, borne away to a Dead March, slowly and sorrowfully enough
for the house to see in the lifeless, blood-stained hero the estimated
7,000 British that rumour said lay on the field of Waterloo.

Another popular revival given at Cirencester in 1815 was
Valentine and Orson.[12] The plot was well known for it was to be
found in innumerable little chap-books sold at fairs as well as in
pretty editions for children to be had from the booksellers. The story
of twin brothers, one reared as a wild man by a bear and the other
brought up at court as a prince, existed with variations all over
Europe. The troubadours of medieval France had taken it up and in
the course of time this piece of universal folk-lore had found its way
on to the stage. Miss Hudson was listed as Valentine's Princess
Eglantine, daughter of Pepin, King of France (Jones), Miss Shuter
as Agatha, Eglantine's confidante, and Mrs Moore as the beautiful

Florimenda, daughter of Duke Savary of Acquitaine. Livid villainy was assured with Roberts as the Green Knight, Agramant, and behind the scenes there would have been Quantrill with his thin box carefully meting out powered magnesium and preparing a barium chlorate mixture to light the Pavilion of the Green Knight in appropriate flash and hue. On the same evening the company gave the Polynesian romance *Inkle and Yarico* by George Colman the Younger compressed into two acts with music by Samuel Arnold.[13]

Notes

1   *Gloucester Journal*, 10 August 1807.
  The Gamester was first staged at Drury Lane in 1753. John Philip Kemble and Sarah Siddons appeared in it together at the same theatre in 1783. Notices on the play are given in *Biographia Dramatica* (1812).
  According to John Doran, *'Their Majesties' Servants', Annals of the English Stage* (1864), Sarah Siddons first played in Cheltenham in 1773 when Chamberlain and Crump were the managers. She took the title role of Belvidera with costumes lent by Miss Boyle, Lord Dungarvon's daughter. 'The Cheltenham "propertys",' Siddons remarked, 'were of the poorest'.
  Siddons' season of 1806–7 was a busy one at Covent Garden. She then went on tour, playing at Liverpool in July and she subsequently appeared at the Gloucestershire theatres in August 1807.
2   For Sarah Siddons' letters at this time of trial see James Boaden, *Memoirs of Mrs Siddons* (1827), pp 354 ff.
3   William Charles Macready, *Macready' Reminiscences*, ed. Frederick Pollock (1875), I, 55.
4   *Blue Beard* was first presented at Drury Lane in 1798. In 1811 the play was revived at Covent Garden with several interludes for a troupe of horse added and the importation of Astley's Stud. Some provincial managers, such as Samuel Russell at Oxford, introduced horses into their small playhouses (*Jackson's Oxford Journal*, 17 June 1815). Had Watson done this, however, he would have made capital of the fact in the newspapers. *Blue Beard* contains Colman's elaborate stage directions and it is on these that Anthony Denning bases his descriptions of the scenes.
5   *The Times* and the *Morning Post*, 22 October 1813. The play was staged at Covent Garden with music by Henry Bishop (1786–1855) and scenery by John Henderson Grieve (1770–1845) and Charles Pugh (fl 1786–1828).
6   The blow-up was achieved in the London production by the stage hands

hoisting sections of the mill, which jig-sawed together, into the flies; further parts were knocked flat and the machinist catapulted life-size rag dolls into the air. Rough edges of this activity were in part hidden by flashes and smoke. Such London stage effects, many of which were similar in the country theatres, are described in Percy Fitzgerald, *The World behind the Scenes* (1881) and Mitchell Wells, 'Spectacular Scenic Effects of the Eighteenth Century Pantomime', *Philosophical Quarterly*, XVII (1938), 67–81.

7   *The Castle Spectre* by Matthew Gregory Lewis was first presented at Drury Lane in 1797. *The Monk*, also by M G Lewis (1775–1818), received its first publication in 1796; a recent reissue in the *World's Classics* (1980) is edited by James Kinsley. For a detailed description of the play on the London stage see Paul Ranger, *Terror and Pity Reign in every Breast* (1991).

8   *Pizarro* by Richard Brinsley Sheridan was first staged at Drury Lane in 1799.

9   A bill dated 10 July 1815 for the Cirencester production is in the Gloucestershire Collection, Gloucester Public Library. Jack Watson had already some experience of mounting the scenery for this plot as he gave *The Virgin of the Sun* in June 1812 at Cheltenham. This entertainment was based on Marmontel's *Incas* and Kotzebue's *Rolla*. One of the settings was for the Temple of the Sun in which the interior 'lighted up'. See: playbill in the collection of the Cheltenham Museum and Art Gallery.

10   Kotzebue's text was closed to Sheridan who could not read German; instead he worked from translations by M G Lewis, *Rolla, or The Peruvian Hero* (1799) and Anna Plumtre, *The Spaniards in Peru, or The Death of Rolla* (1799). As Sheridan's title implies he shifted the focus from the Peruvian leader to the Spanish conquistador, Pizarro. An informative article on these sources is to be found in the *Critical Review*, July 1799. Thomas Dutton, in his pamphlet *Pizarro in Peru or the Death of Rolla* (1799), deals with the staging at some length.

Although George III may not have liked *Pizarro*, he commanded it for a performance at Covent Garden in 1804 as part of the celebrations for his temporary recovery from porphyria. James Fittler (1758–1835) made an engraving of the theatre interior, clearly showing the stage and the scene of the Valley of the Torrent in which Rolla rescues Cora's child.

11   There was an irony in Betty speaking lines to which John Philip Kemble had given a definitive rendering. The Kemble family had scant respect for the juvenile. In tackling the cited speech, Kemble declaimed loudly 'we serve a monarch' and then dropped his voice dramatically in speaking of 'a God whom we adore'. Charles Mayne Young (1777–1856) who later played the role carried on this tradition of delivery. See:

Enchiridion Clericum (1912) and the *Stage* (1815–6).

Playbills in the Gloucestershire Collection, Gloucester Central Library, and the playbill collection of the Cheltenham Museum and Art Gallery indicate that other roles played by Betty in his 1815 visit to Cirencester were Alexander the Great in *The Rival Queens*, Nathaniel Lee's tragedy first staged in 1677, Selim in Dr John Brown's *Barbarossa* and the title role in *Hamlet* with Shuter as Polonius and Miss Shuter as a most feminine Osrick.

12   *Valentine and Orson* by Thomas Dibdin was first performed at Covent Garden in 1804. A bill for the play, dated 25 August 1815, is to be found in the Cheltenham Museum and Art Gallery collection.

13   The operetta *Inkle and Yarico* was first given at the Haymarket Theatre in 1787.

Chapter 17:
Theatrical Visitors to Cirencester

Every Georgian theatre manager invited a bevy of London performers to his theatres. These served to attract full houses. Many of the people John Boles Watson drew to Cirencester in its early days have already been considered and in this chapter the focus is on the nineteenth-century visitors.

Amongst the novelties Watson introduced in 1802 was

the New and Popular Exhibition, called Phantasmagoria, or, Wonderful Display of Optical Illusion, which has engrossed and still continues to attract the attention of the Fashionable World, having drawn together all last winter more Crowded Audiences in London, Dublin, Edinboro', York, Bath, Liverpool, Ec., Ec., than any other species of entertainment. It is absolutely necessary that the Theatre should be entirely darkened during the Exhibition, which (for that reason) will precede the Play and commence precisely at 7 o'clock, after which no person can be admitted until the Phantasmagoria is closed, which will not exceed 20 minutes. This Spectralogy, which professes to expose the practices of artful Imposters and pretended Exorcists, and to open the eyes of those who still foster the absurd belief in Ghosts, or dismembered Spirits, will, it is assumed, afford to the spectator an interesting and pleasing Entertainment.[1]

Awed into silence by the gloom and shuddering of approaching thunder, the distant clanging of bells and the heavy clank of chains which usually accompanied these exhibitions, the audience would have waited breathless until a cry of fright and relief went up as the Castle Spectre appeared in a burst of smoke and glided around the walls and boxes, eventually to settle, shimmering, in front of them.

The patrons knew the lady in white from Lewis's romantic drama but she was never so eerily diaphanous before. She retreated gradually until she vanished in a flicker, followed by a Skeleton too realistic to be as congenial as the mischievous bag of bones in the Harlequinade. Into the pitch darkness were

> introduced Phantoms and Apparitions of the Dead and Absent, in a way more completely illusive than has ever been offered to the Eye in a Public Theatre, as the Objects freely originate in the Air, and unfold themselves under various Forms and Sizes, such as imagination alone has hitherto painted them, occasionally assuming the Figure and most perfect Resemblance of several distinguished Characters of the past and present.

Then was seen a shade which changed to the recently deceased Lord Howe, First Lord of the Admiralty, recognisable from a popular print as the victor at sea over revolutionary France on 'The Glorious First of June', 1794. Next followed Shakespeare, depicted leaning against a pillar, a pile of his works at his feet, for all to acknowledge in the stance so well known from Scheemaker's statue niched in Stratford-upon-Avon Town Hall. The figure of the Duke of Bedford 'recently dead' appeared. Some might remember him as the young man of much character and little education (he discovered books at the age of twenty-four) who finished his reckless early years as one of the two seconds supporting the fainting Prince of Wales during his marriage to Caroline of Brunswick. Others might recall him as Francis Russell, fifth of the line, protesting in the House of Lords against the brutal means used to put down rebellion in Ireland at the time of Napoleon's threatened invasion of England, the rebellion that colonel Kingscote and the Royal North Gloucester Militia had helped suppress. He remained in the public eye while his girth increased as a figure of caricature and lampoon:

> Thou Leviathan on ocean's brim,
> Hugest of things that sleep and swim,

until he retired to his seat at Woburn, there to achieve lasting renown as a revolutionary agriculturalist and stock breeder. The audience would know of the festivities at his model farm each year which attracted farmers from all over the country with sheep shearing demonstrations, wool sampling, prizes for ploughing and similar rural competitions.[2]

Finally shone a portrait of Lord Nelson, already with eye patch and empty sleeve, the hero of Cape St Vincent, Aboukir and Copenhagen, guardian of the uneasy peace then reigning after the Treaty of Amiens. Even with Trafalgar undreamed of, he was depicted 'in the Arms of Victory and Crowned by Fame'. The newspaper reported:

> The Effect of this Exhibition was equally new and astonishing, the spectres seemed to emerge from total darkness, and float, in empty space, gradually or suddenly expanding themselves at the pleasure of the operator, approaching within a few paces of the spectator, in whatsoever part of the theatre he is placed; nay, so strange is the illusion, that several persons in the gallery at Gloucester were fully persuaded the figures were there also, and actually attempted to grasp them. The manner in which they recede is also wonderful, retiring seemingly to an immense distance, yet preserving their perfect forms until they become a mere speck, and fully disappear.

At the end delight was enhanced by 'superb Optical FIREWORKS (on true Philosophical Principles – occasions neither Smoke nor smell) replete with a Variety of Brilliant and fanciful Changes'. Both amusements were achieved by projecting transparent coloured engravings or hand paintings on glass with the surrounding field blacked out, some revolving to produce the simulation of cascading fireworks. This imaginative use of the magic lantern, or of two machines to achieve the dissolving of one figure into another, was done by extending and retracting the lens with the aid of a ratchet and screw in the casing.

William Henry West Betty made several visits to Cirencester. In 1807 the sixteen-year-old, by then past the most wonderful of his days, arrived in the town. In an age of wars and upheaval, youth, the embodiment of hope, received extraordinary adulation and it was undoubtedly the bloom of the boy's physical endowments that repeatedly drew a large part of his ardent, unreasoning London following. He was gifted with an angelic face. His fair hair had to be pinned up with a comb by day. His blue eyes ingenuously captivated anyone they settled on. In addition he moved and posed with extreme physical grace at a time when 'attitudes' were the convention and his genuine ability to declaim in a melodious boy's voice gave support to the fable that he acted quite naturally, as from intuition.[3] 'A wonderful genius in Theatric Oratory,' the *Belfast Newsletter* (16 August 1803) had proclaimed him. In the last resort his winning, unaffected self-confidence conquered all. His childlike sincerity and precocious earnestness, coupled with the charm of his person and his expressive voice, enabled the boy to fill a vast theatre for five or six nights a week. At the height of the demand he was so exploited by his father, socially as well as on the stage, that he had to be sustained with milk and rum during performances. For the duration of one season Master Betty was the darling of the highest ranks of society who even declared his Hamlet as surpassing that of Garrick. In the role of Young Norval (*Douglas*), he was certainly an ideal realisation of the character as the author of the play, John Home, himself found but it could not have been unadulterated love of the arts of the theatre that brought crowds to see him play Romeo to a full-blown Juliet. Mrs St Leger acted opposite him in the play and she was six foot tall. When he attempted Richard III the boy was admitted to be out of his depth. From being a sensation and a revelation he became a craze and a toy of fashion.[4] After the collapse of the London success the provinces continued to welcome him and as prices at Cheltenham were raised to 5s., 2.6d and 1s.6d to meet the high fee exacted by his father, no doubt the same demands were made at Cirencester.

The piece selected to unfold the boy's genius was the gloomy play *The Earl of Warwick* which Dr Thomas Franklin, when engaged on translating Voltaire's works, had taken from a French play by J F de la Harpe.[5] The piece concerns the latter years and death of the Kingmaker and features the intrigues during the Wars of the Roses of Margaret of Anjou, Henry VI's queen, to thwart Warwick's love for Lady Elizabeth Grey. Margaret of Anjou had been one of Mrs Siddons' strongest roles. That same year in his provincial progress Master Betty acted Warwick at Dumfries, Macready, only two years his senior, was in the company. The future tragedian, later the equal in power to Kean and second only to Garrick, remembered the performance well and in his *Reminiscences* wrote that he could

159

bear witness to the very clever acting of my opponent. In the scene where Warwick renders his sword to the King, he displayed an energy and dignity that well entitled him to the fervent applause lavished on him.

Sarah Siddons, the great tragic actress arrived soon after Betty's departure.[6] Her art rested in a dignified and imposing style of acting which in lesser hands had already begun to deteriorate into sing-song declamation and a drawing-room strut. Thomas Davies wrote of her stage presence:

She walks and moves like a woman of superior rank. Her countenance is expressive, her eye so full of information that the passion is told from her looks before she speaks. Her voice, though not so harmonious as Mrs Cibber's, is strong and pleasing; nor is a word lost for want of due articulation. She excels all persons in paying attention to the business of the scene, her eye never wanders from the person she speaks to, or should look at when silent. Her modulation of grief, in her plaintive pronunciation of the interjection, 'Oh!', is sweetly moving and reaches the heart. The many accidents of spectators falling into fainting fits in the time of her acting bear testimony to the effects of her exertions.[7]

Cirencester saw Mrs Siddons in Edward Moore's domestic tragedy *The Gamester*, the plot of which has been described in chapter 16. She played Mrs Beverley, a part she had made her own despite the author's having left it a weak, almost monotonous role. Her triumph in it is a great testimony to her powers as an actress, for the part is inessential to the action. Mrs Beverley is a mood rather than a character and represents at most only half a personality, the complementary half being her sister, Charlotte. Mrs Beverley, moreover, appears in only seven of the play's sixteen short scenes and in the climax at the end she is given nothing to say. The final scene caused Garrick as Beverley endless trouble in the original production and it had to be curtailed in the prompter's book. Even this was of little avail for the great actor could not save the ending from a sense of tedium. Mrs Siddons, with her intensity of grief and, in the absence of words, the power of her acting, brought the curtain down successfully. She was so compelling as the long-suffering wife that Charles Mayne Young, overcome when acting Beverley

160

opposite her, lost his power of speech for a moment and before the play could go on Mrs Siddons had to murmur a sharp, 'Mr Young, recollect yourself!'

Macready, while still in his teens, also played opposite her at Newcastle just before her London farewell and, he remembered, apart from his nerves and her having to prompt him and suggest a dose of hartshorn, that in the part of Mrs Beverley the image of conjugal devotion was set off with every possible charm of grace and winning softness. It was however, Siddons' intellect, rather than her heart, which presented clearly to her audiences the unity of the character:

> Throughout the tragedy of *The Gamester* devotion to her husband stood out as the mainspring of her actions, the ruling passion of her being; apparent when reduced to poverty in her graceful and cheerful submission to the lot to which his vice has subjected her, in her fond excuses of his ruinous weakness, in her conciliating expostulations with his angry impatience, in her indignant repulse of Stukely's advances, when in the awful dignity of outraged virtue she imprecates the vengeance of Heaven upon his guilty head.[8]

One of the few child performers who could be compared with Master Betty with any degree of seriousness was 'The Young Roscia', Miss Fisher, who came to the Cirencester Theatre in October 1807.[9] She had been engaged to follow Betty's Richard III at Drury Lane in the early part of 1805 as soon as he had finished his first season there. Indeed John Philip Kemble is said to have engaged her in order to surfeit the public with juvenilia and so cause a revulsion in theatre-going taste. In the event she did not give her Richard then, but it was claimed for her that she drew overflowing houses for seven successive nights as Little Pickle in The Spoil'd Child.[10]

It was not until the July of 1805 that she presented her Richard to the public, at Cheltenham. In an age when newspaper reports tended to be so utterly prejudiced or so fulsomely partisan as to sound as if written by the subjects themselves an account in the *Gloucester Journal* (8 July 1805) of the young girl's stage performance is given at length as it seems to be based on first-hand experience and to have an unusual air of restraint. It also gives a glimpse into the hard life imposed on a child prodigy:

> The first soliloquy of Richard was delivered with judgement and force; and the scene, in which he murders King Henry, was played with peculiar skill and discrimination, and drew down loud and deserved applause. In the celebrated scene with Lady Anne, she was uncommonly happy; though perhaps occasionally too loud. – Where Richard presents her with his sword to stab him, we think she mistook the meaning of the author, and was not sufficiently plaintive and pathetic; for, it is under tenderness of manner and external feeling, that he best conceals his perfidious hypocrisy. The expression of 'To the Tower! aye, to the Tower!' was admirably delivered; and in the soliloquy, after the young princes are sent thither, she was uncommonly happy in describing the vices of men, and the ambition of Richard. The quarrel with Buckingham, a very difficult scene, was excellently played. – The news of his defection, and of the invasion of Richmond, was received in a manner which astonished the audience; and the celebrated exclamation, 'Off with his head! – so much for Buckingham!' drew down thunders of applause. The Tent Scene and the Battle Scene closed the life of the Usurper; and these were played in a very superior style of excellence. Perhaps her action is rather too sudden, and her utterance, at times, too voluble; but the spirit, the energy, and the fury of a disappointed Usurper, were never more admirably delineated. In her dying scene she was eminently successful.
>
> Upon the whole, the talents of Miss Fisher suffer no diminution from comparison. The voice of approbation was loud and general; and the present commendation will receive a support from every one who was fortunate enough to witness her exertions.
>
> It is but fair to mention that she had travelled the whole of the preceding night, without the refreshment of slumber; that her father declares she never saw the play of Richard acted before! Let these things be considered, and they will justify in asserting with Johnson, that she is 'not the greatest, only because she is not the first'. Her performance of Richard was allowed, by those who had seen both of them, greatly to exceed that of her well-known rival.

The text used, a concentration of all the Shakespearean scenes in several plays showing Richard's villainy, was by Colley Cibber under the title, *The Tragical History of King Richard III*. Cibber himself appeared with success in the part for nearly forty years despite nature's having ordained him a brilliant comedian.[11] By 1807 his version had held the stage against Shakespeare's original for over a century and was to continue to do so into the middle of the twentieth century. Laurence Olivier's film of 1955 gave a credit to Cibber. 'Off with his Head! So much for Buckingham!' the best known line Cibber ever wrote, pales before the tyrant's later supremely triumphant, 'Richard's himself again!'

By way of contrast after the play one evening Miss Fisher sang the song of 'Crazy Jane' in character to pianoforte accompaniment 'in tones at times remarkably brilliant and her ear very correct'.[12] Crazy Jane was a favourite folk character made familiar by countless penny histories sold by shopkeepers and song sheets broadcast by ballad sellers and hawkers at fairs and markets. The original Jane was the youngest daughter, remarkable from childhood for her beauty, of a substantial farmer named Arnold in the neighbouring county of Wiltshire. She fell in love with the faithless Henry Percival and became the victim of his seductive charms. Having surrendered her virtue to the importuning of the deceitful Henry she lost her reason and used to wander the paths she had walked with her betrayer, her girdle loosened and her head, Ophelia fashion, bedecked with straws, sprigs of willow and meadow flowers. Monk Lewis had produced a Crazy Jane ballad, 'The Maniac', in 1774 which gave rise to a fashionable 'Crazy Jane' hat that swept the kingdom, a straw tied with ribbon under the chin and bedecked with poppies, wheat ears and corn flowers, a head-dress Miss Fisher may have worn 'in character'. This fashion in millinery persisted into the early nineteenth century as 'a gypsy bonnet'. At the time Miss Fisher appeared in Cirencester, a painting by Henry Fuseli of the subject was being shown in London.[13] The stage showed its love of the girl in repeated melodramas and the ballad of Crazy Jane was to become a favourite party and recital piece of Ellen Terry's. It was even recorded on cylinder by Sir Henry Irving in August 1888 with grave tones in a heightened melodramatic style:

> I'll rave no more in proud despair,
> My language shall be calm, though sad;
> And yet I firmly, truly swear
> I am not mad, I am not mad.[14]

Between the acts of one evening's entertainment Miss Fisher gave the Pas Seul which had been specially composed for her and danced it with grace and agility. With reference to her Norval the *Journal* conceded that 'perhaps it is not quite fair, to compare a studied and finished performance, as Master Betty's may be called, with the first attempt of Miss Fisher made without any study or reflection; for this, indeed, was the fact'.[15] She showed her versatility as Emily Tempest in *The Wheel of Fortune* and acted Lucy in the farce of *The Virgin Unmasked* but a cold reduced the volume of her voice and a stirring of criticism must have been felt because it was arranged that a letter of special pleading be delivered to the *Gloucester Journal*, penned possibly by the father whose hand may have sent in the earlier reports.[16] Theatre comment like this is rare in the pages of the *Journal*.

> Sir – As the little phenomenon who has been exhibiting at our Theatre, has continued, without intermission, to surprise and amuse an audience which certainly may be ranked in respectability with any out of the metropolis; and as there are circumstances attending her with which I have become acquainted – from the sincere pleasure and satisfaction I, amongst others, have experienced in being often in her society, I request you will have the goodness to permit the introduction of my sentiments. I could have wished that one more able had furnished you with what I now offer; yet the circumstance of Master Betty being about to appear at Worcester, impels me to the task, in order that criticism may not, for want of proper data draw comparisons which might be injurious to the little girl, whose private demeanour has not less captivated those who know her, than her extraordinary talents. I shall but little criticise her performance at present, both because I will not take up too much of your room, and because your two former Papers have contained critiques which render it in a great measure unnecessary. What I wish to have generally known are facts, on which, I believe, you may place implicit reliance.
>
> Miss Fisher's appearance makes it hardly necessary to say, she is not yet 13 years of age, not having completed them until October next. She made her first appearance at Cheltenham on Saturday, the 6th July, in *Richard III*. She arrived but that morning, she had been sick and deprived of sleep all the night, and never had attempted the character before. How she succeeded is best exemplified by the loud

and unanimous cry to have it repeated, which it accordingly was, on Tuesday, the 9th. to a crowded audience. On Thursday 11th. she performed, and also for the first time, Rosalind, in *As You Like It*, in which performance her sportiveness occasioned as much delight as her Richard had astonishment; both which sensations received no diminution from the elegance of her dancing, and the sweetness of her songs. On Saturday, the 13th., she appeared as Young Norval, in *Douglas*, in which her father took the part of Lord Randolph. In this she was certainly greatly inferior to Master Betty (except in some scenes, where superiority over her manner was impossible). When the public is appraised that this child has no instructor, her father's diffidence preventing his undertaking the task – that the book is put into her hand, or, as is generally the case, only the part she is to perform, and that her own ideas alone are to direct her, candour will not be at a loss to see the evident disadvantage under which she labours in comparison with her rival, to show every other performer, and every other thing, has been made subservient. But there is another circumstance not to be unknown – Her father's extreme agitation and attention to her throws her off her guard; of which, the difference between her manner when he was on the stage with her, and when not, afforded a palpable proof. I do not, for myself and many others, scruple to assert, that she will be inferior to Betty in any thing, only while she wants the advantages he has received; and that an uncommon strength and brilliancy of tone, added to most interesting countenance, will afterwards give her a decided superiority.

On Tuesday, the 16th., she repeated Rosalind with unbounded applause; and, on the following night, Richard III and Cowslip [in the Musical Entertainment of *The Agreeable Surprise*], at Gloucester; this latter part she had never looked at when she left Cheltenham at three o'clock; and the public may rely on the fact, that it was learned, without assistance, during her ride there. She was brought home in a friend's carriage, after midnight; and her habitual sickness while travelling rendered it necessary for her to have as much air as possible, she caught a severe cold and hoarseness. This most materially affected her in the delicate and tender Juliet, a part she played the next night at Cheltenham, for her benefit, to the greatest audience this place has ever witnessed, the receipts being nearly one-third more than Munden, that old favourite of the public, had at his benefit.

I am just returned (twelve o'clock at night) from witnessing her Juliana, in *The Honey-Moon*, a performance of which I may have

165

more to say hereafter; but, for the reasons mentioned above, I cannot avoid sending you this now, contenting myself, for the present, with remarking, that she has in it outshone herself, and enabled the public to ascertain her prominent walk – a walk hitherto almost exclusively possessed by Mrs Jordan; but for which, whatever Miss Fisher may have to contend against with rivals, she will, I confidently predict, never be beaten off by a superior. – I have almost forgotten my subject – reminding myself and the public, that it is a girl under 13 years of age, acting under her own ideas, and hitherto without instruction or patronage.

I am, Sir, your most obedient servant,

T.P.

Cheltenham; July 20, 1805[17]

The letter gives a glimpse into the daily life of the gifted child of an unsparing father. Some will have said that she was terrified of him. Others will have assumed that he himself was 'T.P'.

By the time Miss Fisher finally acted at Cirencester, after two more years of night journeys and travel sickness, the ambitious parent was exhibiting a younger daughter, four years old, billed as 'Miss M Fisher'. The elder girl had grown up in the intervening years and when she appeared at the Cirencester Theatre in October 1807, on the first night of a new season, it was on her fifteenth birthday, by which she was old enough to play adult roles convincingly. She began in *The Will*, a sentimental comedy dating from 1797.[18] *The Will* was almost melodramatic with its old Gothic chamber as one of the scenes in which Mrs Rigid intercepted letters addressed to her daughter, Albina, by an admirer by name Mandeville. *The Spoil'd Child* was the farce that evening, in which Miss Fisher could show her growing charms in the sailor suit of the lead, Little Pickle. This farce was universally loved and had been the vehicle for her initial success at Drury Lane. It was in the nautical plaits and pigtails of this part that Dorothy Jordan caught the eye of George III's sailor son, the Duke of Clarence, later King William IV, and led to her bearing him a brood of ten children. It was claimed that the author of *The Spoil'd Child* was the father of her four earlier offspring, Richard Ford, MP. In this farce it was customary for the performer to interpolate a hornpipe and one or two nautical airs. The piece served Miss Fisher well as it finished the evening of her benefit at the end of the 1807 visit to Cirencester.

The hardships which the last young actress endured give an indication of the hazards of touring. Whatever their status, almost all of the performers of the London stage undertook this arduous adventure each year when the patent theatres closed for the long summer recess; others took to the provinces when employment in London was not available. For most, the need to make money was the prime incentive to set out but for some a tour of the provincial playhouses was an opportunity to try out roles denied them in London. Regular appearances in a round of country theatres could be a welcome way to extend one's repertoire. The audiences, for their part, welcomed these new faces to augment those of the regular company: with many roles to play in a nightly changing programme, faces could easily become over-familiar.

Notes

1 *Gloucester Journal*, 8, 15 and 22 February 1802. 'Phantasmagoria' was a name invented by Philipstal in 1802 for an exhibition of optical illusions produced by a projection lantern. Images shown would increase or decrease in size, dissolve into other images or vanish. A brief description of a phantasmagoria is given in the *Gentleman's Magazine*, LXXII (1802), 544. See also a reference in S. Ryley, *The Itinerant* vol. 3 (1808), Thomas Frost, *The Lives of the Conjurers* (1874), and George Speaight, 'Professor Pepper's Ghost', *Theatre Notebook XLIII* (1989). A working projector is exhibited at the Museum of the Moving Image, South Bank, London.

2 Francis Russell, 5th Duke of Bedford (1765–1802) had passed strictures on the proposal to award a state pension to Edmund Burke (1729–97) and in retaliation Burke published *A Letter to a Noble Lord on the Attacks made upon him and his Pension in the House of Lords by the Duke of Bedford and Earl of Lauderdale early in the present Sessions of Parliament* (1796). In the course of this Burke stated:

> The duke is the leviathan among the creatures of the crown . . . Huge as he is, he is still a creature.

'The New Morality' was a versification of the letter which appeared in the

Anti-Jacobin Review. The lines cited are to be found in Edmond's edition (1890).

3   The pencil and chalk drawing made in 1805 by Samuel de Wilde of William Henry West Betty as Frederic in Elizabeth Inchbald's *Lover's Vows* gives a good impression of his feminine, frail appearance; the drawing is in the collection of Victor Glasstone. The portrait by John Opie (1761–1807), painted in 1804 (National Portrait Gallery), of Betty as Young Norval in John Home's *Douglas*, illustrates Denning's remarks about his graceful attitudes.

4   *Douglas*, written by John Home (1722–1818), a minister of the Church of Scotland, received its first performance at the Cannongate Theatre, Edinburgh, in 1756; the first London production was at Covent Garden in 1757.

5   *The Earl of Warwick* received its first presentation at Drury Lane, 13 December 1766.

6   For information on Betty's popularity in the provinces and Siddons' hopes of raising funds on the 1807 tour, see Thomas Campbell, *The Life of Mrs Siddons* (1834).

7   Thomas Davies, *Dramatic Miscellanies* (1783–4).

8   Charles William Macready, *Reminiscences*, ed. Frederick Pollock (1875).

9   Miss Fisher is a shadowy figure. Watson advertised on his bills that she was trained by 'Madame de la Croix of the Opera House [ie the King's Theatre in the Haymarket], London'.

10   *The Spoiled Child* by Isaac Bickerstaff was first performed at Drury Lane, 22 March 1790.

11   Colley Cibber (1671–1757) made his version of *Richard III* in 1700. He was an actor, mainly in humorous roles, a playwright and a poet, made Laureate in 1730. His autobiography, *An Apology for the Life of Mr Colley Cibber* (1740), gives a picture of the post Restoration stage.

12   *Gloucester Journal*, 5 and 12 October 1807.

13   Montague Summers in *The Gothic Quest* (1968) gives an account of M G Lewis on a visit to Inverary Castle walking with Lady Charlotte Campbell when they met with a 'poor maniac girl', which encounter inspired him to write the ballad 'Crazy Jane'.

Henry Fuseli (1741–1825), Swiss by birth, studied painting in Rome and then resided in England. Many of his paintings show the horror and fear that works beneath the surface of the human imagination. In domestic mood, Fuseli was fascinated by his wife's elaborate hair styles and wide-brimmed hats; examples of his recording of the latter are 'Mrs Fuseli in a Big Hat' (c1792) in the Ulster Museum, Belfast, and 'Mrs Fuseli seated in the corner of a Sofa in a wide-brimmed Hat' (1792–5) at the Kunsthaus in Zurich. A 'Crazy Jane' is not recorded as a descriptive name for a hat in the Oxford English Dictionary.

14   Sir Henry Irving (1838–1905), an English actor manager, was based from 1878 at the Lyceum Theatre.

Dame Ellen Terry (1847–1928), actress, was Irving's leading lady.

15   *Gloucester Journal*, 12 October 1807.

16   *The Wheel of Fortune* by Richard Cumberland was first staged at Drury Lane, 18 February 1795; *The Virgin Unmasked* is a version of Henry Fielding's comedy *An Old Man Taught Wisdom*, first staged on 24 January 1786 at Drury Lane.

17   *Gloucester Journal*, 12 October 1805.

18   *The Will* by Frederick Reynolds was first given at Drury Lane, 19 April 1797. Cirencester saw a number of his plays including *The Dramatist* and *The Rage*. Many sidelights on the contemporary stage are to be found in Reynolds' autobiography, *The Life and Times of Frederick Reynolds* (1826).

Epilogue:
The Changing Fortunes of the Cirencester Theatre and the Watson Family

Anthony Denning ended his account of the Cirencester Theatre at 1819. In this year, with the expiry of the lease, the connection with John Boles Watson II was severed. But the ending is too abrupt and leaves many loose threads. In this epilogue I want to trace the subsequent history of the building in Gloucester Street, Cirencester. I shall also look in general terms at the circuit in relation to the declining fortunes of the Watson family's management.

For several years before 1819 the theatre had been rarely opened and could hardly have been a profitable investment. Visiting performers tended to use the assembly rooms at the King's Head Hotel as their venue. On the expiry of the lease the cottages standing at the front of the auditorium were converted into a public house which opened in 1820 as the Loyal Volunteer. This did not preclude future theatrical activity, however, and may possibly, if only temporarily, have fostered it by providing a ready made group to form the nucleus of an audience.[1]

In March 1821 Henry Bennett, after making 'thorough repairs', reopened the theatre. The manager, without the availability of the attached accommodation, resided in Dyer Street, south of the Market Place. Bennett's company played from March until June. Shakespeare appears to have been popular. An early production was *Macbeth* in which there were several spectacular interpolations; the murder of King Duncan was shown on stage and one also saw the coronation of Macbeth. Amongst the cast the Kennedy family was strongly represented. Later followed the documentary *The Mysterious Murder of Maria Ashfield*. A degree of fantasy entered into the production at the end when 'the Murdered Maid, [was] attended by

171

celestial bodies, who hail her approach into the abode of peace and happiness'. As a benefit for the manager and a Mrs Beahan (she herself seems to have acted as co-manager but it is unknown whether this implies more than a solely professional relationship) *She Stoops to Conquer* was given with the two beneficiaries playing Young Marlow (in itself not necessarily an indication of the youthfulness of the performer) and Mrs Hardcastle. Two nights later the Kennedy family enjoyed its benefit. *Romeo and Juliet* was chosen with Kennedy playing Friar Lawrence, Mrs Kennedy the Nurse and one of their daughters a page. Shakespeare was further augmented with the help of some of the 'Young Ladies of Cheltenham', this time in the form of a 'Solemn Procession to the Monument of the Capulets, and a Funeral Dirge'. Town involvement with the production was also seen in *Douglas* when a 'Young Gentleman' was advertised as Norval; by way of identification 'Mr R Hawkins, Grocer', is pencilled on a bill in the Bingham Library. A production of *Brutus or The Fall of Tarquin* (a benefit for the Charteris family) reveals that the scene painter was kept busy with new drops representing an 'Equestrian Statue of Tarquinius which is destroyed by Lightning', the Roman forum, a royal banquet, a tribunal and the 'Court of Tarquin's Palace – shattered by Roman Soldiers'. The season finished with a further performance of *Douglas*.[2]

The season was enlivened by the arrival of two visiting performers. Henry Erskine Johnston, popularly but over-optimistically nicknamed the Scottish Roscius, made a return visit and there was a Miss James, who seems to have been 'useful' in a varied selection of roles. The pair appeared opposite each other in a number of pieces: thus, in the *Merchant of Venice* they appeared as Shylock and Portia respectively, and in *Hamlet* Johnston played the title role to Miss James' Ophelia. Similarly Johnston took Petruchio and Miss James Katharine in Garrick's version of *The Taming of the Shrew*. Of the non-Shakespearean offerings *Rugantino* was popular as this allowed Johnston in his part of the 'Bravo of Venice' the opportunity to appear in a number of disguises and the listing of these featured in the play's advertising.[3]

The play titles given in the two previous paragraphs indicate the conservative nature of the repertoire. Here was a diet of the pieces which had been seen in Cirencester during the management of

Watson I. It is difficult to tell whether this is a reflection of the taste of Bennett and Beahan or the townspeople, the 'I like what I know' syndrome. Certainly there must have been an acceptance of the choice in order to support the stay of the company from the beginning of March until the early days of June.

William Cobbett, after addressing a meeting in the Tewkesbury Theatre, came to Cirencester in November 1826 and spoke in the evening to a gathering of about one hundred and fifty people in the theatre. Sixpence admission was charged with a rise to a shilling for a seat in the boxes.[4]

By 1826 John Boles Watson II had died and his son, John Boles Watson III, took over the remains of the once flourishing theatre circuit; finances dictated that some of the theatres, including those at Cheltenham and Gloucester, should pass into the hands of trustees. Watson gathered a company together and attempted unsuccessfully to lease these two playhouses as a joint base for his activities when the managers, Thomas Gladslane and Daniel Terry, were detained in the King's Bench Prison for debt. He had regained the proprietorship of the Cirencester Theatre but the town was hardly a lively enough location from which to conduct his operations. However, some advantage accrued to him when he leased the building to Davenport who brought his company to Cirencester in November 1828.[5]

It is difficult to be certain whether this Davenport is the same as the manager of a 'set of unfortunate strollers' who in Robert Dyer's estimation left 'such a stigma on the name of player that we were looked upon with painful suspicion' at Chepstow in 1829. He seems to have been a Freemason which possibly gave him some credibility in Cirencester. Several bills help to fill in a few details. The juvenile phenomenon Master Burke arrived as a visitor and played Romeo. The last but one of the benefits was for the Dillons who staged the popular play by Thomas Holcroft, *A Tale of Mystery*, together with the melodrama *Warlock of the Glen*. But in spite of this the company's exertions met with indifferent success.[6]

The theatre was again open in 1830, visited by Maria Foote, the daughter of Samuel Foote the actor and dramatist of the Haymarket Theatre. She performed Letitia Hardy in *The Belle's Strategem*, and Rosalind in *As You Like It*. Watson and his wife both took minor roles in the plays and were joined by a company drawn from a number of the provincial theatres. Servants, the bills advised, must be sent in advance to keep the box places for families. In a lecture Anthony Denning hazarded that the final performances occurred in the theatre four years later.[7]

The subsequent fate of the building can be briefly told. By 1842 the theatre was used as a barrel store, presumably in connection with the Loyal Volunteer. The lease of this became available in 1855 when the manager of some twenty-five years standing retired. An advertisement speaks of 'Extensive Premises' but no mention is made of the theatre building. Earnest Whately of Watermoor obtained permission to go into the theatre building in 1874 and described the drab sight:

[The theatre] had a tier of private boxes, and a gallery approached by a stair. The gallery remained, and the boxes were still here, tho' their once gay adornment of painted floral wreaths and gilding was sadly faded . . . part of the pit had been utilised as a bowling-alley, and the stage formed the floor of the club-room of the Inn.

By this time part of the auditorium had been floored over and the town band practised in the upper section of the building. Over the following fifty years there was a mix of disintegration and demolition. The boxes and gallery were removed with the resulting space turned into further rooms for the inn; the rear of the original building disappeared in the 1920s and flooding, in 1929, aggravated the poor condition as water gathered in the area where the pit had been. Strangely, as late as 1930 an old back-cloth could still be seen hanging on the stage. This, and much else, was destroyed by fire when the building was gutted in the 1930s. In 1955 the Loyal Volunteer closed and the whole building, both original cottages and the theatre, were converted into a private dwelling, now numbered 27 Gloucester Street. Very little of the feel of a theatre can be discerned any longer. The passage-way leads past an interior window reputed to be the aperture of the box office. For a while a trace of original decoration, rope swags within a painted arch, could be seen in one of the bedrooms of the house, an area thought to have been a (or more likely, *the*) dressing room of the theatre. The painting has now been lightly covered with emulsion.[8]

174

The Cirencester Theatre building in its last stage as a public house before its conversion into a private residence.

As a theatre the building suffered a slow and apathetic demise. It reflects the changing fortunes of Gloucester Street. In this, the present attractive Georgian buildings give little indication that once the area was rough and cheerful: now a tone of quiet gentility broods the length of the street. When an observer stands in front of the residence the playhouse has become, an effort has to be made to recapture the spirit of gaiety, excitement and crowded anticipation which was once the hallmark of the small building during its theatrical seasons.

After the death of John Boles Watson I the fortunes of the family were still inextricably linked with those of the theatres on the circuit. Each individual theatre, of course, had its own subsequent history and to clarify this the Gazetteer is provided. Anyone restructuring the careers of the second and third John Boles Watson must however be aware that a lack of business adroitness as well as a lack of will-power sapped strength from their enterprises. The imagination, the ability to sustain and expand a vast circuit of theatres, was no longer present but the Watsons were not solely to blame. The introduction to this work has pointed out some of the social, economic and religious movements which vitiated any hope of theatrical success after the 1820s, not just on the Boles Watson circuit, but on numerous others throughout Great Britain.

At the end of his account of the chronology of the Cirencester Theatre (Chapter 14) Anthony Denning left a picture of John Boles Watson II immersed in debt and failing enterprises. His foray to the Theatre Royal at Bristol had not proved a success. After his departure the lease of that theatre reverted to M'Cready but two years later, in 1821, solicitors were still attempting to coerce Watson to pay his arrears of rent. Indeed, during the first half of this decade letters to Watson's Cheltenham solicitors, Guinnett and Newman, betray the serious extent to which he was in debt. Visiting artists, including William Henry West Betty, had not received their fees. The economic recession after the Napoleonic Wars had drained Watson's sources of income: numbers of his theatres were leased to other managers who similarly failed in their payments. The Crisp brothers (managers of the theatres at Cheltenham, Gloucester, Hereford and Wolverhampton) made their payments in instalments as low as £2.00 and in 1822 their scenes and properties were seized yielding a mix of scene-drops (Berkeley Castle amongst them), a couple of deal thrones and canopies, gas burners and branches, a box of scripts and four basins and ewers. It was a paltry collection. Frederick Yates and Charles Farley (managers of Cheltenham and Gloucester following the Crisps as well as the theatre at Tewkesbury) suffered the same fate. These managers' lack of interest in a prompt payment of debts can hardly be blamed. The theatres they had leased were disgracefully in need of repair and redecoration. It was one of John Crisps's first tasks to decorate the theatre at Kidderminster on taking a lease of it.[9]

Contrary to appearances Watson II had not abandoned either the charge of a company or his own theatrical career. From 1821 he had a hankering to take up management again and seems to have maintained touch with a company nucleus. Within the next five years touring became a reality. Both he and his wife appeared in various productions. Strangely, it was Mrs Watson who headed the company on a visit to Worcester and Hereford. At other times, with Watson at the helm, the group travelled vast distances, making its way in May 1822 to the westernmost point of the circuit, Carmarthen, where the manager quickly engaged himself, according to the newsapaper puff, in 'fitting up the Theatre, in a style *superior* to what has *hitherto* been witnessed'. Performing such old stand-bys as *The Stranger*, *George Barnwell* and *Warlock of the Glen*, his choices nevertheless appealed to the local people and the newspaper declared that this was the most eminent company seen in the town since the days of Andrew Cherry's management.[10]

Still in debt in 1826, Watson II was forced to sell the Theatre Royal, Bath Street, Cheltenham. Business seems to have carried on as before for actors linked with the Watson company such as Charles Kemble and Charles Farley were appearing at the theatre during August. Farley was responsible for presenting the spectacular musical play *The Knights of the Cross* with the canine wonder Bruin from Drury Lane.[11]

The death of John Boles (Jack) Watson II *c*1826 passed with few recorded remarks. When he had made his will in February 1821 he strove to ensure that after his death his wife held the control and rent of the Warwick and Hereford theatres independently during her lifetime. He set aside £50 per annum for clothes for his

177

disadvantaged, illegitimate son, David, and, in the event of his wife's death, his eldest son, John Boles Watson III, was to be responsible for the boy. Of other property and effects, half was bequeathed to his wife and the other half to his other three children, John, Louisa and Henrietta. Furthermore, he authorised his wife, in consultation with John, to raise money by mortgage or annuity or to liquidate in order to pay his debts. As a result of his parlous financial circumstances a body of trustees was formed to administer funds. These appropriated a number of the theatres with the result that Watson III was seriously in need of money by the middle of 1827. He yearned to open the Cheltenham and Gloucester Theatres, the starting point of his grandfather's circuit in the Cotswolds. Dealing with the trustees was a slow and difficult process and by 1829 Watson was still making his applications to them.[12]

Suddenly Watson's company took to the road. 1830 seems to have been an auspicious year for him. The doors of the Cheltenham Theatre opened. Recently redecorated, the building was further graced by Spencer's painted rideau depicting the new spa at Pittville. In May James Robinson Planché's highly successful melodrama *The Brigand*, first presented in 1829 at Drury Lane, was staged with Watson playing Rubaldo. The company included his wife and daughter. Considerable resources would have been needed to stage the drama convincingly for its principal attraction was that the scenes and groupings should resemble a series of 'banditti' pictures painted by Sir Charles Lock Eastlake. For the managerial benefit at the end of June *The Foundling of the Forest* was mounted. In September Edmund Kean, in spite of frequent illnesses (he was accompanied by Douchez, his London physician), rejoined the company in which he had played as an unknown youth and took at Cheltenham the title role in *King Lear* on the last night of his engagement. Watson was irked that the nearby Gloucester Theatre, a useful place of transfer, was closed to him by the trustees in spite of the fact that in the previous nine years it had been rarely let. However, by the end of the year he was able to lead his company onto the Gloucester stage and discovered too late that during a recession the town made only a slight response to the presence of the players: nine nights of playing brought in less than £7.00.[13]

For the next couple of years Watson together with three families

Charles Eastlake's paintings of Italian banditti had inspired James Robinson Planché to write *The Brigand* in 1829. In return the Drury Lane management introduced tableaux based on Eastlake's paintings into the stage production. John Boles Watson III incorporated these into his repertory the next year.

in his company (those of Egerton, Angel and Waldron) toured energetically. After appearing at Lichfield and again at Gloucester he followed his father's example and leased the Theatre Royal, Birmingham, for a spell of two years. Here he presented amongst other plays, *Speed the Plough* (with his daughter playing Miss Blandford), *Pizarro* (Miss Watson as Cora), *The Stranger* and *The Miller and His Men*, conservative but nevertheless enterprising choices. Edmund Kean appeared for a week in his celebrated characterisations of Richard III, Shylock, Othello, Sir Giles Overreach, and Mortimer in *The Iron Chest*. George Shuter, presumably the grandson of the comedian who had given such long service to Watson I, arrived for several weeks from the Theatre Royal, Dublin. Other theatres in which Watson and the company performed were Kington (*Nell Gwynne* was one play here), Warwick (Kean played here and Shuter appeared for the first time for four

Theatre Royal, Cheltenham.

In consequence of the recent national calamity, the Entertainments announced for this present MONDAY, 28th inst. will not take place as intended.

For the BENEFIT of

MR. J. WATSON,
MANAGER,

Who earnestly solicits the countenance and support of the Nobility, Gentry, Inhabitants, and Public generally; sensible of the MANY FAVOURS bestowed on his late Grandfather and Father for a series of upwards of 40 years; with a grateful acknowledgement of such, he presents himself a candidate for their support, and humbly trusts his early endeavours will meet on this occasion, a proportionate share of encouragement and success.

First performance of *Mr. SPENCER,* from the Theatre Royal, Norwich.

On WEDNESDAY, June 30, 1830,
Will be presented, the admired Drama, in three acts, called—The

Foundling of the Forest.

Florian, the Foundling, Mr. SPENCER, his first appearance on this stage.
Count de Valmont, Mr. W. H. SIMPSON—Baron Longueville, Mr. BELMONT—L'Eclair, Mr. DANBY
Betrand, ... Mr. J. WATSON—Sanguine, ... Mr. ADDISON
Gaspard, ... Mr. LANGLEY——Lenoir, ... Mr. TANNER——Servants, &c.
Eugenia, ... Mrs. J. WATSON——Geraldine, ... Miss JOYNER
Rosabelle, ... Mrs. POWIS— ——Monica, ... Mrs. DANBY

End of the Play, a favorite Song, by **Miss Thompson**

To conclude, with the musical Farce,

THE POOR SOLDIER.

Patrick, the Poor Soldier, Miss TALLENTIRE
Captain Fitzroy, Mr. LANGLEY—Bagatelle, Mr. SPENCER—Father Luke, Mr. DANBY
Dermot, ... Mr. ADDISON——Darby, ... Mr. J. WATSON
Norah, ... Miss THOMPSON——Kathleen, ... Mrs POWIS

Doors to be opened at seven o'clock, to begin precisely at twenty minutes past.
Boxes 4s.--Pit 2s.--Gallery 1s.--Admission for Children under 12 years of age, Boxes 2s 6d.--Pit 1s
Second Price at 9, Boxes 2s. 6d.—Pit 1s.—no half price to the Gallery

Miss Foote.

The Managers of the Theatre with all submission and respect to the Nobility, Gentry, Visitors, Residents, and Public generally, invite attention to the circumstance of that popular and fascinating Actress performing so near as Gloucester, Tewkesbury, and Cirencester; and it being their anxious wish to afford so rich a treat to the Patrons of the Drama, as would be the case, if Miss FOOTE be prevailed upon to visit Cheltenham *professionally;* they humbly suggest, and earnestly solicit those Ladies and Gentlemen, who may feel disposed to witness Miss FOOTE's performances on the boards of our Theatre, to be so kind as signify their pleasure of such at the Box Office, where memorandum will be taken of Places required, and Tickets will afterwards, in due time, be issued to the parties to *secure their Places,* if the arrangement with Miss FOOTE can be effected.

Shenton, Letter-press and Copper-plate Printer, Rose and Crown Passage,

In 1830 John Boles Watson III thanked his public for their support for himself, his father and his grandfather 'for upwards of forty years'. It was to be almost the end of the theatrical dynasty.

years), Monmouth at the theatre in Monk Street and Stourbridge (with *A Man of Straw* and *The Green Ey'd Monster*). In fact his only recorded rebuff was at the Northampton Theatre where he was refused tenure.[14]

Suddenly the name of John Boles Watson III disappears from the playbills although his daughter's name crops up at a variety of theatres. The manager had been confined in Warwick Gaol for debt. Although conditions were passable after fifty years of humane improvements – the prisoners' lodgings were grouped around a courtyard and they were provided with a dayroom – Watson spent three years there in great pain. His mother sent a begging letter to Rowland Paul of Cheltenham in 1838 asking him for £5.00 with the explanation that, not only was her son confined, but also that he needed an operation on his back. In this pitiable state Watson, after only one brief spell of touring, disappears from the records.[15]

As the 1830s gave way to the following decade events connected with the former theatres of the circuit occurred marking the rapid passing of the Georgian theatre manager. At Wrexham, one of the rowdier theatres on the circuit, Stanton's company – referred to by a critic as 'buskined strollers' – was disbanded. The Tewkesbury Theatre, capitulating to evangelical pressure, was converted into a Sunday School. Abraham Seward, the son of Samuel, sold his Cheltenham puppets. Charles Farley retired and sold his stage wardrobe which included a 'low comedy coat' and waistcoat, a Spanish jacket and tabbs and one gaberdine. The props for the company amounted to little: five shields ('various'), 4 sham tambourines, 4 broken guns and a 'quantity of old keys and rubbish'. The Wolverhamton Theatre closed. Robert Hoy died. The greatest disaster in this dismal listing of the effects of mutability was the destruction of Watson's proudly named Theatre Royal in Cheltenham's Bath Street. Flames were discovered burning through the roof early one morning which, in spite of the efforts of firemen, police and townsmen, gained enough of a hold to send the superstructure crashing through the building which continued to burn for four hours. Little remained:

> The building, as it now stands, has an exceedingly desolate appearance, the four outer walls, the wall which divided the boxes from the lobby and a large stack of chimneys, and a quantity of half

burned beams, being all that remain. . . . The Theatre was insured in the Phoenix Fire Office to the extent of £2000 which will just about half cover the loss sustained by the proprietors of the Theatre.

No regular theatre replaced this ruin until 1854.[16]

Patterns of theatre management are continually changing. When John Boles Watson I began his career it was as a stroller. During his time the life changed to the more settled one of a seasonal stay at one of the theatres on the manager's circuit. By a happy chance the first Watson was just the person to create a large empire of lively theatres. Its gradual decline after his death was not due solely to the ineptitude of his son and grandson for the pattern had changed again and the theatre looked forward to the time when a manager would strive to build up the reputation of a single playhouse, directing all of his energies in that focused pursuit.

Notes

1   The information given in this paragraph is based on a newspaper cutting, undated and unassigned, given to me by the present residents of 27 Gloucester Street. It is an account of a lecture which Anthony Denning gave to the Cirencester and District Archaeological and Historical Society.

2   The playbill collections at the Bingham Library, Cirencester, the Art Gallery and Museum, Cheltenham, and the Gloucestershire Collection, Gloucester Central Library, furnish the details of the 1821 season.

3   A brief record of the career of Henry Erskine Johnston (1777–1845) is given in Phyllis Hartnoll, *The Concise Oxford Companion to the Theatre* (1972).

Rugantino, or The Bravo of Venice by Matthew Gregory Lewis was first performed at Covent Garden in 1805. Rugantino, the true Prince of Milan, disguises himself as a beggar, a friar, a brigand and a law enforcement officer clad in glittering armour. In the preface to his edition of the play, William Oxberry noted that the text was but one of numerous versions based on the German romance of Abalino. Lewis's version, although 'in defiance of reason', was nevertheless an imaginative example, coming into its own, of the 'Literature of the North'.

4   Substance of a lecture by Anthony Denning given in the *Annual Report and Newsletter of the Cirencester Archaeological and Historical Society*, III (1980–81), 7–16.

5   Gloucestershire Record Office, Gloucester: D2025, Box 73.

6   Robert Dyer, *Nine Years of an Actor's Life* (1833), pp 125–6; Cecil Price, *The English Theatre in Wales* (Cardiff, 1948), pp 147–8; Ernest Whatley, 'A Stage Story', *Wilts and Gloucestershire Standard*, 26 January 1876; Gloucestershire Collection, Gloucester Central Library: playbills.

7   Bingham Library, Cirencester: playbill; unidentified newspaper cutting reporting a lecture given by Anthony Denning. Ernest Whately, *op cit.*

The Belle's Stratagem by Hannah Cowley was first presented at Covent Garden in 1780 and was popular for over a century. Maria Foote (1797–1867), the year after her appearance at Cirencester, retired from the stage in order to marry the Earl of Harrington.

8   The advertisement referring to the lease of the Loyal Volunteer appears in the *Wilts and Gloucester Standard*, 28 July 1855; Ernest Whatley's description of the state of the theatre appears in his article 'A Stage Story', *op cit*; Richard Barry O'Brien, 'A Memorable Night at Cirencester Theatre – 150 years ago, Tonight', *Wiltshire Herald and Advertiser*, 14 December 1951; Corinium Museum, Cirencester: 'Report of the Area Museum Council of the South West' refers to the painting at 27 Gloucester Street, Cirencester. Verbal information from Mrs Peter Davies and Mrs Jenkins, both residents of Cirencester, and from Mr Trevor Allen of the Bingham Library, Cirencester, has also been used.

9   Some of the correspondence between John Boles Watson II and his firm of solicitors is preserved in the Gloucestershire Record Office, Gloucester, D2025, Box 73. The inventory of the Crisps' theatrical property is also to be found here. Information about the Kidderminster Theatre appears in W H Gwilliam's typescript 'The Theatre in Worcestershire' in the Worcester City Library.

10   *Carmarthen Journal*, 3, 10, 31 May 1822; Theodore Hannam-Clark, *Drama in Gloucestershire* (1928), pp 93–4.

11   Cheltenham Museum and Art Gallery: playbill collection; Gloucestershire RO: D2025, Box 73.

12   Gloucestershire RO: D2025, Box 73.

13   Gloucestershire RO: D2025, Box 73; Warwickshire Record Office, Warwick: materials relating to the Warwick Theatre, CR 1596, Box 93; Cheltenham Museum and Art Gallery: playbill collection; Hannam-Clark, *op cit*, p 93; Clifford Leech and T W Craik, *The Revels History of Drama in English*, VI, 219–220; Giles Playfair, *The Flash of Lightning. A Portrait of Edmund Kean* (1983), pp 161 and 165; Giles Playfair, *Kean. The Life and Paradox of the Great Actor* (1950), p 300; Harold Newcomb Hillebrand, *Edmund Kean* (New York, 1944), p 313. A more extended study of the re-creation of Eastlake's paintings on the stage is George Speaight, 'The

Brigand in the Toy Theatre', *The Saturday Book 29*, ed. John Hadfield (1969).

14   Gloucestershire and Warwickshire RO, *op cit*; Worcestershire Record Office, St Helen's, Worcester: Foley Scrapbook, IV; Birmingham Central Library: Theatre Royal, Birmingham, Archive, playbill collection; British Library, Playbills 288 (bills of the Warwick Theatre); Keith Kissack, *Monmouth – the Making of a Country Town* (Chichester, 1975), p. 259.

15   Gloucestershire RO, *op cit*; J Nield, *An Account of the Rise, Progress and Present State of the Society for the Discharge and Relief of Persons Imprisoned for Small Debts throughout England and Wales* (1802), pp 275–7; William Field, *A Historical and Descriptive Account of the Town of Warwick* (Warwick, 1815), pp 144–5.

The name of Watson, playing Guildenstern, appears on a playbill for *Hamlet* given at the Gloucester Theatre on 18 May 1859; he also appears as a servant in the afterpiece, *Good for Nothing*. One wonders whether this is a member of the John Boles Watson family. See: Cheltenham Museum and Art Gallery: playbill collection.

16   For notes on the Wrexham Theatre see: Samuel Lewis, *Topographical Dictionary of Wales* (1833), II, entry on Wrexham; Cecil Price, *The English Theatre in Wales* (Cardiff, 1948), pp 143–4; *Bye-Gones*, 1878–9, p 34. For the Tewkesbury Theatre see: *Victoria History of the Counties of England, Gloucestershire* (1968), VIII, 123. For the Wolverhampton Theatre see: Wolverhampton Central Library: newspaper cuttings, 'Old Wolverhampton Sixty Years Ago' by J B Hardcastle. On Seward see: *Bristol Mercury*, 9 April 1838; on Farley and his effects see Gloucestershire RO, *op cit*.

The cited description of the fire at the Theatre Royal, Cheltenham, is taken from the *Cheltenham Chronicle*, 9 May 1839; another description is given in the *Looker-On*, 4 May 1839. In 1854 the recently rebuilt Pump Room of the Royal Old Wells Spa opened as the Theatre Royal; here Samuel Onley and Capt Disney Roebuck ran a stock company. See: Roger Beacham, *The Early History of the Theatre in Cheltenham* (Cheltenham, nd) and Hannam-Clark, *op cit*, p 102.

Gazetteer of the Theatres
on the Watson Circuit

Towns and villages in which John Boles Watson I set up a theatre are listed in this Gazetteer. The brief history of each of Watson's theatres is usually followed to the eventual close of the building, occasionally long after the management of the Watson family ceased. Some towns, of course, possessed more than one theatre (Gloucester is an example) and, unless the additional theatre was connected with the Watsons or the Cheltenham company, then these non-Watsonian playhouses are ignored. The distinction between Watson as leasee or as proprietor of a building is usually noted but joint proprietorships and part-shares present problems especially as the variable arrangements could be short-lived. It is noted if the building is still existence, although rarely are any of the Watson theatres now in use as such.

Each entry is followed by a list of printed source material and also a note of collections possessing relevant material on the playhouse. The figure after each place name refers to its placing on the accompanying map.

1	Holywell	16	Bewdley	31	Swansea
2	Wrexham	17	Ludlow	32	Merthyr
3	Oswestry	18	Llandrindod	33	Abergavenny
4	Welshpool	19	Kington	34	Monmouth
5	Lichfield	20	Leominster	35	Ross
6	Tamworth	21	Worcester	36	Tewkesbury
7	Leicester	22	Alcester	37	Cheltenham
8	Hinckley	23	Stratford-upon-Avon	38	Gloucester
9	Coventry	24	Warwick	39	Stroud
10	Birmingham	25	Daventry	40	Minchinghampton
11	Walsall	26	Banbury	41	Cirencester
12	Wolverhampton	27	Evesham	42	Abington
13	Dudley	28	Hereford	43	Wotton Under Edge
14	Stourbridge	29	Brecon	44	Bristol
15	Kidderminster	30	Carmarthen		

185

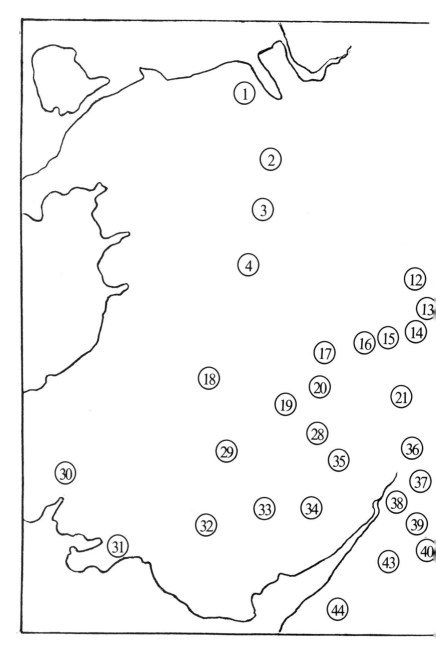

Places with Theatres

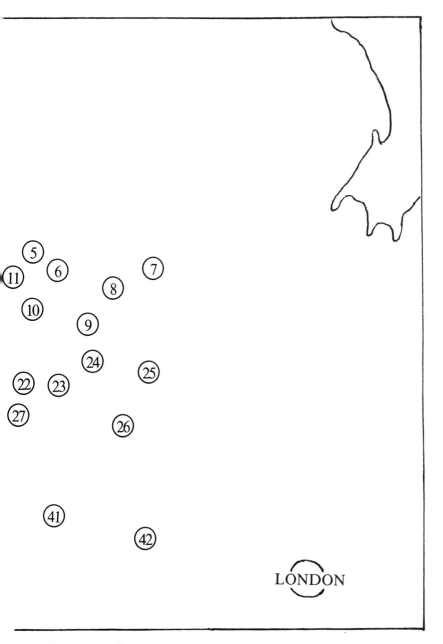

on the Watson Circuit

Abergavenny (33)

The only recorded eighteenth-century theatre in Abergavenny was a building later known as the 'Old Playhouse' situated on the corner of Cross Street and Lower Castle Street. However, documentary evidence is lacking which would connect the visits of the following companies with this particular building.

Charles and Mary Morison, co-founders and members of an actors' commonwealth, in 1741 played in Abergavenny. Receipts brought in nine shillings between them. Hopefully the couple then hired a drummer to advertise the repertory. At about 1747 Richard Elrington's company played in Abergavenny; Charlotte Charke was one of the players.

By 1761 the town featured on John Ward's circuit; in the July of that year his company played for ten weeks. The theatre would have passed, through Roger Kemble, to John Boles Watson I. Henry Masterman held the lease from 1799 (at which time Edward Cape Everard was a player in the company) until his death in 1803. Masterman met with a decrepit town: '[It] has a few good houses scattered in it, but in general the streets are narrow, ill paved and ill built'. When in the region this manager played three nights of the week at Crickhowell and three at Abergavenny.

In March 1813 (the year of the death of the thespian paterfamilias) John Boles Watson II took the theatres at Merthyr, Brecon and Abergavenny for displays of rope walking by his brother-in-law, John Richer. A series of plays ensued at the latter town, which included the popular melodrama *The Castle Spectre*, and the tragedy of *Zara*. In 1819 and 1822 the magistrates at Usk issued licences for Watson II to perform in Abergavenny.

Later theatres were fitted up in the rackets court of the George Commercial Hotel: performances here in 1841 are recorded. Rackets courts made a convenient theatrical location in some towns in the eighteenth century (Oxford, for example) and this building was possibly used earlier as such. The Cymreigyddion Hall (demolished 1959) was also used for theatrical performances.

Principal sources:
A Collection of Tours in Wales (1799); Edward Cape Everard, *Memoirs of an Unfortunate Son of Thespis* (Edinburgh, 1818); Cecil

Price, *The English Theatre in Wales* (Cardiff, 1948).

Abergavenny Museum: Patricia Neal, 'Travelling Companies and Theatres in Newport and Monmouthshire in the Eighteenth and Early Nineteenth Centuries' (typescript); 'Town Centre Survey, 1979–1980', Abergavenny Local History Society (typescript); Gwent Record Office, County Hall, Cwmbran: OS/MB 0004 and 0005.

Abington (42)

Abington, now subsumed within Northampton, in the eighteenth century was a hamlet to the north-east of the town. Although Anthony Denning includes the place in his list of Watson's theatre locations in Chapter 2 of his work, next to nothing is known of a theatre here. As the village consisted simply of a manor house and a couple of sets of cottages there seem to be only two possible sites for a theatre: one could have been a temporary fit up in the hall of the manor; alternatively some sort of pavilion may have been set up in the surrounding fields drawing an audience mainly from Northampton.

The manor has a couple of theatrical connections. Elizabeth Nash, Shakespeare's grand-daughter, married John Bernard in 1649 and so became lady of the manor. The actor David Garrick was an acquaintance of Anne Thursby, lady of Abington Manor in the eighteenth century. To mark their friendship he planted a tree in the garden which still stands and is marked by a brass plaque.

The Manor is now one of the Northampton Museums.

Principal sources:
Nikolaus Pevsner, *The Buildings of England. Northamptonshire*, revised by Bridget Cherry (1973).
Verbal information from Judith Hodgkinson, Keeper of Social History at Abington Museum.

Alcester (22)

At the time of leasing his theatres to George Collins Gibbon and Edward Ray in 1803 Watson listed the Alcester Theatre as a part of his circuit.

Principal source:
Warwickshire County Record Office: Draft of indenture of co-partnership (CR 1596 Box 93).

Banbury (26)

There were two principal theatres in Banbury. The earlier was built above the slaughter-houses and next to the lock-up and gaol in Butcher's Row, a lane running parallel with the High Street and leading from the Market Place. This location may be compared with a playhouse above a meat market in the Square at Winchester. In 1802 a 'New Theatre' was built in Church Lane by James Hill, a leather cutter, and was used for plays, lectures and public meetings. Jackman managed both of these theatres with the help of his wife; from 1835 a son continued the family business. A playbill of 1861 for *As You Like It*, presented immediately before the theatre's final closure, mentions Jackman and Morgan as the lessees of the theatre. The building is now incorporated into a street of shops.

Henry Jackman visited Banbury for a three month season every two years and seems to have sublet the building occasionally. According to Horace Walpole a company came to Banbury in 1780, playing *The School for Scandal* and 'all the new pieces'; whether this was Watson's is not clear. A bill notes that Kemble and his wife arrived in September 1790 to perform *Jane Shore* in a theatre which Kemble fitted up in Parson's Lane. Watson's company certainly came to Banbury in the spring of 1798, presenting *Don Juan* for the last time on 18 April before the scenery and costumes were sent to Worcester.

Principal sources:
Banbury Guardian, 1 October 1953; Alfred Beesley, *A History of Banbury* (1841); George Herbert, *Shoemaker's Widow*, ed C S Cheyney (Chichester, 1971); William Potts, *A History of Banbury* (Banbury, 1958); Paul Ranger, *The Lost Theatres of Winchester, 1620–1821* (Winchester, 1976); Horace Walpole, *The Yale Edition of Horace Walpole's Correspondence*, ed W S Lewis (1936–80).
Bodleian Library, Oxford: John Johnson Collection of playbills, 18 March 1861; British Library: Burney Collection of playbills, 23 September 1790; Cheyney and Son, printers, Banbury: playbill collection; New York Public Library: the William Douglas notebook.

Bewdley (16)

It is difficult to state categorically whether one of the theatres at Bewdley was managed by John Boles Watson I. The town was on Roger Kemble's circuit and thereby possibly was handed on to Watson.

In the spring of 1776 a company which appears to have been jointly managed by Butler and Phillips was performing at a makeshift theatre ('fitted up in the most elegant manner its situation wou'd admit of') in the yard of the Angel Inn. Attendances were good. Encouraged, Phillips returned in 1778 to the same base, but this time he was 'disappointed in every effort made' and the stay was a short one. On the first visit each performance was advertised as a 'Concert of Music' and 'a Lecture' was the euphemism employed on the second.

Another Butler, possibly the son of the manager mentioned above, appeared in the town in 1819, opening a theatre in Load Street, the district traditionally connected with circuses, menageries and theatricals at market time.

However, the Angel Yard theatre ('compact and warm') was still in use by 1829 – in spite of the fact that the assembly room in the inn was also available – when Melville and Turner brought a company to the town. Turner found the going hard and retired leaving Melville in charge; the latter decamped with the takings a couple of weeks later.

In addition to the theatrical locations at the Angel Inn and in Load Street, the assembly rooms in the George Inn and the Wheatsheaf Inn were regularly used for small scale performances.

Possibly somewhere within the earlier years of this development Watson would have had a place. The name of Masterman crops up on a bill advertising the visit to Bewdley of Henry Baker's company in 1811. Henry Masterman, who also acquired some of Kemble's theatres, died in 1803, leaving an actor son, perhaps the person billed.

Principal sources:
Barry Duncan, 'A Worcestershire Company', *Theatre Notebook*, II (1947-8), 76-8; Susan I Brown, 'Markets and Fairs of Bewdley', Lawrence S Snell, ed, *Essays Towards a History of Bewdley* (Bewdley,

1972); Frederick T Wood, 'Notes on English Provincial Playhouses in the Eighteenth Century', *Notes and Queries*, CLX (1931), 147–150. Society of Antiquaries of London: Prattinton Printed Papers, vol 2 (playbill collection).

Birmingham (10)

For a while John Ward was manager of a theatre in Moor Street, Birmingham, constructed at about 1740.

The Theatre Royal, New Street, built by Thomas Saul at a cost of £5,600, opened under the management of Richard Yates in 1775, replacing an earlier booth on the same site but then standing in the meadows. The interior had a gallery and a row of upper boxes which gave it, said John Byng, 'a snug and comfortable look'. The following year the management transferred to M'Cready, the father of William Macready, the tragic actor. By 1792 Yates was again manager but Byng was dissatisfied with his company: 'I never saw a coarser company than this . . . but he gets them very cheap, I suppose'. Yates has a bearing on the Watson story as he worked with Shuter, a mainstay of the former's ensemble, in a theatre booth at Smithfield, London, during the Bartholomew Fair before 1762.

The theatre was rebuilt in 1794 with a large stage (48 feet deep by 53 feet wide) and illuminated at first by tallow candles and then by Argand lamps and wax candles; the auditorium seated 2,000 and the total cost was £14,000.

In November 1808 the proprietors of the Theatre Royal let the building to Jack Watson for a twelve-month period at a rent of eight hundred guineas. Previously one of the Watsons had entered into a deal with the proprietors when, in 1805, the deeds of the Tamworth Theatre were mortgaged to the Theatre Royal, Birmingham, in order to secure £330. During his residency Watson upset M'Cready by using some of the theatre's scenery to which the earlier manager lay claim. Not a model tenant, Watson resented having to pay twenty guineas for the Lamp and Scavenger Levy and his use of tallow candles for illumination dirtied the paintwork of the auditorium. Presumably damage was also caused to the scenes some of which, made for the opening of the theatre, were by the eminent painter Thomas Greenwood, senior. The audience at this theatre contained a rough element: 'many things' were thrown from the gallery into the pit and peace keepers had to be stationed in the house. During this tenancy Edmund Kean was a youthful member of Watson's company. His performance in the pantomime *Alonzo the Brave* was seen by M'Cready's son whose remarks on the playing of both Kean and Mrs Watson (Imogine the heroine), a large, ungainly woman, are entertaining.

> As if in studied contrast to this enormous 'hill of flesh', a little, mean-looking man, in a shabby green satin dress (I remember him well) appeared as the hero, Alonzo the Brave. It was so ridiculous that the only impression I carried away was that the hero and the heroine were the worst in the piece.

The proprietors were ready to extend the let for a further year at the same rent but Watson, in consultation with his father, refused the terms.

In 1820 the theatre was badly damaged by fire and replaced by a stylish building with an interior in which 'warm pink' was the prevailing colour. *Aris's Gazette* (7 August 1820) describes further comforts.

> Under a door of each box in the dress circle will be perceived an iron plate, perfected for the purpose of admitting warm and cold air through every part of the theatre . . .

John Boles Watson III, styling himself proprietor of the theatres at Cheltenham, Gloucester, Hereford, Warwick, 'etc.', leased the Theatre Royal together with the scenes, props and library in January 1831. He had but slight professional acumen (the refreshment saloon was still to let after the season opened) and when Joseph Woods arrived to play in *Cinderella* he was horrified by the company's lack of preparation. He refused to sacrifice his reputation by appearing in the piece. The repertoire consisted of such well-tried plays as *Speed the Plough, Pizarro, The Iron Chest* and *The Castle Spectre*. Highlights of the year were the visits of Kean and Du Crow's Stud. Watson copied the tradition of Robert William Elliston (one of the earlier managers) of having a mid-week 'Fashionable Night'; this was no longer commercially viable however. Financially Watson was inept. Unable to pay the rent, he followed the earlier example and offered the deeds of the Tamworth Theatre as security when the debt reached £267. Although small sums of money were sent by Watson from his home in Warwick, the proprietors demanded that he should quit the theatre on 1 January 1833, addressing the notice to his wife. The manager who followed, Fraser, decamped with the takings and in 1833 Watson's name again appears as manager for part of the year. A succession of feckless men then took on the office for short periods of time.

Principal sources:
Aris's Gazette, 7 August 1827; John Byng, *The Torrington Diaries*, ed C Bruyn Andrews (1970); John E Cunningham, *Theatre Royal* (Oxford, 1950); T Edgar Pemberton, *The Theatre Royal, Birmingham* (Birmingham, 1901); Derek Salberg, *Ring Down the Curtain* (Luton, 1980).
Birmingham Central Library: Theatre Royal, Birmingham, playbill collection; Birmingham Central Library, Archives: Minute Book of the Proprietors of the Theatre Royal, Birmingham (Lee 387); Hereford and Worcester Record Office, Worcester: Foley Scrapbooks (b899.31 BA3762/9).

Brecon (29)

In his younger days John Boles Watson had played in Roger Kemble's company, walking the Welsh circuit. Having, at Kemble's retirement in 1783, with Kemble's blessing formed his own company from the nucleus, he seems to have attempted to travel to many of the Welsh theatres of the circuit regularly, as well as maintain his growing empire in the region of the Cotswolds.

Losing no time, Watson's company arrived in Brecon in the year of the transfer complete with scenery by West. The following year a purpose built theatre (still standing as a warehouse) was erected in Danygaer Road. This may have been unconnected with Watson for in 1787, a year when he visited the town, the Cheltenham manager decided to build his own theatre. The Hon John Byng attended the new playhouse and found it 'neat'. It may, however, have merely been an improvement of the 1784 building, fitted up and decorated by Abbot. Whichever, Watson's company gave performances in it from February to April, and among the plays presented were *Alexander the Great*, *The School for Scandal* and *The Heiress*.

Watson informed his public that he was getting Hinde of Whitechapel to make scenery and machinery which would interchange with the Cheltenham Theatre and some of his other playhouses, including that at Brecon. On this visit to the town John Boles Watson's son of the same name was baptised in St Mary's Church.

The town continued to receive visits from the Cheltenham company once in two years, although this was a flexible arrangement. Curiously, only one of the company, Mrs Hudson, came to Brecon in December 1789, giving an entertainment called 'As You Like It', a lecture interspersed with recitations. This was not held at Watson's theatre (one wonders if there had been a disagreement between manager and employee) but in the Great Room of the Bell Hotel, so spacious that it was fitted up as a complete playhouse. Brecon seems to have had ample accommodation for the drama.

Later in the same month the Cheltenham company arrived and stayed until April 1790, presenting amongst other works *Don Juan, or The Libertine Destroyed* (a dance with music by Gluck which originated from the Royalty Theatre and the patent houses) and *The English Merchant*. For eight weeks from January 1793 Watson was again in the town.

Two managers from the Swansea area took short leases on the theatre, Phillips in February 1805 and Andrew Cherry in November 1807.

In 1813, the year of Watson's death, his son took the Brecon theatre so that Richer might give a display of rope-walking in it. There were no other entertainments.

Charles Crisp, who took over many of Jack Watson's theatres in Wales and the west of England, became the manager of the Brecon Theatre in 1822. For the next eight years he played regular seasons of four months in the town. In 1824 he lit the theatre by gas, yet he still maintained the old conventions of presentation:

> We must not pass unnoticed the great care that is taken in arranging things brought on and off the stage, which is always done by a person in full livery.

The full livery, of course, was a symbol of the 'royal' status of the Cheltenham company.

Crisp died in October 1832. The theatre functioned until the 1860s.

Principal sources:
Cambrian, 6 March 1813; *Hereford Journal*, 25 August, 4 September 1783, 4 January–22 February 1787; *Gloucester Journal*, 21 January, 5 March, 30 April, 7 May, 10 October 1787; Iain Mackintosh and Michael Sell, *Curtains* (Eastbourne, 1982); *Notes and Queries*, 29 February 1868; Cecil Price, *The English Theatre in Wales* (Cardiff, 1948); Cecil Price, 'Eighteenth-Century Playbills of the English Theatre in Wales', *Journal of the National Library of Wales*, VI (1949–50), 270.
Warwickshire County Record Office, Warwick: materials relating to the Warwick Theatre; British Library: Burney Collection of Playbills, 4 December 1789 and 21 January 1790.
Information received from Sister Bonaventure Kellehan of St David's Ursuline Convent, Brecon.

Bristol (44)

In July 1817 Jack Watson leased the Theatre Royal, King Street, Bristol, giving the proprietors a number of underakings: the auditorium would be given new chandeliers, a new foyer would be built and new refreshment rooms would be provided for the patrons of the upper boxes. None of this materialised nor was any rent paid. Richard Smith complained of the gloom of the house and the stench of tallow. The proprietors seized Watson's scenes and wardrobe but the sale of these effects realised only £48.16s 9d. Watson was forced to go into hiding and ultimately went bankrupt. In May 1841 an entry in the Accounts Books reads: 'To Cash and received Dividend in the Estate of John Boles Watson . . . £25.3s'.

William M'Cready was selected as the next leasee in 1819.

The full story of Jack Watson's sojourn at Bristol is narrated in Chapter 14.

Principal sources:
Kathleen M C Barker, *The Theatre Royal Bristol. The first Seventy*

Years (Bristol, 1961); Kathleen M D Barker, 'The Theatre Proprietor's Story', *Theatre Notebook*, XVIII (1963–4), 81–2; G Rennie Powell, *The Bristol Stage* (Bristol, 1919).

Carmarthen (30)

John Boles Watson fitted up a theatre in Little Water Street, Carmarthen, in 1780. It was 'an old place fitted up in the old way' and when full the box office takings amounted to £30. By 1787 Watson was advertising that he had bought land for a new theatre; nevertheless Henry Masterman, visiting the town in 1795, used a temporary theatre as did Andrew Cherry who took over the management in 1807 and arrived in Carmarthen the following year.

On a playbill for a performance of *The Heart of Midlothian* given at the theatre in 1820 the name of Miss Fisher, playing Madge Wildfire, appears. Is this the child prodigy or her sister who visited the Cheltenham and Cirencester theatres in the first decade of the century (see Chapter 18)?

By 1822 Jack Watson was announcing his intention of 'fitting up the theatre [possible that in Little Water Street] in a style *superior* to what has *hitherto* been witnessed'; after performances of *The Stranger* and *The Spectre* the *Carmarthen Journal* compared the high standard attained with that of Cherry's less successful company. This was the year in which Charles Crisp took over part of the circuit. On his coming to Carmarthen in 1828 the *Journal* suggested that it was high time to set up a subscription scheme to raise the £600 needed to build an elegant theatre but nothing seems to have come of this.

By the 1830s the Evangelical Movement held powerful sway locally against the theatre.

Principal sources:
Carmarthen Journal, 3 and 10 May, 1822; John Genest, *Some Account of the English Stage from the Restoration in 1660 to 1830* (Bath, 1832), Vol VII; *Gloucester Journal*, May 1780 and 7 May 1787; Cecil Price, *The English Theatre in Wales* (Cardiff, 1948).
County Record Office, Carmarthen: Carmarthenshire Antiquarian Society, scrapbook (1934); Carmarthen Theatre playbill, 24 April 1820.

Cheltenham (37)

The earliest theatre building in Cheltenham was a converted malthouse in Coffee House Yard, Pittville Street, in which Roger Kemble's company performed. Here the Hon John Byng in June 1781 saw John Boles Watson's players who came over from Tewkesbury act *Love in a Village* which, as a comedy peppered with songs, left him unimpressed: 'Sing-song performances are generally ill-performed . . . I feel for their want of abilities', although he tempered this judgement: 'The actors here were tolerably good with decent dresses and decorations: Mr and Mrs Fullam the best performers'.

Watson realised the inadequacies of the Coffee House Yard Theatre and in 1782 he opened a playhouse in Grosvenor Terrace, off the High Street, which became the headquarters of his company. This was dubbed a Theatre Royal in 1788 on the occasion of the visit of George III to the spa to take the waters (see Chapter 2). Visitors to this small theatre included Michael Kelly and Anna Maria Crouch (so great was their popularity that the pit was railed into additional boxes) and Sarah Siddons; they generated a ferment of excitement as the following newspaper cutting suggests:

> We have here in the course of the season all the excellencies of London. The theatre is managed with great spirit and deserves encouragement.

As is shown in a drawing by James Winston, the theatre suffered from the disadvantage of having no frontage on the street. This necessitated entering through the passageway of a domestic dwelling.

In turn the building became inadequate for the numbers of visitors and Watson bought a plot of land (85 feet by 30 feet) on Cambray Meadow (then an area of the town in which few houses had been erected) in 1805, inviting subscribers at £100 each or at 150 guineas with free admission. With its frontage in Bath Street, this large theatre, costing £8000, opened the same year. Admission prices were more expensive than in many country playhouses: box seats at 4/- (20p), pit 2/6 (12p) and gallery 1/- (5p). James Winston, who carped at Watson's management, claims that the interior of the

198

theatre smelt obnoxious as 'kitchen stuff' in place of oil was burnt as an illuminant; the scenery and props were held to be 'very bad' with only one set of wings. The company salaries in the year of opening were said to range from 9/- (45p) to 15/- (75p). Because of his ill-health Watson leased the building to Ray and Gibbon.

From this point the history of the theatre becomes a roll-call of short-lived managerships and mounting debts. John Crisp (also the manager of the Worcester Theatre) held the title in 1819, paying Jack Watson £420 per annum rent. By 1821 he was so seriously in arrears with his payments that his scenes and properties at Cheltenham and Gloucester were seized. He was followed in 1823 by Frederick Yates who in turn soon found some of his property impounded. In 1826 Jack Watson sold the theatre in an attempt to solve some of his own monetary problems, an action he seems to have regretted, for the following year he was making enquiries about leasing the building so that his 'greatly improved' company could be seen in Cheltenham. Possibly the joint proprietors were Daniel Terry and Thomas Gladslane, the latter, also financially embarrassed, soon to be a debtor in the Kings Bench Prison. Nevertheless, in 1829 the external entrance to the boxes was repaved and an act drop by W H Spencer depicting the New Spa at Pittville was hung. By June 1830 John Boles Watson III was manager (we learn from a letter that his father has been 'confined' for sixteen months – whether this means from sickness or has been kept within the debtors' prison is not clear), arranging a benefit in thanksgiving for the favours the town had bestowed upon himself, his father (Jack Watson) and his grandfather (John Boles Watson I). 1831 saw a remarkably brief management, that of D'Ville who decamped with the theatre takings in the same year. Spencer, the actor–painter, became manager in 1835. Tragedy occurred during Grattan's managership in 1839 when the building was totally gutted by fire.

Performers at the Bath Street Theatre included Dorothy Jordan, Harriot Mellon (whose mother kept the Cheltenham Post Office; the actress bought a building plot near to the theatre on Cambray Meadow in 1809), John Richer the rope-walker, Edmund Kean, Joseph Grimaldi, Joseph Munden and John Bannister. Some members of the aristocracy appeared on the stage too: Lady Mary Montagu announced Mellon's benefit night and Colonel Berkeley of

Berkeley Castle hired the theatre for amateur productions.

Samuel Seward (died 1810), who originally hailed from Bristol and Bath and then became a member of Watson's company as actor (a most successful Harlequin) and scene painter, opened his own theatre, the Sadler's Wells or English Fantoccini, in approximately 1795. His son, Abraham, inherited this. Puppet shows were staged from Monday to Friday in the season. James Winston wrote that the shows (string puppets were used in them) were 'well managed' and Samuel Ryley was enthusiastic about this 'real legitimate puppet show . . . [of] the ancient school [which] appeared in all its glory and splendour'. The small theatre building may be seen in a drawing by Winston. On the facade is a notice 'Sadler's Wells House. Fantoccini Exhibition' and in pencil beneath 'Seward's Puppet Show'. This theatre, which continued in use until *c*1850, later became known as the New Clarence. It still stands, now a garage. The puppets were inherited by Rebequi in 1838.

Principal sources:
Bristol Mercury, 9 and 23 April 1838; John Byng, *The Torrington Diaries* ed C Bruyn Andrews (1970); *Cheltenham* (Cheltenham, 1810); *Cheltenham Chronicle*, 9 May 1839; *Cheltenham Directory* (Cheltenham, 1800); *Cheltenham Looker-On*, 4 May 1839; *The Cheltenham Guide* (Cheltenham 1805); *Gloucester Journal*, 23 July 1810, 22 March 1813; John Goding, *Norman's History of Cheltenham* (Cheltenham and London, 1863); Theodore Hannam-Clark, *Drama in Gloucestershire* (1928); Eric Irwin, 'More Drawings for Winston's Theatre Tourist', *Theatre Notebook*, XIX (1964–5) 120; S W Ryley, *The Itinerant*, vol VI, chap. 24 (1817); George Speaight, *The History of the English Puppet Theatre* (2nd ed. 1990); George Speaight, 'Wire or Strings?' *Theatre Notebook*, XXXVII (1983) 63–6; Margaret Cornwell Baron Wilson, *Memoirs of Harriot, Duchess of St Albans* (1839).
Birmingham Central Library: the Winston Collection; British Library: Richard Percival Collection, III, fol 65 (Crach 1 Tab 4 b 4); Cheltenham Museum and Art Gallery: playbill collection; Gloucester County Record Office, Gloucester: various papers relating to the theatre (D2025), Box 73); undated note (D214 F1/193); indenture of 1803 (D6075); National State Library of New South Wales, Sydney, Australia: drawings by James Winston in preparation for *The Theatric Tourist*.

Cirencester (41)

Since the early days of the eighteenth century visiting players arriving at Cirencester used a barn in the yard of the Three Cocks Inn, Castle Street, as their theatre.

When John Boles Watson succeeded to the Kemble circuit he also used this makeshift accommodation, regularly bringing the Cheltenham company from its base in the nearby spa town until 1794. In that year, in a location now unknown but presumably superior to the yard, he 'fitted up a Play-house', a phrase implying an adaptation rather than a new building. The brief use of the location also suggests an impermanent arrangement.

Watson put up a permanent purpose-built theatre in Gloucester Street. This opened in 1799. Doubt seemed to exist amongst the townspeople about the numbers this held; some claimed five hundred whilst others doubled the figure. The Cirencester Theatre was amongst the batch leased to Ray and Gibbon in 1803. In 1807 Watson reclaimed the management.

John Boles Watson died in 1813 and his son Jack Watson took up the management of the circuit. His reaction to the arrival in 1816 of the Fenton family – past members of the Cheltenham company – staging plays in the Assembly Rooms of the King's Head Hotel, Cirencester, may only be guessed. Throughout much of the 1820s, although Jack Watson was the proprietor, Davenport saw to the management of the playhouse. A notable, non-theatrical visitor was William Cobbett who spoke at a meeting in 1826 to an audience of about 150 people; he had previously spoken at the Tewkesbury Theatre.

By the 1830s John Boles Watson III was manager of the company, performing in Cirencester together with his wife.

However by that time the cottages at the front of the building had been turned into a tavern, the Loyal Volunteer, opened in 1820. The theatre gradually faded away from disuse. A floor was built across the theatre; the lower part became a bowling alley and the upper a function room in which, amongst other activities, the town band practised. Flooding and fire in turn damaged the building during the twentieth century. In 1955 the premises were further adapted and became a private residence. The building still stands in use as such at 27 Gloucester Street.

Principal sources:
Annual Report and Newsletter of the Cirencester Archaeological and Historical Society, No. 23 (Cirencester, 1981); *Gloucester Journal*, passim; Theodore Hannam-Clark, *Drama in Gloucestershire* (1924); Richard O'Brien, 'A Memorable Night at Cirencester Theatre', *The Wiltshire Herald and Advertiser*, 14 December 1951.
Bingham Library, Cirencester: playbill collection; Cheltenham Museum and Art Gallery: playbill collection; Gloucester Public Library, Gloucestershire Room: playbill collection.
Information from Mr Trevor Allen of the Bingham Library, Cirencester; Mrs Jenkins and Mr and Mrs Peter Davies.

Although Theodore Hannam-Clark gives a useful history of the Cirencester Theatre, there are a number of errors in the summary. For example, he runs the fit up and the permanent theatre into one in his account. In the recounting of detail he is valuable, however.

Coventry (9)

Although Roger Kemble fitted up a hall in the town gaol as a playhouse in 1780, St Mary's Hall was used in 1797 by John Boles Watson and his partner Robert Hoy (the company's acting manager), formerly of the Theatre Royal at Bath. According to W T Parke, Watson gained financially and the benefits pleased the actors.

The 1797 season – opening with a rhymed prologue by Watson – was long, lasting for five months with acting on three nights of the week. Mrs Siddons visited for a week and played Zara in *The Mourning Bride*, Isabella in *The Fatal Marriage*, Lady Randolph in *Douglas* and the title role in *Jane Shore*. These roles are described in detail in the anonymous tract *The Beauties of Mrs Siddons* (1786). At an evening benefit in aid of military associations formed to defend the town against 'the enemies of this country' a Coventry citizen wrote a prologue (spoken by Hoy) warning of the dangers of 'proud imperious France'. On the last night Hoy would seem to have suffered some sort of indignity from a section of the audience. What happened is not made clear by the newspapers.

Jack Watson brought the Cheltenham company to the town in 1810 and found St Mary's Hall commodious enough to install a prefabricated gallery and boxes. The taste of the town was conservative, preferring *Oroonoko, Cymbeline* and *Isabella* to such pieces as *Don Juan, Gustavus Vasa, The Honeymoon, The Wags of Windsor, Ella Rosenburg* and *Adelgitha,* all dismissed as 'slight dramas' by a writer to the newspaper.

The following year Watson and the company together with John Richer and his rope walking returned to be joined by Mrs Jordan making something of a provincial comeback. Later in the year she described the Cheltenham company as 'wretched' and claimed that her audiences found her 'ill-supported'. The makeshift theatre in Coventry intrigued her:

> [It] is made out of the town hall, and a curious looking place it is. How it will look at night I don't know. It is entirely surrounded by high painted windows which press up behind the Boxes and look so odd. This is the hall where Lady Godiva dined with the Corporation.

The audience won her heart after her first performance when she played the Widow Cheerly in *The Soldier's Daughter* by Andrew Cherry.

> They received me very greatly, and continued their civility during the whole Play, and when it was over the old hall shook again with their approbation.

On a visit in 1826 Robert William Elliston (later manager of Drury Lane) joined the players, appearing as Dr Pangloss in *The Heir at Law.* Jack Watson took the role of Zekiel Homespun.

The following year the management of the theatre passed to the Penley family and then to Melmoth of the Theatre Royal, Birmingham. The *Coventry Mercury* remarked that

> we know our townspeople can and will support him . . . if he will but bring good performers, and not insult their understandings by bringing such companies as we, for these few seasons, have been accustomed to see in Coventry.

Principal sources:
A Aspinall, *Mrs Jordan and her Family* (1951); *Coventry Mercury*; William Hickling, *History and Antiquities of the City of Coventry*

(Coventry, 1846); W T Parke, *Musical Memoirs* (1830); George Raymond, *Memoirs of Robert William Elliston Comedian* (1844); Thomas Sharp, *The Coventry Guide* (Coventry, 1824); *Victoria History of the Counties of England, Warwickshire*, vol. VIII.
Central Library, Coventry: Arthur Heap, 'Plays, Players and Playbills in Coventry', newspaper cuttings from the *Coventry Herald*; Arthur Heap, 'Compilation', newscuttings from the *Coventry Herald* (Arthur Heap was a reporter on the staff of the local paper).

Daventry (25)

Early in 1799 the theatre at Daventry was made ready for the visit of the Cheltenham company which arrived, headed by John Boles Watson and his co-manager Richards, in February; this was to be a 'short season' of eight weeks as the new Cirencester Theatre was due to open at Easter. The repertoire, according to the advertisements, consisted of the plays which had won applause at the 'Cheltenham, Gloucester, Coventry and Leicester' theatres, namely such pieces as *Wild Oats*, *King Richard the Third*, *The Mountaineers*, *The Stranger*, *Jane Shore*, *As You Like It*, and *The Belle's Strategem*.

On an evening in February 1803 a fire broke out in the theatre consuming scenery and premises. Another playhouse was quickly built: it measured 78 feet by 39 feet, adjoining the Fold (or Boddering) Yard, near to the west end of Tavern Lane. The building was leased to Gibbon and Ray in October 1803.

Northampton Mercury, 15 December 1798; 23 February, 2 March, 20 April 1799; 5 February 1803.
Warwickshire County Record Office, Warwick: Materials relating to Warwick Theatre.

Dudley (13)

After a season at Stourbridge during March and April 1783 John Boles Watson and the Cheltenham company went on to Dudley for five nights in May.

Jack Watson appears to have inherited either the Dudley Theatre or its lease from his father. In an undated note to his solicitors (Guinnett and Newman of Cheltenham) he proposed to let a Mr Wright hold the key to the building so that he could attempt to let it occasionally and so defray some of his debts.

Principal sources:
H E Palfrey, *Some Account of the Old Theatres at Stourbridge*
(Stourbridge, 1936).
Gloucestershire Record Office, Gloucester: note from Jack Watson
to Guinnett and Newman (D 2025, Box 73).

Evesham (27)

Old Drury Lane Theatre at Evesham was a converted barn situated
in the town between Bewdley Lane and Merstow Green.

The Cheltenham company under John Boles Watson's management performed here in February and March 1792 giving, amongst
other entertainments, *The Jubilee* (a stage reproduction of the
procession David Garrick organised at Stratford-upon-Avon in
honour of Shakespeare), *Scrub's Travels* rendered by Shuter and, at
the request of the Friendly Society of the Vale of Evesham, *The
Farmer*, chosen by Watson for his benefit. The company reappeared
for a Christmas season, 1793. The Evesham Theatre was on the list
of the Watson theatres leased to George Collins Gibbon and
Edward Ray in 1803.

Principal sources:
Gloucester Journal, 6 February 1792.
Warwickshire County Record Office, Warwick: Draft indenture of
co-partnership (CR 1596 Box 93); Worcester County Record Office,
St Helen's Worcester: Foley Scrapbooks, III, 204.
Information from Mrs S Williamson, Librarian; Anthony Denning's
typescript.

Gloucester (38)

A theatre was opened, fashioned from a disused malthouse, in
Barton Street, Gloucester, in either 1763 or 64. This was a
'melancholic, inconvenient place, which, when filled, would not
hold more than £35' (in Ryley's words) although it was rare for the
'dungeon' to take this amount at a performance. Inconveniently the
building was entered through a domestic dwelling. Sarah Siddons
played here on the night one of her daughters was born. To this
building John Boles Watson brought the Cheltenham company.

Possibly because of the unsuitability of the place, in 1789 Watson
moved into the Booth Hall for the season. This was a timber

construction which lay behind the Booth Hall Inn in Westgate Street. It had served as guildhall, market hall and, since the mid-sixteenth century, playhouse. The Revd Thomas Rudge described the part used for theatricals as a 'large, unornamented room, possessed of some conveniences, but on the whole too mean for the respectable and opulent county of Gloucester'. H Y J Taylor had fonder memories:

> Vestiges of the old Bothall may still be seen and I can remember when it was used for a theatre. The stage faced South. The drop scene was a green baize curtain . . . I can still hear the music of that primitive orchestra.

Watson purchased a plot of land in Westgate Street in February 1791, demolished the standing property and opened his new theatre by June. The authorities had decided not to licence another theatre, but as the building was within ten miles of the Cheltenham playhouse, the venue was put up 'under sanction of lease from the Corporation'. By August 1797 ill health forced Watson to take Hoy as co-manager and the following year he became so infirm that Hoy took over the management of the Gloucester Theatre completely.

By 1808 Edmund Kean, during Beverley's managership, was a member of the company and played here before an apathetic citizenry for three months. A noble roll call of performers appeared here whilst the Watsons were proprietors; among them were Sarah Siddons, John Philip Kemble, Charles Mayne Young, Charles Incledon, Daniel Terry and William Farren.

In 1819, having promised his patrons the benefit of gas lighting, an unfulfilled boast, Jack Watson let the theatre, together with that at Cheltenham, to Crisp at a yearly rent of £545. The latter fell heavily into arrears and John Boles Watson III was complaining by 1830 that the Gloucester Theatre was 'not thought of' by the townspeople during the then current recession.

In 1835 a new manager, Belville Penley, announced that the theatre was no longer lit by tallow candles or 'train oil lamps' but by gas. It is interesting that, despite the many changes of management, the Watson family was still connected personally with the theatre, a Miss Watson appearing in 1836 in *Gustavus III*. Holmes was manager in the 1840s, a hapless man who had brought both the Winchester and the Newbury theatres to ruin by his incompetence. The theatre appears to have been used only sporadically for presentations and by 1844 Mrs Watson (presumably the wife of John Boles Watson III) was advertising the building to let as a warehouse.

In 1857 the place was sold for £450 to John Blinkhorn, a railway contractor. At a cost of £9000 he reconstructed the building and William Beverley, the son of the earlier manager, risen to a scene painter's position at Drury Lane, painted a new drop depicting an Italian landscape. The theatre was ready for reopening in March 1859.

Blinkhorn, in turn, sold the building to a local company for £3150 in 1887. Four years later the centenary of the building was celebrated by a visit from Henry Irving, Ellen Terry and the Lyceum Company; two of the plays staged were *The Bells* and *Nance Oldfield*. A banquet was also held at the Bell Hotel.

The notices for the 1902 auction supply details of the building: the theatre could accommodate 1890 people and had a holding capacity of £75 a performance. The stage was 36 feet deep with an opening of 34 feet by 35 feet in height. The stage was equipped with a vampire trap and two star traps. Charles Poole bought the place, running it as a theatre, variety hall, opera house and cinema under the name of the Palace; mail for the Bishop of Gloucester was sometimes inadvertently delivered here. The first film shown was of Sir Herbert Beerbohm Tree's company in *Henry VIII*.

The building was dismantled in 1922 although a doorway surmounted by a bust of Shakespeare remains in Westgate Street and below ground a door in the adjoining building, the Theatre Vaults Public House, was used as the pit entrance.

Principal sources:
Gloucester Journal, 14 June 1819; Theodore Hannam-Clark, *Drama in Gloucestershire* (1928); Alan Moore, *The Picture Palaces of Gloucester and Cheltenham* (Sutton Coldfield, 1989); Paul Ranger, *A Catalogue of Strolling Players* (Newbury, 1990); Thomas Ridge, *The History and Antiquities of Gloucester* (Gloucester, 1811); Samuel Ryley, *The Itinerant or Memoirs of an Actor* (1808); *The Victoria History of the Counties of England, Gloucestershire* (1988) vols IV and VII.

Gloucester Public Library, Gloucester Collection: Programme for the Centenary of the Theatre Royal, Gloucester ((H) E. 15.4 (15)); plan of the Theatre Royal, 1902 (NX29.2); playbills for 22 November 1834, 21 December 1835, 16 March 1836, 9 and 17 January 1844 (NX29.3); playbill for 23 December 1835 (NR29.6); Gloucestershire County Record Office, Gloucester: papers relating to Jack Watson (D2025, Box 73).

Information supplied by Miss B Drake and Brian Frith FSG of Gloucester; Anthony Denning's typescript.

Hereford (28)

Hereford was one of the theatres on Roger Kemble's circuit which John Boles Watson took over. He arrived in Hereford with the Cheltenham company in 1783, presumably acting in makeshift premises. The venue must have been unsatisfactory for Watson promised to build a playhouse in the town. News of this was given in the *Hereford Journal* (21 September 1786); a brief note describes the building in Broad Street, possibly on the site of a former playhouse, as 'handsome', but a correspondent to *Notes and Queries* (CLX (1931) 301) claimed it was not only pokey but poorly attended. The exterior of the building was graced with a pediment ornamented with busts of Shakespeare, Powell and Garrick, the latter two born in the town. The builder was a Mr Parker who in the first season received a benefit consisting of half the receipts of one night to which he was entitled by contract. Watson's own announcement in October assured patrons the scenery was 'quite new', that 'nothing under full price' would be taken and that the backstage would be kept clear of visitors (*Hereford Journal*, 26 October 1786). For the last three months of 1788 Watson played in the town. The acting was acceptable but the band fell below par and there were insufficient playbills. A benefit was held for Samuel Day and his wife: the couple were fruit sellers in the theatre. The comedian Shuter received a benefit night on 5 December 1788 playing in *A New Way to Pay Old Debts*.

On Jack Watson assuming the management in 1819 a series of improvements were undertaken: the interior was painted, lamps and chandeliers introduced and the seats provided with stuffed cushions; the pit passage was also widened. The new manager had intended to raise the roof above the gallery, but time precluded this. The *Hereford Guide* of 1827 is noncommittal in describing the interior as 'neat'. At that date Watson only visited the Hereford Theatre once every three years. Takings usually amounted to £40 per night.

Between the managements of John Boles Watson I and that of his son, John Crisp took charge, followed by his brother Charles, an able artist. In addition to Gloucester and Cheltenham, they also managed the theatres at Leominster, Bridgenorth and Ludlow. Charles Crisp played a variety of roles including Richard III, the Ghost in *Hamlet*, Macbeth, Shylock, Liston in *Paul Pry* and Rambler in *Wild Oats*.

In 1831 John Boles Watson III was manager for a brief span.

A Miss Faulkland took charge of the theatre in 1853 and W Peters the following year. The building was demolished and replaced by the Corn Exchange in 1857. This continued the theatrical tradition, becoming the Kemble Theatre in 1911 and then a cinema. It was finally demolished in 1963.

Principal sources:
Gloucester Journal, 21 January 1787; *Hereford Journal*, 21 September and 26 October 1786; 28 July 1819; *Notes and Queries*, I (1868), 141–2, 206, CLX (1931), 301; Cecil Price, *The English Theatre in Wales* (Cardiff, 1948); W J Rees, *Hereford Guide* (Hereford, 1827). Birmingham Central Library: Theatre Royal, Birmingham, playbill collection; Johannesburg Public Library: the William Douglas Notebook.
Typescript and information supplied by R J H Hill of Hereford City Library.

Hinckley (8)
In 1774 Chamberlain led the Cheltenham company in a visit to Hinckley. During this Burton, a stock low comedian, died and was buried in St Mary's churchyard; burial and headstone were paid for by the actors in the company.

A playbill informs that the company were again in Hinckley at the 'New Theatre' in August 1800 with Colley Cibber's version of *King Richard III* (Marshall playing Richard) and *Lock and Key* (Chamberlain as Old Brummagem).

209

Principal sources:
Helen and Richard Leacroft, *The Theatre in Leicestershire* (Leicester, 1986).
Leicestershire Record Office, Wigton Magna: playbill collection.

Holywell (1)

Having played successfully at Wrexham for four months at the beginning of 1785, John Boles Watson progressed to Holywell, performing there during May and June. According to *Adams' Weekly Courant* he drew crowded houses supported by the Bagillet Lads who patronised *A Bold Stroke for a Wife*. In a glow of success Watson outlined his proposals for the future:

> Mr Watson's Comedians are so liberally encouraged in the town of Holywell that he had contracted for a spacious building, purposing to pay his respects there again.

He then went on to say that on his next visit to Wales he would include the towns of Welshpool and Denbigh.

A bill for a Phelps' benefit in which *Henry IV* is advertised, under the patronage of Master Mostyne of Talacre, is held at the County Record Office, Hawarden. The playhouse is referred to as the 'New Theatre', Holywell, suggesting that Watson had lived up to his word. The actor receiving the benefit does not appear to be a close forbear of Samuel Phelps, the later manager of Salder's Wells.

Principal sources:
Adams' Weekly Courant; Cecil Price, *The English Theatre in Wales* (Cardiff, 1948).

Kidderminster (15)

Richard Baxter (1615–91), the Puritan divine, was curate to the incumbent of Kidderminster and thereby it is only to be expected that the townspeople would be averse to players and performances. The actor John Henderson (1747–85) told of the reaction of a Mr Watson to a group of strollers who were received favourably by the townspeople; he nailed a card with the following lines to the door of the barn which served as the 'Summer Theatre Royal':

How art thou fallen, Oh! Kidderminster;
When every spulster [winder], spinner, spinster,
Whose fathers lived in Baxter's prayers,
Are now run gadding after players;
Oh, Richard, could'st thou take a survey
Of this vile place for sin so scurvy,
Thy pious shade, enraged, would scold them
And make the barn too hot to hold them.

In 1821 Charles Crisp's company played at the barn.

Principal sources:
Worcester at Leisure (Cheltenham and London, nd).
Worcester City Library, Local History Collection: typescript by H W Gwilliam, 'The Theatre in Worcestershire'.

Kington (19)

Roger Kemble was manager of the Kington Theatre (originally the barn of the Sun Inn in Morris' Square and later a barn behind the Talbot Inn, Bridge Street) and here his daughter Sarah is said to have first performed at the age of three. His son, Stephen, was baptised in Kington in April 1758.

Although John Boles Watson acquired the theatre, along with most of the others on the Kemble circuit, he rarely appeared in the town, concentrating on the more populous areas. It was a drawback that the theatre would only hold £20 in box office takings and the magistrates were inclined to limit their permission to thirty-six nights. However, Watson and the Cheltenham company were playing in November 1785 and Mr H Beavan wrote to Nathaniel Winchcombe of Stroud: 'We have been very agreeably entertained since our arrival here by Watson's company from Cheltenham, which have received great encouragement and I think [illeg] the best travelling company I ever saw'. Two months later, making his way northwards, Watson played a season there before going to Leominster. The Cheltenham company were next in Kington in 1791. John Richer appeared during the first half of November 1802 and then the full company arrived in December when the players included Shuter and Tony le Brun. Hoy performed in 1802–3 and Waldegrave arrived in 1818.

211

A playbill in Hereford Museum tells of John Boles Watson III and his wife appearing in Kington in November 1832 in *Nell Gwynne*.

Principal sources:
W H Howse, *Kington, Herefordshire. Memorial of an Old Town* (Kington, 1953, reprinted 1989); W H Howse, *Radnorshire* (Hereford, 1949); Philip H Highfill, jnr *et al*, *A Biographical Dictionary of Actors* etc (Carbondale and Edwardsville, 1973–); *Notes and Queries*, I (1862), 268; Richard Parry, *The History of Kington* (Kington, 1845); Cecil Price, *The English Theatre in Wales* (Cardiff, 1948); Carl Willmott, 'The Theatre in Kington, Herefordshire', *Theatre Notebook*, V (1951), 44–6.
Gloucestershire County Record Office, Gloucester: Letter from H Beavan (D149 E 85).

Leicester (7)

The Cheltenham company provided a season during the 1797–8 winter at which time Watson described himself as the manager of the Leicester Theatre. Presumably playing was at the Assembly Rooms, Coal-Hill, which were fitted up with boxes and gallery. In earlier days William and Sarah Siddons and John Philip Kemble had appeared here. This building ceased to be used for the drama on its sale in 1805. Sanderson, the box keeper, a 'cross-grained queer old codger' remarked an actor writing to James Winston, had held office since the middle of the eighteenth century, residing in the makeshift playhouse.

John Boles Watson advertised on his Warwick playbills of 1799 that he was about to open a new theatre in Leicester. A theatre in Horsefair Street adjoining the Assembly Rooms was then erected by John Johnson. This was a brick building, very small, with an exterior so plain 'as to approach meanness'. Yet surprisingly when full, the takings would amount to £76.

A further theatre was put up in 1836 by Samuel Beazley, a celebrated builder of theatres whose designs included such London houses as the St James's and the Lyceum. He was also a prolific dramatist.

Principal sources:
Charles James Billson, *Leicester Memoirs* (1924); Phyllis Hartnoll,

The Concise Oxford Companion to the Theatre (1972); Helen and Richard Leacroft, *The Theatre in Leicestershire* (Leicester, 1986); Jack Simmons, *Leicester Past and Present* (1974); *Victoria History of the Counties of England, Leicestershire*, vol. IV.

Birmingham Central Library: the Winston Collection; Johannesburg Public Library: William Douglas Notebook; Warwickshire County Record Office, Warwick: materials relating to the Warwick Theatre; Worcester County Record Office, St Helen's, Worcester: Foley Scrapbook, IV.

Leominster (20)

A small theatre was in use during the first half of the eighteenth century in Leominster. From 1754 onward the Schoolhouse (employed as chapel, sessions house and playhouse) was often used by groups of actors and it was here that 'Ward the Player' performed in season on Mondays, Wednesdays and Fridays.

The Cheltenham company performed in the town in the early months of 1786 and 1789. Another season was held in 1794 when William Miell spoke a prologue written by a 'Miss T H-S' about the various usages of the building. The text is given in the *Gentleman's Magazine*, LXIV (1794), 458.

When John Ward handed his company over to Roger Kemble he and his wife settled in Leominster. Their grave is in the Priory.

Principal sources:
Gloucester Journal, 9 January 1786; *Hereford Journal*, 31 December 1788; Cecil Price, *The English Theatre in Wales* (Cardiff, 1948); N C Reeve, *Town in the Marches* (Leominster, 1972).

Lichfield (5)

Roger Kemble's company visited Lichfield in 1770, probably playing in the Guildhall, a building in which six years earlier Samuel Johnson and James Boswell had sat watching Stanton's company perform *Theodosius* by Nathaniel Lee. One of the plays given during Kemble's season was *The Recruiting Officer* written by George Farquhar whilst staying in the city at the George Inn. William Siddons, the future husband of Kemble's daughter Sarah, was playing in the company on this visit.

In 1790 John Miller of London designed a theatre to stand in Bore

Street on the site of the White Hart Inn. The theatre was purchased in 1793 in joint stock by subscribers for £7155s. 8d. The *Staffordshire Advertiser* described the building as neat 'with a stucco front, the interior spacious and boxes, stage, etc. neatly decorated'. Alfred Parker, who probably saw the building before its demolition in 1875, mentions its 'four large dressing rooms . . . boxes, upper boxes . . . a fairly commodious pit and a good gallery'. The gallery however suffered the inconvenience of a large central beam three or four feet away from the seats.

Companies usually played for a week or less at the times of the races in March, September and during the Yeomanry Week. One of the first people to be granted a sixty day licence was James Miller, the manager of the Worcester Company; whether he was the manager here or had merely taken a short lease on the building is not clear.

It was to this theatre that the Cheltenham company made a number of visits: one such season was from the beginning of February until mid-March 1809. If Anna Seward's earlier made remark were correct, the neglect of the residents would have afforded Watson slight reward.

John Boles Watson III brought the Cheltenham company to Lichfield in 1831.

Principal sources:
Aris's Birmingham Gazette, 5 January 1767; Howard Clayton, *Coaching City* [Didsbury, 1977]; John Jackson, *History of the City and Cathedral of Lichfield* (1805); Alfred Parker, *A Sentimental Journey in and About the Ancient and Loyal City of Lichfield* (Lichfield, 1925); Charles Ryscamp and Frederick A Pottle, *Boswell, the Ominous Years, 1774–76* (Yale, 1963); *Victoria History of the Counties of England, Staffordshire*, vol XIV.
Birmingham Central Library: the Winston Collection; the Theatre Royal playbill collection; Archive: Minute Book of the Proprietors of the Theatre Royal, Birmingham (Lee 387).

Llandrindod (18)

The new spa at Llandrindod with its waters, Great House, Long Rooms and race weeks attracted large numbers of visitors. Once merely a few farmhouses, the place rapidly became a stylish resort:

Let England boast Bath's crowded springs,
Llandrindod, happier Cambria sings!

John Ward (with Roger Kemble, his son-in-law, in the company) visited the town for a week in 1755, fitting up his playhouse in a barn in Trevonen. The visit may have been prompted, suggests Cecil Price, on hearing of the success of Glenn's Company of Comedians which had played in their 'New Theatre' at the conclusion of each day's races the previous year.

This station on the circuit passed via Roger Kemble to John Boles Watson although his visits here seem to have been extremely rare.

Principal sources:
T P Davies, 'Llandrindod Wells in the Eighteenth Century', *Radnorshire Transactions*, IV (1934) 10–16; *Gentleman's Magazine*, XVIII (1748), 469; W H Howse, *Radnorshire* (Hereford, 1949); Cecil Price, *The English Theatre in Wales* (Cardiff, 1948); Cecil Price, 'A Welsh Spaw', *Welsh Review*, V (1946), 42–4.

Ludlow (17)

John Ward presented plays at the Ludlow Guildhall and this station on the circuit, as with others, succeeded to John Boles Watson via Roger Kemble; Watson styled himself as the manager of the theatre on several occasions.

In use by 1775, a new theatre was situated on the west side of Mill Street, opposite the Grammar School. According to a playbill, the building appears to have had no boxes but these had been built when the Hon John Byng visited the theatre in June 1784:

> . . . seeing a crowd at a door, and enquiring the cause, [we] were told it was the theatre, and that the play [*A Bold Stroke for a Husband* by Hannah Cowley] was just began; in we sallied, took our places in the boxes, amidst a numerous and well-dress'd audience, and were sufficiently amused; though it lasted too late [after 11 pm] . . . Some of the performers play'd with judgement and spirit . . . the company consist of 28 persons, including the band, and perform 3 times a week; and the gay men of the place subscribe £1.1 for a transferable ticket for 20 nights.

Names in the company at this time which crop up in the story of the Cirencester Theatre are those of Ryley (the manager who played Don Vincentio in Cowley's comedy), Durravan and Mrs Jackson. Ryley spoke of the theatre as 'a miserably poor place', holding only £20; audiences were sparse and often a mere £5 would be taken at the box office. During some of the race weeks performances started at 11.00 a.m. when, said Ryley, it was 'irksome' to have to shut out the daylight.

George Frederick Cooke played at the Ludlow theatre in August 1803, teaming with Henry Siddons (the son of Sarah Siddons) and his wife for a performance of *Othello*. Immediately prior to his appearance there he had played at two other Watsonian theatres, Cheltenham and Worcester.

Seasons tended to start with the races at the beginning of July and then continued for about ten weeks.

Three names connected with Watson's company crop up: Carleton was playing Morcar in Dr Thomas Franklin's *Matilda* in 1775; Mr G Shuter took part as Montano in the *Othello* mentioned above, gave a song and took the role of Davy in the afterpiece, *Bon Ton* by the Revd James Townley; William Miell, who managed some of Watson's theatres, did so at the Ludlow.

Principal sources:
John Byng, *The Torrington Diaries* (1934); Arnold Hare, *George Frederick Cooke; the Man and the Actor* (1980); David Lloyd and Peter Klein, *Ludlow: a Historic Town in Words and Pictures* (Chichester, 1984); H E Palfrey, *Some Account of the Old Theatres at Stourbridge* (Stourbridge, 1936); Cecil Price, *The English Theatre in Wales* (Cardiff, 1948); Samuel Ryley, *The Itinerant* (1808).
Ludlow Museum: playbill, 15 August 1803.

Merthyr (32)
Anthony Denning lists the Merthyr Theatre as one managed by John Boles Watson I. In the absence of a local newspaper detailed documentation is difficult to come by. For a few years Henry Masterman was manager of the purpose-built theatre in Merthyr and on his death in 1803 R Phillips, one of his company and a former Drury Lane actor, took over part of the company and retrod a section of Masterman's walk: Merthyr, Brecon, Swansea, Haverford-

west and Milford Haven. Phillips played in Merthyr from May to July in 1805 but later that year, when he failed to gain the permanent management of the Swansea Theatre (Andrew Cherry the playwright and former Drury Lane light actor was the selected candidate), he disbanded the company. Possibly it was at this juncture that Watson I was able to add Merthyr to his circuit.

In the year of Watson I's death (1813) his son visited the town to present a season of plays and these were followed by exhibitions of rope walking by John Richer, Watson II's brother-in-law.

There is little further to report. Cecil Price notes that Williams of the Bath Theatre led a company here in November 1814; Roy of the Aberystwyth Theatre visited the town in 1832, J Collier, manager of a fugitive company, was playing here two years later and Glover, a London actor, appeared with a company in 1835.

Another theatre, a fit-up, was opened by Maddocks in the Market House in June 1839. The company played here until September.

Principal sources:
Cambrian, May to July, 1805; Cecil Price, *The English Theatre in Wales* (Cardiff, 1948).
Theatre Museum: Peter Davey's manuscript notebooks.

Minchinhampton (40)

Only three miles from Stroud (the location of one of John Boles Watson I's theatres) and on the main London–Stroud–Cirencester Route, Minchinhampton would have been an ideal location for another of Watson's theatres. Many of its inhabitants, the potential audience, were connected with the wool, yarn and cloth industry.

A Market House for the wool sellers, eventually one of three in the town, was built in 1698 by Philip Sheppard, Lord of the Manor. This consisted of an open ground floor with a hall above supported on pillars. At the beginning of the next century Tetbury took the lead as the principal wool town of the Cotswolds and the market house was deprived of its main function. Instead it became used for entertainment, town business and festivities.

As early as 1732 the Bath Company of Comedians gave a two week season in the House, setting up a stage and benches. The repertoire included *The London Merchant*, *The Provok'd Husband*

and *The Beggars' Opera*. Later Richard Elrington (child actor in Dublin, manager of a south of England company of strollers and eventually a player at the patent theatres) visited the town whilst working the West Country and here was gaoled for a day for infringing licensing regulations.

There was a popular tradition that Sarah Siddons played here and a portrait now hangs in the building. Siddons was acting at Bath from 1778 until 1782 from whence she made forays to Stroud and Cheltenham. Members of the Sheppard family were great patrons of the drama and may possibly have invited her to perform.

Theatrical usage seems to have ended by the early years of the nineteenth century when the upper floor was used as a school.

Principal sources:
Theodore Hannam-Clark, *Drama in Gloucestershire* (1928); Arthur Twixden Playne, *History of the Parishes of Minchinhampton and Avening* (Gloucester, 1915); Cecil Price, *The English Theatre in Wales* (Cardiff, 1948); *A Short History of Minchinhampton Market House* (Minchinhampton, 1986); *Victoria History of the Counties of England, Gloucestershire*, vol XI.

Monmouth (34)

Roger Kemble had made a number of attempts to play in Monmouth and was disgruntled that 'little Parties . . . such as disgrace the Stage' were obtaining permission whilst his own company was refused. However, in June 1775 he obtained a licence and was to be seen at Baker's theatre, possibly a building in St Mary's Street.

John Boles Watson seems to have had no difficulty in gaining permission to play at the Shire Hall in 1784 where he staged *The Beaux Strategem*. He returned to the same venue ('a theatre equal to almost any in the Kingdom in point of size and accommodation', he advertised) in April 1790. On this visit *Captain Cook* was given, but over two nights as the scenes were 'too numerous to use and remove in one night, without many unpleasant delays'. A feature of the tour was the appearance in May of Charles Lee Lewes on his return from the East Indies. Lewes was remembered as the originator of the role of Young Marlow in Oliver Goldsmith's comedy *She Stoops to Conquer*.

218

Watson was succeeded towards the end of the century by Henry Masterman. A subsequent manager of some note was Andrew Cherry, actor and prolific playwright, who began his work in the town in 1803. Cherry would possibly have been based at a theatre in Monk Street.

In 1834 John Boles Watson III brought the Cheltenham company to Monk Street for a series of 'Plays, Interludes and all other Entertainment'.

Principal sources;
Gloucester Journal, 19 April, 17 and 31 May 1790; K Kissack, *Monmouth – The Making of a Country Town* (Chichester, 1975); Cecil Price, *The English Theatre in Wales* (Cardiff, 1948).

Oswestry (3)

Although a theatre existed in Oswestry since 1775 in the renamed Victoria Road, when John Boles Watson and the Cheltenham company visited in September 1782 they played in the Town Hall. Subscription tickets for eighteen nights were available.

The Oswestry Theatre was taken into the orbit of Charles Stanton's circuit near the beginning of the nineteenth century: descended from several generations of theatre managers, Charles inherited playhouses in most of the main towns of Shropshire and Staffordshire. In Oswestry his theatre stood in Lower Brook Street where he performed for a few weeks each autumn. He then opened a theatre next to the White Lion Hotel in Willow Street which had a short-lived financial success as the balcony became unsafe, and the building was utilised as a malthouse.

Principal sources:
William Cathrall, *History of Oswestry* (Oswestry, 1855); Cecil Price, *The English Theatre in Wales* (Cardiff, 1948); William Price, *The History of Oswestry* (Oswestry, 1815); *Shrewsbury Chronicle*, 28 September, 23 November 1782.

Ross (35)

The connection of John Boles Watson with the theatre at Ross appears to be slight. Anthony Denning mentions the town as a station on the circuit.

Ross was on the walk of a band of players in the 1750s, under the management of Richard Elrington.

James Winston noted a playhouse here in 1803. It is difficult to ascertain whether this is identical with the very small permanent theatre existing in July 1829. For this the manager of the Carmarthen company, T Mildenhall, staged his documentary drama based on the life of John Kyrle, the town's benefactor, as well as his account of a recent murder, *The Red Barn or Midday Murder*. Robert Dyer, in the company, noted, 'We were not attractive at Ross . . .'.

Principal sources
Robert Dyer, *Nine Years of an Actor's Life* (Plymouth, 1833); *Monmouthshire Merlin*, 21 November 1829: Cecil Price, *The English Theatre in Wales* (Cardiff, 1948).
Harvard University, Theatre Collection: James Winston's manuscript notes in preparation for *The Theatric Tourist* (1805).

Stourbridge (14)
For several years Sarah Kemble went to school in Stourbridge and local tradition holds that as a child she performed in a barn-like building set between the Bell Hotel and the Drill Hall in Bell Street. Tradition has it, too, that this building was the theatre in which both Roger Kemble and John Boles Watson played a number of seasons.

Watson led the Cheltenham company here in March 1783. The announcement that 'the playhouse . . . is fitted up in a most pleasant manner' suggests that a temporary theatre was used. As at other theatres on this tour *Matilda*, 'dressed in superb habits of the times and country' was played, to which was added the romance of *Cymon*. Once the fair opened, nightly performances were given. During *The Tempest* elaborate machinery was used for flying and sinkings. *Hamlet* was another Shakespeare play given during the season, after which Mrs Watson sang a 'favourite hunting song'. *All for Love* and *The Recruiting Officer* were two other plays presented. After a break at Dudley the company returned on 26 May for Watson's benefit at which was given *The Quaker's Wedding*. Watson did not appear in this but he gave a comic lecture on the art of acting, sung a ditty and spoke the rhymed epilogue thanking the patrons for their support.

At another highly successful season in 1786 Lord and Lady Westcote sponsored *The Heiress*; *The Young Quaker* and *The Flitch of Bacon* were also performed. Watson's expectations led him to advertise that he would build a 'complete new theatre against the next time he attends'. But three years later Watson was still playing in the old building. He brought with him the Charltons from Norwich and the Chalmers from Covent Garden. Shuter, whose name figures on many a Cirencester bill, received a benefit, playing *The Fashionable Lover* in which he was assisted by his wife and son; in masonic gear he spoke a prologue commending the order.

Not until 1792 was the foundation stone of the new theatre laid by John Halliday of the Leasowes and the opening in 1793 was delayed so that the place might be 'perfectly dry and safe in all points'. It stood near to the Talbot Hotel (itself the venue for plays) in what was to become Theatre Road. The yearly rent for the building was £6. 6s. To celebrate the opening of the new playhouse an augmented company was formed by combining the Cheltenham with the Worcester; the manager of the latter, William Miell (as a partner of Watson's also part owner of the Worcester and Wolverhampton theatres) performed in the repertoire.

The death of Miell in 1797 brought the Stourbridge Theatre to the auction room in both that and the following years. The sale advertisement gives an impression of the premises:

The [playhouse was] erected under the judicious management of Mr Watson, whose taste is well known, and comprises a very substantial and lofty theatre, with dressing rooms, and suitable offices attached to such a concern; there is excellent cellaring and vaults under the premises, and the interior may easily be converted into warehouses . . .

By May, 1799, Hoy added Stourbridge to the list of theatres at Worcester, Wolverhampton, Hereford and Ludlow he managed.

Some names which have cropped up in the narrative of the Cirencester Theatre surface again here. Seward, painter at Astley's Amphitheatre, was engaged to produce scenes for *Pizarro*; the Shuter family were members of the company as was Mrs Cresswell; William Betty visited the theatre. G F Cooke, the London tragedian, visited Stourbridge in 1805, acting Othello to Shuter's Cassio.

By 1813 Crisp was the proprietor of the theatre. He let it to a Mrs Nunns for two years and then again took up the managerial reins.

Bills exist for John Boles Watson III's visit in 1831. Although Henrietta Watson, his daughter, was assuming roles (Louise in *The Green-Eye'd Monster*, for example), Watson remained off stage but in the town. One of the Shuter family played such roles as Zekiel Homespun in *The Heir at Law* and Solomon Sharpwit in *Sharp and Flat*.

Principal sources:
H E Palfrey, *Some Account of the Old Theatres at Stourbridge* (Stourbridge, 1936).
Warwickshire County Record Office, Warwick: materials relating to Warwick Theatre; Worcester County Record Office, St Helen's, Worcester: The Foley Scrapbooks, IV; the Palfrey Collection.
Information supplied by Ms S R Wallin.

Stratford-upon-Avon (23)
John Ward, a staunch 'bardolator', was visiting Stratford-upon-Avon as early as 1744 with his company. In 1746 he gave a performance of *Othello* at the Town Hall using the proceeds to renovate with paint (described as 'disfiguring' by a contemporary diarist) the bust of Shakespeare in Holy Trinity Church. A satisfied citizen, claiming to be a descendant of the poet, presented Ward with a pair of gloves, reputed to be Shakespeare's. His son-in-law, Roger Kemble, brought his company frequently to the town between 1761 and 1782. One can only speculate on where their theatre was: it may have been the barn theatre by the Unicorn Hotel near Clopton Bridge.

Ray and Gibbon led the Cheltenham company to Stratford in February 1805. Again, the whereabouts of the theatre are in doubt: possibly a timber-framed barn in Chapel Lane was used. Watson's name appears on a playbill, the roles suggesting that this is Jack. Just before the end of the season, in April, *Romeo and Juliet* was given; Ray played Romeo and some 'Young Ladies of Stratford' formed the procession of mourners.

A sketch of the barn theatre was made by Captain James Saunders, a local antiquary in 1823. A permanent theatre, the Shakespearean, was erected in the same street, but on a different site, in 1827.

Principal sources:
W Hutchings, *Past Dramatic Performances in Stratford-upon-Avon* (Stratford-upon-Avon, 1895); *Notes and Queries*, CLX (1931), 186; Cecil Price, *The English Theatre in Wales* (Cardiff, 1948); Philip Styles, *The Borough of Stratford-upon-Avon and the Parish of Alveston* (1946).
The Shakespeare Birthplace Trust, Stratford-upon-Avon: playbill collection.
Information supplied by Mr Charles Calvert.

Stroud (39)
As early as 1732 the Bath Company visited Stroud, setting up a stage and benches in the Market House. By 1779 the company converted a brewery in the neighbourhood of Webb's Almshouses into a theatre. The following year Sarah Siddons, at the age of twenty-four, performed here. A resident, Paul Hawkins Fisher, saw her in a number of roles, including that of Lady Macbeth:

> Her noble face and figure – her fine voice, – her perfect conception of, and complete identification with, the characters she represented, – fully entitled her to the honour of being the subject of that sublime personification of the Tragic Muse, which Sir Joshua Reynolds painted, in the very attitude she first assumed when sitting for her portrait.

Stroud had been on Roger Kemble's circuit and, footprint-wise, John Boles Watson I visited the town regularly once every three years in the spring for a season lasting from six to twelve weeks. Watson fitted up his theatre in the garden workshop belonging to a carpenter, Edward Keene. The premises were situated at the north-east angle of Bedford Street and patrons entered via a private passageway running alongside Keene's house. Plays at the 'New Theatre, Stroud' were advertised from 1794. A playbill for 30 June of that year lists in the company Mr and Mrs Stanton (this was their benefit), Mr and Mrs Carleton and Shuter. Mrs Shuter made a transparent painting of George III which was flanked by a triumphal arch. In 1799 Watson, together with Robert Hoy, was again seeking a licence to stage performances.
Watson's Cheltenham company arrived in the town in May 1808

under the sub-management of Beverley. One of its members was the young Edmund Kean who had been engaged at Gloucester. There he took a disastrous joint benefit: the returns for himself and his fellow actor Jack Hughes amounted to 1/6d (7p). Receipts at Stroud were poor in the extreme too. Normally Beverley played the tragic roles but at Stroud he relinquished them to Kean. Also in the company were two sisters, lately arrived from Waterford in Ireland, Mary and Susan Chambres, or so they spelt their surname. On the company's move to Cheltenham, Kean married Mary Chambres, returning to Stroud for the ceremony on 17 July 1808 and dashing back for a wedding breakfast in Cheltenham.

Watson obviously thought highly of his young performer. At Stroud he was paid one guinea per week. Ten shillings was later added on condition that Kean took the role of Harlequin in the afterpieces. Lord Broughton (John Cam Hobhouse) claimed that in one evening he had seen Kean at Stroud playing Shylock, perform rope dances, sing 'The Storm', spar with Mendoza and act the role of Three Finger'd Jack in *Obi*. Broughton, too, told the story of Kean forgetting his lines on one occasion at Stroud and substituting Milton's 'L'Allegro' without a reaction from the audience.

During the 1808 season William Henry West Betty also played in Stroud, taking from Kean the role of Hamlet. For the several days of Betty's engagement a displaced Kean hid in the neighbouring fields living off root crops.

On a map of 1839 the workshops are shown and designated a playhouse.

A later theatre consisted of a fit-up in the Victoria Rooms, King Street and the Subscription Rooms (opened 1834) housed companies for a week at a time.

Principal sources:
Paul Hawkins Fisher, *Notes and Recollections of Stroud* (1986); Raymund Fitzsimons, *Edmund Kean* (1976); *Gloucester Journal*, 3 March 1794; Theodore Hannam-Clark, *Drama in Gloucestershire* (1928); Giles Playfair, *Kean* (1939); Cecil Price, *The English Theatre in Wales* (Cardiff, 1948); Cecil Price, 'Some Movements of the Bath Company, 1729–34', *Theatre Notebook*, II (1947–8), 55–6; *Victoria History of the Counties of England, Gloucestershire*, vol XI; F T Wood, 'Notes on English Provincial Playhouses in the Eighteenth

Century', *Notes and Queries*, CLX (1931), 183–7.
Gloucestershire Record Office, Gloucester: playbills; Birmingham Central Library: Winston Collection.

Swansea (31)

At the beginning of the second chapter of this book Anthony Denning lists Swansea as one of Watson's theatrical locations although it must be said the manager would appear not to have owned or leased a playhouse here on any sort of regular basis.

The first Swansea Theatre (a gimcrack place with boxes left open to the draughts of the pit passage) situated in Wind Street was opened in 1780. Numbers of companies visited this: on several occasions the Bath and in 1795 Henry Masterman's company put on *Hamlet* in which Charles Mathews the Elder played Polonius. The building closed at the end of 1806 when preparations were under way to open the new Theatre Royal with entrances in Goat Street and Bank (later Temple) Street. This theatre was built from the proceeds of a tontine. The Committee of the Tontine in 1807, prior to the opening of the theatre, appointed Andrew Cherry, for five years a popular comedy actor at Drury Lane as well as a playwright of note, to undertake the management. A professional rivalry existed between Cherry and Watson, making it unlikely that the Cheltenham company would have visited the Theatre Royal, Swansea. Cherry built up a widely flung circuit encompassing Watson's previous location of Carmarthen, as well as Haverfordwest and Waterford on the south coast of Ireland.

A single playbill exists in the collection of Swansea Public Library containing the name Watson. This is for a benefit on 17 September 1806 at which the historical drama *The English Fleet in 1342* was presented. Watson took the role of Fitzwater. According to Denning, 1806 was one of the years in which Watson was lying fallow after a succession of illnesses; the name may therefore refer to John Boles Watson II or there is the possibility that this Watson is not a member of the Boles Watson family. At this time the Swansea manager was R Phillips, a member of the Swansea company, who had assumed the position on the death of Henry Masterman, its manager, in 1803.

Principal sources:
David Boorman, *The Brighton of Wales: Swansea as a Fashionable Seaside Resort, 1780–1830* (1986); Raymund Fitzsimons, *Edmund Kean* (1976); Alan Jones, *The Story of the Grand* (Llandybie, 1983); Cecil Price, *The English Theatre in Wales* (Cardiff, 1948); Peter Stead, 'The Entertainment of the People' in Glanmore Williams, ed, *Swansea, an Illustrated History* (1990); *The Swansea Guide* (Swansea, 1813).
Bodleian Library, Oxford: Volume of Autographs (MS Autogr. d.10 (235)); Swansea Public Library: playbill collection.

Tamworth (6)
The Town Hall built by Thomas Guy, Tamworth's Member of Parliament, in 1701 was used as the first theatre here. The chamber was approached by an external flight of stone steps.

The Tamworth historian Charles Ferrers Palmer refers to 'a large and commodious barn' near to the end of Lichfield Street and it was possibly this which John Boles Watson adapted as a playhouse in 1796. A playbill (28 July 1800) reveals that Richards was manager, Mrs Edwin was the visiting celebrity and the company consisted of such well-known Watsonian names as Field, Chamberlain, Wharton and Le Brun.

A new, purpose-built, large theatre at the corner of Church Street (then Butcher Street) and Lower Gungate opened in 1803. The following year Watson leased the building to Ray and Gibbon; in 1805 he mortgaged the deeds to the proprietors of the Theatre Royal, Birmingham in an attempt to raise money and in 1812 his son leased the playhouse to Mrs Nunns, an actress whose late husband had also been on the stage.

Following his grandfather's example, John Boles Watson III in 1831 again assigned the mortgage of the Tamworth Theatre to the Birmingham Theatre Royal in order to secure the rent for his lease of the latter.

The building in which Sarah Siddons and Harriot Mellon had played became a four-storey malt house until in 1870 it was presented by its then owner, Sir Robert Peel, to the trustees of the Baptist Chapel for use as a place of worship. The building has, appropriately, since become the Tamworth Arts Centre.

Principal sources:
H Charles Mitchell, *Tamworth Tower and Town* (Tamworth, 1936); C
F Palmer, *The History of the Town and Castle of Tamworth*
(Tamworth, 1845); Mabel Swift, *The Peels of Tamworth* (Tamworth,
1988); Henry Wood, *Borough by Prescription* (Tamworth, 1958).
Birmingham Central Library, Archives: Minute Book of the
proprietors of the Theatre Royal, Birmingham (Lee, 387); Tamworth
Castle: playbills; Tamworth Central Library: collection of newspaper
cuttings, H C Mitchell, vol IV; Warwickshire County Record Office,
Warwick: materials relating to the Warwick Theatre; William Salt
Library, Stafford: playbill collection.

Tewkesbury (36)

Members of Roger Kemble's company, when playing in Cheltenham,
would sometimes walk over the fields to Tewkesbury to perform. An
early venue was a temporary building set up in a meadow called the
Pantry which lay to the east of the road to Bredon. A rival concern,
in the Rails Meadow, was under the management of Henry
Thornton who later in life became manager of a prestigious theatre
at Windsor, frequented by George III and his family.

Hearing that John Boles Watson wished to build a theatre in the
town, in 1789 Quakers petitioned the magistrates to refuse him a
licence. Coming to Tewkesbury in 1796 (he had arrived three years
earlier, but his place of playing is uncertain), he performed in the
well-established – but not purpose-built – playhouse, situated
behind the Wheatsheaf Inn. This opened during the races in the
second or third week of August with boxes and 'front seats' selling at
3/- (15p), and pit and gallery at the usual prices of 2/- (10p) and 1/-
(5p) respectively.

The Watson term of management was short lived as in 1802
Stanley took charge.

In 1823 the theatre was completely refitted (some Tewkesbury
writers suggest rebuilt) and Charles Farley, who plays a part in the
Cirencester Theatre narrative, became the manager. Farley was
partnered by Abbot for the first two years and in 1825 by Yates. He
continued the Watsonian custom of commissioning scenes from
John Henderson Grieve a member of the famous family of stage
designers. Tewkesbury appears to have been uninterested in the

227

drama, however, and in 1827 the building was turned into a silk mill.

Principal sources:
James Bennett, *A History of Tewkesbury* (Tewkesbury, 1830); John Goding, *Norman's History of Cheltenham* (Cheltenham and London, 1863); Michael Kelly, *Reminiscences of Michael Kelly* [ed Theodore Hook] (1826); *Notes and Queries*, CLX (1931), 186; *Tewkesbury Yearly Register* (Tewkesbury, 1850); *The Victoria History of the Counties of England, Gloucestershire*, vol VIII.
Birmingham Central Library: Winston Collection; Gloucestershire Record Office, Gloucester: prohibitions of theatre performances, 1775 and 1777 (Q/TS, addl), petition by local Quakers against granting a licence (D1340/B2/M3), licences to perform, 1825 and 1827; New York Public Library: William Douglas manuscript notebook.

Walsall (11)

Walsall's early theatre situated in Lime Pit Bank consisted of a malthouse belonging to Samuel Wood. In this playhouse Samuel Stanton frequently appeared with his itinerant company which included a local lad from Pelshall, Thomas Holcroft, the future playwright and author of the popular gothic melodrama, *A Tale of Mystery*. Here too William Siddons, later the husband of Sarah Kemble, played in Roger Kemble's production of *Douglas*. Siddons was born in Rushall Street at his father's tavern, the London Apprentice. The theatre appears to have fallen into disuse.

In September 1802 John Boles Watson petitioned the Mayor for permission to play in the town. He pointed out

> . . . it is in his [ie Watson's] power to attend more eligibly and keep a better Dramatic establishment for the amusement of the place, than if the concern lay more remote.

Possibly this is an oblique reference to Stanton. He went on to propose that he should erect a 'new and commodious Theatre' as soon as possible in a central location. His theatre in Old Square was completed the following year from cash raised by subscriptions of £50 with each subscriber obtaining interest and a transferable silver ticket which would admit the bearer to performances. The interior consisted of the usual boxes, pit and gallery. Takings at the box office produced £50 to £60 per night.

The lease passed to Edward Ray and George Collins Gibbon in 1803 and by 1805 they were petitioning the magistrates for a forty day licence to play during and after the races. In March 1812 Mrs Elizabeth Nunns, Stanton's daughter, leased the theatre (and those at Warwick and Walsall) from Jack Watson.

Few people of note arrived to augment the company; mention should be made of Harriot Mellon and Edmund Kean. Although performances were still held until 1841, not enough interest in the theatre was expressed to warrant it being kept open. The proprietors were evicted for arrears of rent in 1845 and the building converted into shops.

Principal sources:
Aris's Birmingham Gazette, 17 September 1787; Thomas Pearce, *The History and Directory of Walsall* (Birmingham, 1813); Stebbing Shaw, *The History and Antiquities of Staffordshire* (1798–1801); *Victoria History of the Counties of England, Staffordshire*, vol. XVII; *Walsall Chronicle No 1. A Review of the Work of Walsall Metropolitan Borough Archives Service during 1978–9* (Walsall, 1979); *Walsall Observer*, 4 March 1966.
Walsall Local History Centre: petition to erect a theatre (Acc 277/204/3); petition of Ray and Gibbon (Acc 277/05/1,2); typescript copy of 'The Life and Times of James Gee'; Warwickshire County Record Office, Warwick: materials relating to the Warwick Theatre (CR 1596, Box 93).

Warwick (24)
In 1801 objections of the Warwick residents prevented John Boles Watson opening a new theatre in the Market Place and he was forced to make use of the site of the existing makeshift theatre of 1786 at Cocksparrow Hall, as he had on a former visit in 1799. This he rebuilt. Although the exterior of the new playhouse was unpromising, William Field noted that the 'interior affords ample space and convenient accommodation, for all who usually resort to theatrical amusements'. For the opening night in September 1802 Watson

composed a rhymed address which was spoken by Richards. A drop curtain showed a townscape within which Warwick Castle occupied a prominent position and to this Richards pointed as he declaimed:

> Here might he view the battle's proud array,
> And tilts and tournaments, and pageants gay;
> Yon 'gorgeous palace, and those cloud-capt Towers'
> Where now no storm of civil discord lowers,
> But antique state, and shades of mellow'd art,
> And peaceful grandeur sooth the soften'd heart.

The company, Field judged, was averagely provincial but the visiting performers were eminent.

In 1803 the theatre, in common with many others on the circuit, was leased to Gibbon and Ray. This transaction did not prevent Jack Watson appearing regularly throughout the season and holding a benefit at which Richer performed on the rope. An advertisment in the *Warwick Advertiser* of 1807 gives Watson and Buckle as the managers.

In 1831 John Boles Watson III briefly undertook the management, inviting Kean to play Shylock. In January 1832 the company visited Warwick as soon as its lease of the Theatre Royal, Birmingham, expired. Miss H Watson's name appears regularly on the Warwick bills for 1832 and 1833.

Principal sources:
John Britton *et al*, *The Beauties of England and Wales* (1814), vol XV; *European Magazine*, XLII (1802) 458–9; William Field, *An Historical and Descriptive Account of the Town and Castle of Warwick* (Warwick, 1815); Thomas Kempe, *A History of Warwick and its People* (Warwick, 1905); *Victoria History of the Counties of England, Warwickshire*, Vol VIII; *Warwick Advertiser*, 22 August 1807.
Birmingham Central Library: Theatre Royal, Birmingham, playbill collection; Warwick Public Library: typescript, Jane Osney, 'The Theatre and Related Entertainments in Warwick, *c*1800'; Warwickshire County Record Office, Warwick: draft of co-partnership (CR 1596, Box 93); Warwick Theatre playbills (M1 284).

Welshpool (4)

In the early years of the nineteenth century a theatre existed in the Bear Yard (the Bear was the principal inn, situated in the High Street) at Welshpool. Entrance was by a narrow passage at the side of the hostelry. Anthony Denning lists the Welshpool Theatre as one of the places leased by John Boles Watson I but his connection seems to have been a fleeting one. A note in the *Chester Courant* advertises his intention of visiting Welshpool on an impending visit to Denbigh. This latter town is not mentioned by Denning as part of the regular Watson circuit.

There is an entry in the diary of Viscount Grimston dated 25 September 1769: on this day he attended the theatre (maybe the building mentioned above) in Welshpool and, strange sum, paid five shillings and sixpence in admission for his companion and himself.

Principal sources
Bye-Gones, IV (1896), 275, 284; *Chester Courant*, 7 June 1785; Cecil Price, *The English Theatre in Wales* (Cardiff, 1948); Ion Trant, *The Changing Face of Welshpool* (Welshpool, 1986); *Verulam* (Historical Manuscripts Commission Reports, 1906).

Wolverhampton (12)

Wolverhampton, a stopping point for London traffic heading to North Wales and Ireland, was an ideal location for a theatre. Roger Kemble arrived regularly with his company, using the Town Hall, then situated at High Green – the market area of the town – as a theatre. Here the youthful Sarah and John Philip Kemble both played. Bills exist for a performance of *Love in a Village*, by Isaac Bickerstaff, given in 1770 with Roger Kemble as Sir William Meadows, William Siddons as Young Meadows, Mrs Sarah Kemble as Madge, Sarah as Rosetta and Fanny as the Housemaid and for *The School for Scandal* by Richard Sheridan given in 1778 with Roger Kemble, William Siddons and his wife Sarah.

By 1778, however, the Town Hall, unsatisfactory as a theatrical venue, was in disrepair. A new playhouse was opened in 1779, situated at the extreme end of the yard of the Swan Inn, a building lying on the east side of High Green. A writer in the *Wolverhampton Chronicle* noted:

231

The building was a substantial brick structure about eighty feet long by thirty-six feet in breadth, with two entrances – one to the boxes (or dress circle) facing down Swan Yard, and the other, leading to the pit and gallery, being opposite the opening, or gateway entrance from Wheeler's Fold.

The interior was almost as plain as the exterior, there being little attempted artistic embellishment or decoration, except in the vicinity of the stage, which occupied the entire breadth of the building at the east end. It was not more than eighteen feet to twenty feet in depth, flanked with Grecian capped pillars supporting the proscenium, and a nicely painted drop scene, representing a pastoral subject from one of Shakespeare's comedies.

In front of the stage was a small orchestra for the accomodation of some half dozen musicians, and the auditorium was arranged in semi-circular form, with pit, boxes and gallery, capable of seating altogether an audience of about six hundred persons.

This theatre was incorporated into John Boles Watson's circuit; he held an annual winter season in the town, playing for four evenings a week. By around 1784 he had sublet the building to Perry and Pero. Mrs Nunns, who appears in the Watson saga, was acting during their management, referred to by Samuel Ryley as a 'tragedy queen'.

By 1790 Miell was the manager. The following year a young playwright, Edmund John Eyre, became a member of the company. Eyre was to advertise himself 'of the theatres of Shrewsbury, Worcester and Wolverhampton' on the fly leaf of his works. Given a benefit night on 26 March 1792 under the patronage of the Rose Club, he spoke an elaborate address, bemoaning his lack of fame, yet in his misfortune 'shelter'd by the friendly – Rose' just as 'Royal Charles' had found a hiding place in the sacred oak.

Crisp shouldered the management from 1809 until 1820. He was followed in the lesseeship by one of the Shuter family, who unfortunately proved to be a failue as a manager, lasting only two years. Bennett (who, according to Robert Dyer, had made enough money running a public house theatre in Wales to buy several playhouses) and Mrs Beahan, reopened the theatre after a brief closure. The pair were also managers of the theatres at Lichfield and Worcester. Their first task was to install 'the gas' but the Wolverhampton Gas Works unfortunately used tubing too narrow for the amount required with the result that the stage was only dimly illuminated.

In the early 1840s the theatre was dark for a while and then in 1844 converted into a two-storey building, the lower used as stabling and the upper as a billiard room.

Principal sources:
J B Castle, 'Old Wolverhampton Sixty Years Ago', *Wolverhampton Chronicle*, 28 November 1894; Robert Dyer, *Nine Years of an Actor's Life* (1833); Edmund John Eyre, *The Fatal Sisters with a Variety of Poetic Essays* (1797); Gerald P Mander, *A History of Wolverhampton to the early Nineteenth Century* (Wolverhampton, 1960); Gerald P Mander, *Early Wolverhampton Books and printers with a Note on some Playbills* (Wolverhampton, 1922); Frank Mason, *The Book of Wolverhampton* (Buckingham, 1979); Frank Mason, *Yesterday's Town: Wolverhampton* (Buckingham, 1982); Samuel Ryley, *The Itinerant* (1808).
Johannesburg Public Library: William Douglas Notebook; Wolverhampton Central Library: Susan Fletcher, 'A History of the Grand Theatre, Wolverhampton' (typescript).

Worcester (21)

The original Worcester Theatre was a small timber building ('a barn with a stage three yards wide' the Revd Henry Bate described it) in a yard between the King's Head and the Golden Lion in the High Street; it opened in 1764. John Ward was at first the manager and then Roger Kemble appeared here with his company from February until April 1767. In 1778 he remodelled the theatre, providing the rough barn with a new ceiling.

On taking over the management, James Augustus Whiteley abandoned the barn theatre and built a new structure in Angel Street at a reputed cost of £1000, opening it in 1781. The Worcester historian Valentine Green described the building:

> It is about 66 feet long and 36 feet wide. The pit contains an ascending range of 12 benches, gently incurved towards the stage. These are screened by twelve large boxes, three on each side below and the same number above. There are also three boxes fronting the stage, and one at each of the corner angles of the pit. Over these is the gallery. Of interior decorations it cannot boast; all we can justly say of it is that it is sufficiently neat and commodious for the intended purposes.

After Whitely a succession of managers followed: Powell and Pero (two actors in the company), Ryley, Baker and Miller. One of the managers, William Miell, died in 1797 and before that date Watson had joined forces with him in management. Miell had been superintendent of a circus before he became manager of the Wolverhampton, Shrewsbury and Worcester circuit. At Miell's death the scenery and costumes at Worcester were sold. By 1798 John Boles Watson and Richard Hoy had entered into a partnership as managers of the Worcester Theatre; Hoy, resident at Worcester, looked after matters there whilst Watson looked after a section of the company in Cheltenham. Amongst others, the company included at the time the Shuter family and M'Cready. In 1798 Hoy engaged Sarah Siddons to play Calista in *The Fair Penitent* and in 1801 her brother, John Philip Kemble, to play Hamlet. Later, in 1805, he engaged Betty to play the roles of Young Norval, Barbarossa, Romeo, Rolla and Tancred but by that time the Watson–Hoy partnership had been dissolved (they parted in 1803) leaving Hoy free to enter into another in 1807 with Crisp, of the York and Liverpool theatres.

Mrs Jordan discovered a great difference between the sections of the company established at Cheltenham and that at Worcester when she visited the theatre in 1811. 'This is a dismal, gloomy theatre and the performers shocking,' she wrote home; three days later she was still disillusioned with the players: 'The performers (if they can be call'd so) put me out of temper with their ignorance and stupidity'.

With the change of management of the company from father to son, the Watsons continued their interest in the Worcester Theatre, occasionally taking a temporary lease on it. In 1821, when the weather was bad and Watson, deeply in debt, had for a while given up management, it was left to Mrs Watson to bring the company to the city.

In 1874 the small theatre was reconstructed at a cost of £2000.

Principal sources:
A Aspinall, *Mrs Jordan and her Family* (1951); *Concise History of the City and Suburbs of Worcester* (Worcester, 1816); Valentine Green, *The History and Antiquities of the City and Suburbs of Worcester* (1796); F Grice, 'Roger Kemble's Company at Worcester', *Theatre Notebook*, April–June 1955; F Grice, 'The Theatre Royal at

Worcester', *Theatre Notebook*, April–June 1956; *Thespian Dictionary* (1805); *Worcester Directory* (Worcester, 1788).
County Record Office, St Helen's, Worcester: Foley Scrapbook, IV; photographs of playbills (989.9.161); series of cuttings of newspaper articles by H W Gwilliam.

Wotton Under Edge (23)

Part of the Market House of Wotton (later known as the Town Hall) was enclosed to form a room and it was this which was prepared for a visiting company in 1751.

John Boles Watson fitted up the Town Hall for theatrical use and prepared to open his season there in April 1795. The Minister of the Surrey Chapel in Blackfriars, the Revd Rowland Hill (1744–1833), was also a resident of Wotton. This fundamentalist cleric

was exceedingly annoyed by the introduction into the town of a company of travelling actors, whom he thought it his duty to oppose, to the utmost extent of his influence. The clergyman of the parish [the Revd W D Tattersall] was favourable to the licence for the performances being granted; and he and another gentleman signed a petition to the authorities for that purpose. A number of respectable inhabitants drew up a counter petition, which had Mr Rowland Hill's entire approbation. Still the first was successful, and the performances were permitted.

Hill proceeded to publish *An Expostulatory Letter* in which he examined the texts of the plays presented which, he claimed, had an 'abominable tendency to corrupt the morals of the people'.

In spite of these strictures on the players, regular forays were made to the town during the early years of the nineteenth century.

Principal sources:
William Jones, *Memoirs of the Life, Ministry and Writings of the Revd Rowland Hill, MA* (1843); E S Lindley, *Wotton Under Edge. Men and Affairs of a Cotswold Wool Town* (1962); R Perry, *Wotton Under Edge. Times Past – Times Present* (privately printed, 1986); Edwin Sydney, *The Life of the Revd Rowland Hill* (1834).
Anthony Denning's draft typescript; information supplied by Mrs Clare Smith of Wotton Under Edge.

Wrexham (2)

In 1785 John Boles Watson brought his Cheltenham company to give a four month season at Wrexham Town Hall. The building would seem to have been limited to a pit and superior type of gallery for which Watson charged 1/- (5p) and 2/- (10p) respectively. At nearby Wynnstay Sir Watkins Williams Wynn was a keen promoter of private theatricals, helped by the amateurs of the town. These players supported Watson's professional first season in Wrexham staunchly. Indeed one of the company, Henry Bunbury, a designer as well as an actor in which latter capacity he was known locally as the 'Wynnstay Roscius', procured permission for Watson to bring his company to this and the neighbouring towns once every three years.

The Stanton company arrived regularly from 1802. Samuel was the founder who had gained Dr Johnson's patronage at Lichfield on a visit there in March 1776. His son John was painter and machinist to the Shrewsbury Theatre before he gained a northern circuit. Captain Nunns, a son-in-law of Samuel, took over the company at the founder's death in 1797 but this management was short-lived and another of old Stanton's sons, Charles, took custody.

A new theatre was built in 1818 by Penson, a local auctioneer, architect and mason with a house next door for the builder. This served the Stanton company until it was disbanded in 1837. In its latter days the company had to resist the opposition of the Wrexham Calvinistic Methodists.

The playhouse was converted into a Temperance Hall in 1875 and later a Salvation Army Citadel.

Principal sources:
R J Broadbent, 'The Stanton Circuit', *The Stage*, 15 September and 3 November 1932; A H Dodd, *A History of Wrexham, Denbighshire* (Wrexham, 1957); *Jackson's Oxford Journal*, 9 February 1785; Alfred Neobard Palmer, *A History of the Town of Wrexham* (Wrexham, 1893); Cecil Price, *The Professional Theatre in Wales* (Swansea, 1984); Cecil Price, *The English Theatre in Wales* (Cardiff, 1948); Sybil Rosenfeld, *Temples of Thespis* (1978).

Sources

Bibliography

Adams, W Davenport, *A Dictionary of the Drama*, (1904)

Adolphus, John, *Memoirs of John Bannister, Comedian* (1839)

Aspinal, A, *Mrs Jordan and her Family* (1951)

Baker, H Barton, *The London Stage* (1889)

Barfoot, P and Wilkes, J, *Universal British Directory of Trade and Commerce* (1790–98)

Barker, Kathleen M D, 'The Theatre Proprietor's Story', *Theatre Notebook*, XVIII (1963–64), 79–91

Barker, Kathleen M D, *The Theatre Royal, Bristol. The First Seventy Years* (Bristol, 1961)

Barker, Kathleen M D, *The Theatre Royal, Bristol, 1766–1796. Two Centuries of Stage History* (1974)

Bathurst A B, *History of the Apsley and Bathurst Families* (Cirencester, 1903)

Beacham, Roger, *The Early History of the Theatre in Cheltenham* (Cheltenham, nd)

Bearman, Robert, *Stratford-upon-Avon. A History of its Streets and Buildings* (Nelson, 1988)

Beauties of Mrs Siddons, The (1786)

[Beecham, W K], *The History and Antiquities of the Town of Cirencester* (Cirencester [1842])

Beesley, Alfred, *A History of Banbury* (1841)

Bennett, James, *A History of Tewkesbury* (Tewkesbury, 1830)

Bergman, Gusta M, *Lighting in the Theatre* (Stockholm, 1977)

Billson, Charles, 'Players and Playhouses', *Leicester Memories* (1924)

Bisset, John, ed, *Critical Essays on the Dramatic Excellencies of the Young Roscius* (1804)

237

Boaden, James, *Memoirs of Mrs Siddons* (1827)

Boaden, James, *Memoirs of the Life of John Philip Kemble, Esq.* (1815)

Boorman, David, *The Brighton of Wales: Swansea as a Fashionable Seaside Resort, 1780–1830* (1986)

Britton, John, *et al, The Beauties of England and Wales* (1814)

Broadbent, R J, 'The Stanton Circuit', *Stage*, 15 September and 3 November 1932

Burney, Frances, *Diary and Letters of Madame D'Arblay*, ed Charlotte Barrett (1891)

Butler, Weedon, *The Cheltenham Guide* (1781)

Byng, John, *The Torrington Diaries*, ed C Bruyn Andrews (1970)

Campbell, Thomas, *The Life of Mrs Siddons* (1834)

Castle, J B, 'Old Wolverhampton Sixty Years Ago', *Wolverhampton Chronicle* (28 November 1894)

Cathrall, William, *History of Oswestry* (Oswestry, 1855)

Chancellor, E Beresford, *Old Q and Barrymore* (1925)

Charke, Charlotte, *A Narrative of the Life of Mrs Charlotte Charke (Youngest Daughter of Colley Cibber, Esq)* (1755)

Cheltenham (Cheltenham, 1810)

Cheltenham Directory (1800)

Cheltenham Guide, The (Cheltenham, 1805)

Cibber, Colley *An Apology for the Life of Mr Colley Cibber* (1740)

Clayton, Howard, *Coaching City* [Didsbury, 1977]

A Collection of Tours in Wales (1799)

Concise History of the City and Suburbs of Worcester (Worcester, 1816)

Copeland, John, *Roads and their Traffic, 1750–1850* (Newton Abbot, 1968)

Cross, Richard, *An Early Diary of Richard Cross, Prompter to the Theatres*, ed H W Pedicord (Manchester, 1955)

Cunningham, John E, *Theatre Royal* (Oxford, 1950)

Darly, Mary, *Comic Prints of Characters, Caricatures, Macaronis, etc* (1776)

Davies, T P, 'Llandrindod Wells in the Eighteenth Century', *Radnorshire Transactions*, IV (1934), 10–16

Davies, Thomas, *Dramatic Miscellanies* (1783–84)

Dawes, Edwin A, *The Great Illusionists* (1979)

Decastro, Jacob, *The Memoirs of J Decastro*, ed R Humphreys (1824)

Defoe, Daniel, *A Tour through the Whole Island of Great Britain* (1724–27)

Denning Anthony, 'Cobbett in Cirencester', *Cirencester Archeological and Historical Society Annual Report*, XXIII (1980–81), 7–16

Denning, Anthony, 'Early Theatricals in Cirencester', *Cirencester Archaeological and Historical Society Annual Report* XIV (1971–72), 5–9

Sources

Dibdin T F, *The History of Cheltenham and Account of its Environs* (Cheltenham, 1803)

Dictionary of National Biography, The, ed Leslie Stephen and Sidney Lee (1908–09)

Dodd A H, *A History of Wrexham, Denbighshire* (Wrexham, 1957)

Doran, John *'Their Majesties' Servants' Annals of the English Stage* (1864)

Duncan, Barry, 'A Worcestershire Company', *Theatre Notebook*, II (1947–8), 76–8

Dutton, Thomas, *Pizarro in Peru, or The Death of Rolla* (1799)

Dyer, Robert, *Nine Years of an Actor's Life* (1833)

Egan, Pierce, *The Life of an Actor* (1825)

Enchiridion Clericum (1812)

Everard, Edward Cape, *Memoirs of an Unfortunate Son of Thespis* (Edinburgh, 1818)

Eyre, Edmund John, *The Fatal Sisters with a variety of Poetic Essays* (1797)

Fahrner, Robert, *The Theatre Career of Charles Dibdin the Elder (1745–1814)* (New York, 1989)

Field, William, *A Historical and Descriptive Account of the Town of Warwick* (Warwick, 1815)

Fisher, Paul Hawkins, *Notes and Recollections of Stroud, Gloucestershire* (Stroud, 1871)

Fitzgerald, Percy, *The World Behind the Scenes* (1881)

Fitzsimons, Raymund, *Edmund Kean* (1976)

Foote, Horace, *A Companion to the Theatres* (1829)

Fothergill, Brian, *Mrs Jordan. Portrait of an Artist* (1965)

Frost, Thomas, *Circus Life and Circus Celebrities* (1875)

Frost, Thomas, *The Lives of the Conjurors* (1874)

Geary, W M N, *The Law of Theatres and Music Halls* (1885)

Genest, John, *Some Account of the English Stage from the Restoration in 1660 to 1830* (Bath, 1832)

Gilliland, Thomas, *The Dramatic Mirror* (1808)

Gloucester Guide (1792)

Goding, John, *Norman's History of Cheltenham* (Cheltenham and London, 1863)

Green, Valentine, *The History and Antiquities of the City and Suburbs of Worcester* (1796)

Grice, F, 'Roger Kemble's Company at Worcester', *Theatre Notebook*, IX (1955), 73–5

Grice, F, 'The Theatre Royal at Worcester', *Theatre Notebook*, X (1956), 83–6

Grove's Dictionary of Music and Musicians, ed Eric Blom (1954)

Hall, Lillian Arvilla, *Catalogue of Dramatic Portraits in the Theatre Collection of Harvard College Library* (Cambridge, Mass, 1931)

Hannam-Clark, Theodore, *Drama in Gloucestershire* (1928)

Hare, Arnold, *G F Cooke. The Man and the Actor* (1980)

Harper's Cheltenham Street Directory (1844)

Hartnoll, Phylis, *The Concise Oxford Companion to the Theatre* (1972)

Hartnoll, Phylis, *The Oxford Companion to the Theatre* (1967)

Haslewood, Joseph, *The Secret History of the Green Rooms* (1790)

Haydon, Benjamin Robert, *Diaries*, ed Willard Bissell Pope (Cambridge, Mass, 1960)

Hazlitt, William, *The Complete Works of William Hazlitt*, ed P P Howe (1930–34)

Herbert, George, *Shoemaker's Window*, ed C S Cheyney (Chichester, 1971)

Hickling, William, *History and Antiquities of the City of Coventry* (Coventry, 1846)

Highfill, jnr, Philip H, Burnim, Kalman A, Langhans, Edward A, *A Biographical Dictionary of Actors, Actresses, Musicians, Dancers, Managers and Other Stage Personnel in London, 1660–1800* (Carbondale and Edwardsville, 1973–).

Hill, Aaron, *Collected Works* (1753)

Hillebrand, Harold Newcomb, *Edmund Kean* (New York, 1933)

Historical and Local Cheltenham Guide (Bath [1805])

Horner, B H, *The Life and Work of Dr Arne* (1893)

Howse, W H, *Kington, Herefordshire. Memorials of an Old Town* (Kington, 1953)

Howse, W H, *Radnorshire* (Hereford, 1949)

Hummert, Paul A, 'The Prompter: An Intimate Mirror of the Theatre in 1789', *Restoration and Eighteenth Century Theatre Research*, III (1964), 37–46

Hunt, Leigh, *Critical Essays on the Performers of the London Stage* (1807)

Hunt, Leigh, *Dramatic Essays* ed William Archer and Robert W Lowe (1824)

Hutchings, W, *Past Dramatic Performances in Stratford-upon-Avon* (Stratford-upon-Avon, 1895)

Irwin, Eric, 'More Drawings for Winston's *Theatric Tourist*', *Theatre Notebook*, XIX (1964–65), 64–66

Jackman, W T, *The Development of Transportation in Modern England* (Cambridge, 1916)

Jackson, John, *History of the City and Cathedral of Lichfield* (1805)

Jones, Alan, *The Story of the Grand* (Llandybie, 1983)

Jones, William, *Memoirs of the Life, Ministry and Writings of the Revd*

Sources

Rowland Hill MA (1843)

Kelly, Michael, *Reminiscences of Michael Kelly*, ed Theodore Hook (1826)

Kempe, Thomas, *A History of Warwick and its People* (Warwick, 1905)

Kissack, Keith, *Monmouth – the Making of a Country Town* (Chichester, 1975)

Kitchiner, W, *A Brief Memoir of Charles Dibdin* (1884)

Knight, Charles, *Passages of a Working Life* (1873)

Lamb, Charles, *Essays of Elia* (1832)

Leacroft, Helen and Richard, *The Theatre in Leicestershire* (Leicester, 1986)

Leech, Cliford and Craik, T W, *The Revels History of Drama in English* (1975–83)

Lewis, Matthew Gregory, *Crazy Jane* (1830?)

Lees-Milne, James, *The Earls of Creation* (1962)

Lewis, Samuel, *Topographical Dictionary of Wales* (1833)

Life of William Henry West Betty, The [1804]

Lindley, E S, *Wotton Under Edge. Men and Affairs of a Cotswold Town* (1962)

Lloyd, David and Klein, Peter, *Ludlow, a Historic Town in Words and Pictures* (Chichester, 1984)

Lynch, Jeremiah, *Box, Pit and Gallery* (Berkeley, California, 1953)

Mackintosh, Iain and Sell, Michael, *Curtains* (Eastbourne, 1982)

Macready, Charles William, *Reminiscences*, ed Frederick Pollock (1875)

Malcolm, J P, *Londinium Redivivium* (1802–7)

Mander, Gerald P, *Early Wolverhampton Books and Printers with a Note on some Playbills* (Wolverhampton, 1922)

Mander, Gerald P, *A History of Wolverhampton to the Early Nineteenth Century* (Wolverhampton, 1961)

Manvell, Roger, *Sarah Siddons* (1970)

Martin, Peter, *Pursuing Innocent Pleasures – The Gardening World of Alexander Pope* (Hamden, Conn, 1984)

Mason, Frank, *The Book of Wolverhampton* (Buckingham, 1979)

Mason, Frank, *Yesterday's Town: Wolverhampton* (Buckingham, 1982)

Merritt, John, *Memoirs of the Life of William Henry West Betty* (Liverpool, 1804)

Mitchell, Charles, *Tamworth Town and Tower* (Tamworth, 1936)

Moore, Alan, *The Picture Palaces of Gloucester and Cheltenham* (Sutton Coldfield, 1989)

Moreau, Simeon, *A Tour of the Royal Spa at Cheltenham* (Bath, 1797)

Morgan, Fidelis and Charke, Charlotte, *The Well-Known Trouble Maker* (1988)

241

Mozeen, Thomas, *Young Scarron* (1752)

Mulock, Dinah Maria, *John Halifax, Gentleman* (1856)

Murray, Christopher, *Robert William Elliston* (1975)

Neild, James, *An Account of the Rise, Progress and Present State of the Society for the Discharge and Relief of Persons Imprisoned for Small Debts throughout England and Wales* (1802)

Nicoll, Allardyce, *A History of English Drama, 1660–1900* (Cambridge, 1955)

O'Brien, Richard Barry, 'A Memorable Night at Cirencester Theatre – 150 Years Ago, Tonight', *Wiltshire Herald and Advertiser* (14 December 1941)

Oxberry, William, *Oxberry's Dramatic Biography and Histrionic Anecdotes* (1826)

Palfrey, H E *Some Account of the Old Theatres at Stourbridge* (Stourbridge, 1936)

Palmer, Alfred Neobard, *A History of the Town of Wrexham* (Wrexham, 1893)

Palmer, C F, *The History of the Town and Castle of Tamworth* (Tamworth, 1845)

Parke, W T, *Musical Memories* (1830)

Parker, Alfred, *A Sentimental Journey in and about the Ancient and Loyal City of Lichfield* (Lichfield, 1925)

Parker, George, *A View of Society and Manners in High and Low Life* (1781)

Parry, Richard, *The History of Kington* (Kington, 1845)

Pearce, Thomas, *The History and Directory of Walsall* (Birmingham, 1813)

Pemberton, T Edgar, *The Theatre Royal, Birmingham* (Birmingham, 1901)

Perry, R, *Wotton Under Edge. Times Past – Time Present* (Wotton Under Edge, 1986)

Petronius Arbiter (pseud), *Memoirs of Elizabeth, Countess of Derby* (1797)

Pevsner, Nikolaus, *The Buildings of England. Northamptonshire*, revised by Bridget Cherry (1973).

Playfair, Giles, *The Flash of Lightning. A Portrait of Edmund Kean* (1983)

Playfair, Giles, *Kean. The Life and Paradox of the Great Actor* (1950)

Playfair, Giles, *The Prodigy. The Study of the Stage Life of Master Betty* (1967)

Playne, Arthur Twixen, *The History of the Parishes of Minchinhampton and Avening* (Gloucester, 1915)

Powell, G Rennie, *The Bristol Stage* (Bristol, 1919)

Price, Cecil, 'Eighteenth Century Playbills of the English Theatre in Wales', *Journal of the National Library of Wales*, VI (1949–50), 270–71

Price, Cecil, *The English Theatre in Wales* (Cardiff, 1948)

Sources

Price, Cecil, *The Professional Theatre in Wales* (Swansea, 1984)

Price, Cecil, 'Some Movements of the Bath Company, 1729–34', *Theatre Notebook*, II (1947–8), 55–6

Price, Cecil, 'A Welsh Spaw', *Welsh Review*, V (1946), 42–44

Price, William, *The History of Oswestry* (Oswestry, 1815)

Ranger, Paul, *A Catalogue of Strolling Players* (Newbury, 1990)

Ranger, Paul, *The Lost Theatres of Winchester, 1620–1821* (Winchester, 1976)

Ranger, Paul, *Terror and Pity Reign in Every Breast* (1991)

Raymond, George, *The Life and Enterprises of Robert William Elliston* (1857)

Raymond, George, *Memoirs of Robert William Elliston, Comedian. 1774 to 1810* (1844)

Rede, Leman Thomas, *The Road to the Stage* (1827)

Reed, Isaac, *Biographia Dramatica* (1812)

Rees, Terence, *Lighting in the Age of Gas* (1978)

Rees, W J, *The Hereford Guide* (Hereford, 1827)

Reeves, N C, *The Town in the Marches* (Leominster, 1972)

Rhodes, R Crompton, *The Theatre Royal, Birmingham* (1924)

Ridge, Thomas, *The History and Antiquities of Gloucester* (Gloucester, 1811)

Rosenfeld, Sybil, *The Georgian Theatre of Richmond, Yorkshire* (York, 1984)

Rosenfeld, Sybil, *A Short History of Scene Design in Great Britain* (Oxford, 1973)

Rosenfeld, Sybil, *Temples of Thespis* (1978)

Rudder, Samuel, *The History and Antiquities of Cirencester* (1780)

Rudder, Samuel, *A New History of Gloucestershire* (Cirencester, 1779)

Ryley, Samuel, *The Itinerant or Memoirs of an Actor* (1808)

Ryscamp, Charles and Pottle, Frederick, A, *Boswell, the Ominous Years, 1774–76* (Yale, 1963)

Saint, Andrew, *et al*, *A History of the Royal Opera House, Covent Garden, 1732–1982* (1982)

Salberg, Derek, *Ring Down the Curtain* (Luton, 1980)

Sharp, Thomas, *The Coventry Guide* (Coventry, 1824)

Shaw, Stebbing, *The History and Antiquities of Staffordshire* (1798–1801)

Short History of Minchinhampton Market House, A (Minchinhampton, 1986)

Siddons, Sarah and William, *The Letters of Sarah and William Siddons to Hester Lynch Piozzi*, ed Kalman A Burnim (Manchester, 1969)

Simmons, Jack, *Leicester Past and Present* (1974)

Snagg, Thomas, *Recollections of Occurrences*, ed Harold Hobson (1951)

Snell, Lawrence S, ed *Essays Towards a History of Bewdley* (Bewdley, 1972)

Southern, Richard, *Changeable Scenery* (1952)

Southern, Richard, 'Trick Work in the English Theatre', *Life and Letters Today*, XXI (1939), 94–100

Southern, Richard and Brown, Ivor, *The Georgian Theatre, Richmond, Yorkshire* (Richmond, 1962)

Speaight, George, 'The Brigand in the Toy Theatre', *The Saturday Book 29*, ed John Hadfield (1969)

Speaight, George, *A History of the Circus* (1980)

Speaight, George, *The History of the English Puppet Theatre* (1990)

Speaight, George, 'Wires or Strings?', *Theatre Notebook*, XXXVII (1983), 63–66

Stochholm, Joanne, *Garrick's Folly* (1964)

Stone, George Winchester, 'Garrick's Long Lost Alteration of *Hamlet*', *Papers of the Modern Language Association*, LXIX (1934), 890–905

Styles, Philip, *The Borough of Stratford-upon-Avon and the Parish of Alveston* (1946)

Swansea Guide, The (Swansea, 1813)

Summers, Montague, *The Gothic Quest* (1938)

Swift, Mabel, *The Peels of Tamworth* (Tamworth, 1988)

Sydney, Edwin, *The Life of the Revd Rowland Hill* (1834)

Tewkesbury Yearly Register (Tewkesbury, 1850)

Thespian Dictionary (1802; enlarged edition 1805)

Trant, Ion, *The Changing Face of Welshpool* (Welshpool, 1986)

Trewin, J C, *The Story of Stratford-upon-Avon* (1950)

Tribute to the Genius of the Young Roscius, A (Wisbech, 1808)

Verey, David, *The Buildings of England: Gloucestershire. 1. The Cotswolds* (1970)

Verulam (Historical Manuscripts Commission Reports, 1906)

Victoria History of the Counties of England:
> *Gloucester*, vol XI, ed N M Herbert (Oxford, 1976)
> *Leicester*, vol IV, ed R A McKinley (1958)
> *Oxford*, vol X, ed Alan Crossley (1972)
> *Stafford*, vol XIV, ed C R Elrington (1990)
> *Stafford*, vol XVII, ed M W Greenslade (Oxford, 1976)
> *Warwick*, vol VIII, ed R B Pugh (1969)

Walpole, Horace, *The Yale Edition of the Correspondence of Horace Walpole*, ed Wilmarth Sheldon Lewis (1937–80)

Walsall Chronicle No 1. A Review of the Work of Walsall Metropolitan Borough Archives Service during 1978–79 (Walsall, 1979)

244

Sources

Wells, Mitchell, 'Spectacular Scenic Effects of the Eighteenth-Century Pantomime', *Philological Quarterly*, XVII (1938), 67–81

Welsford, Jean, *Cirencester. A History and Guide* (Gloucester, 1987)

Whatley, Ernest, 'A Stage Story', *Wilts and Gloucestershire Standard*, 26 January 1876

Williams, David, *Royal Recollections. A Tour to Cheltenham* (1788)

Williams, Glanmore, ed, *Swansea, an Illustrated History* (1990)

Williams, John, *The Life of the Late Earl of Barrymore* (1793)

Williams, John Ambrose, *Memoirs of John Philip Kemble, Esq* (1817)

Willmott, Carl, 'The Theatre in Kington, Herefordshire', *Theatre Notebook*, V (1951), 44–46

Wilson, Margaret Baron, *Memoirs of Harriott, Duchess of St Albans* (1839)

Wilson, Margaret Baron, *Our Actresses* (1844)

Winston, James, *Drury Lane Journal: Selections from James Winston's Diaries, 1819–1827*, ed Alfred L Nelson and Gilbert B Cross (1974)

Winston, James, *The Theatric Tourist* (1805)

Wonderful Theatrical Progress of William Henry West Betty, The (1804)

Wood, Henry, *Borough by Prescription* (Tamworth, 1958)

Wood, F T, 'Notes on English Provincial Playhouses in the Eighteenth Century', *Notes and Queries*, CLX (1931), 147–150, 165–9, 183–7.

Worcester Directory (Worcester, 1788)

Newspapers and Magazines

Adams Weekly Courant

Aris's Gazette

Banbury Guardian

Bath Chronicle

Bristol Mercury

Bye-Gones

Cambrian

Carmarthen Journal

Chelmsford Chronicle

Cheltenham Chronicle

Cheltenham Looker-On

Chester Courant

Coventry Herald

Coventry Mercury

Critical Review

Era Almanac

European Magazine

Felix Farley's Bristol Journal

Gentleman's Magazine

Gleaner

Gloucester Echo

Gloucester Journal

Gloucestershire Notes and Queries

Hampshire Chronicle

Hereford Journal

Jackson's Oxford Journal

Liverpool Advertiser

London Magazine

Morning Post

New Monthly Magazine

Northampton Mercury

Notes and Queries

Public Advertiser

Quarterly Review

Shrewsbury Chronicle

Spectator

Stage
The Times
Walsall Observer

Warwick Advertiser
Wilts and Gloucester Standard
York Courant

Collections

Abergavenny, Museum:
  typescript by Patricia Neale, 'Travelling Companies and Theatres in Newport and Monmouthshire in the Eighteenth and Early Nineteenth Centuries';
  Abergavenny Local History Society's Town Centre Survey, 1979–1980.
Banbury, Cheyney and Son, Printers:
  playbill collection.
Banbury, Museum:
  playbill collection.
Birmingham, Central Library:
  Winston Collection.
Birmingham, Central Library, Archives:
  Minute Book of the Proprietors of the Theatre Royal, Birmingham (Lee 387).
Birmingham, Central Library, Local Studies and History Department:
  playbill collection.
Cambridge, Mass, Harvard College Library, Theatre Collection:
  James Winston's manuscript notebooks and drawings.
Carmarthen, County Record Office:
  Carmarthenshire Antiquarian Society, scrapbook (1934).
Cheltenham, Museum and Art Gallery:
  playbill collection.
Cirencester, Bingham Library:
  local history collection;
  playbill collection.
Coventry, Central Library:
  'Plays, Players and Playbills in Coventry', newspaper cuttings from the *Coventry Herald*; 'Compilation' by Arthur Heap, newspaper cuttings from the *Coventry Herald*.
Croydon, Central Library:
  manuscript notes of J C Anderson referring to the Croydon Theatre.
Cwmbran, Gwent Record Office:
  theatre playbills and licences (QS/MB 0005 and 0007).
Daventry, Moot Hall:
  playbill collection.

Gloucester, Central Library, Gloucestershire Collection:
   playbill collection;
   various newspaper cuttings on the Gloucestershire theatres.
Gloucester, County Record Office:
   pew rent books of the Church of St John the Baptist, Cirencester;
   papers of Gwinnett and Newman, solicitors (D2025, Box 73).
Hereford, Central Library, Local History Collection:
   Scrapbooks of the Kemble and Siddons papers.
Johannesburg, Public Library:
   manuscript notebook of William Douglas on the theatres of the British
   Isles.
London, British Library:
   Richard Percival Collection of Material relating to Sadler's Wells
   Theatre (Crach 1 Tab 4 b 4);
   playbill collection, volumes 288 and 426;
   Burney Collection of Playbills.
London, Public Record Office, Chancery Lane:
   will of John Boles Watson I (PROB 11/1544, 226, folios 65–66).
London, Royal National Theatre:
   Maugham Bequest of Theatrical Paintings.
London, Society of Antiquaries of London:
   Prattinton Printed Papers, vol 2 (playbill collection).
London, Theatre Museum:
   Peter Davey's manuscript notebooks
New York, Public Library:
   manuscript notebook of William Douglas relating to the theatres of the
   British Isles.
Oxford, Bodleian Library, John Johnson Collection:
   playbill collection.
Oxford, Bodleian Library, Department of Western Manuscripts:
   Volume of Autographs (MS Autogr. d. 10 (235))
Stafford, William Salt Library:
   playbill collection.
Stratford-upon-Avon, Shakespeare Birthplace Trust:
   playbill collection.
Swansea, Public Library:
   playbill collection.
Sydney, New South Wales, State Library of New South Wales, Mitchell
Library:
   coloured drawings of British provincial theatres by James Winston.
Tamworth, Castle Museum:

playbill collection.

Walsall, Local History Centre:

petition of John Boles Watson I (Acc 277/204/3); anonymous typescript, 'The Life and Times of James Gee'.

Warwick, Public Library:

typescript by Jane Osney, 'The Theatre and Related Entertainments in Warwick, c1800'.

Warwick, County Record Office:

Papers relating to the Warwick Theatre (CR 1596, Box 93).

Wigton Magna, Leicestershire, County Record Office:

playbill collection.

Wolverhampton, Central Library:

cuttings of newspaper articles by J B Hardcastle, 'Old Wolverhampton Sixty Years Ago';

typescript by Susan Fletcher, 'A History of the Grand Theatre, Wolverhampton'.

Worcester, County Record Office, St Helen's:

Foley Scrapbooks;

newspaper cuttings of articles by H W Gwilliam.

Index